DEAN MARTIN
Recollections

Dean Martin archivist and biographer Bernard H Thorpe was the co-founder, President and Chief Executive of The Dean Martin Association from its inception in 1960.

Bernard spent his life promoting and documenting Dino's life and career, compiling and producing numerous top-selling Capitol and Reprise albums for re-issue. He was most proud to have among them Dino's only Gold album in 1976 for one million+ UK sales of Reprise's 20 ORIGINAL DEAN MARTIN HITS.

His meticulously-researched discography of Dean's entire recording career won the 2023 Association for Recorded Sound Collections Award for Excellence in Historical Recorded Sound Research.

Bernard passed away peacefully in 2015.

DEAN MARTIN
Recollections

BERNARD H THORPE
WITH ELLIOT THORPE

MEMORY HIVE BOOKS

'How would I like to be remembered? Well, I guess that I did my best to hopefully please everybody; that I was a nice guy, and that's about it. What more could anyone want? It's been a grand life.'

DEAN MARTIN

'Cool is as cool does. Dean Martin was the epitome of that statement. A distinctive vocal ability and effortless grace have made Dean an icon for the ages.'

MICHAEL BUBLÉ

'Why do you go on about this Dean Martin chap, son? He's never likely to ever contact you. It's just a phase you're going through. You'll forget all about him in a few months.'

HENRY THORPE

Thank you…

…the family and Estate of Bernard H Thorpe; Thomas Brady, Kent Edens, Ron Iveson, Ed Krzan, Marisa Lavins, Karen Morris, Cindy Williford; Mark Adams, BBC Essex, Becky Banning, Mayor Jerry Barilla, Dave Blyth, BooksMarx Bookstore, Jimmy Bowen, Simon Brett, Michael Bublé, Steve Caldwell, Vincenzo Carrara, Chinbeard Books, John Chintala, Mike Colonna, Rodney Lee Conover, Croydon Advertiser, Graham Daniels, Roger de Courcey, Michelle Della Fave, Peter de Ryk, Rhea Dingess, DRP Touring Ltd, Barnaby Eaton-Jones, Hal Espinosa, Susie Ewing, Tony Fisher, Kevin Fontaine, Dino Forte, Luke Foxwell, Froehlich's Classic Corner, Del Fuller, Ian Gallagher, Grosvenor House Publishing, Kenton Hall, Mark Halliday, Robert Hammond, The Harmonium Project, Nicholas Hollands, David Iannandrea, Kim Johnson, Liz Kelley, Jayne Kempsey, Danny Kissane, Rich Little, George Daniel Long, Malcolm Macfarlane, Jessica Martin, Fred McNamara, Memory Hive Productions, Francie Mendenhall, Jimmy Monaco, Muscular Dystrophy Association, Linda Nagle, Newsmax Media, Jeanne Normandeau, NTVB Media, Barb Oates, Tony Ocean, Ohio Valley Health Center, Marilyn O'Neill, Joeytunes Panzarella, Chris A Phasey, Charles Pignone, Ruth Pulis, Cheryl Radden,   The Rat Pack Music Alliance, Gerald Ravasio, Sharon Reid, Emerian Rich, Rosario Roller, Heather Roulo, Tamsin Rush, Carol Salerno, The Sammy Davis Jr Estate, Sand Castle Communications, Joe Scalissi, Steve Scruton, Matthew Schmitz, *Search Magazine*, Shaken Not Stirred Productions, Richard Shelton, ShowPlanr, Nancy Sinclair, Oliver Slee, Steubenville Cultural Trust, Michael Tingley, Rosemary Tingley, Mathew Todd, Stephen Triffitt; Uckfield FM, Uckfield News, Veritas Entertainment, John Walsh, Gary Williams, Tony Williams, Andy Worden; *Yours Retro* Magazine, Michael Zinno; all of the record, film, television, and production companies, artists, producers, managers, and directors who have ever worked with Dean Martin over the decades; all the organizations and people too numerous to mention individually (or we may have inadvertently - and with apologies!   overlooked) who have assisted us and vice versa over the years…; Dean's fans and admirers wherever you are in the world; DMA members past and present…

…and the entire Dean Martin Family - thank you for all that you have done and continue to do.

For Dino.
In memoriam.

I also dedicate this work to my wife Irene and my children Carole and Elliot, to the memories of my grandparents Maria & Don Pasquale Verrechia, and to those of my parents Florinda & Henry.

Dino

Dear Bernard:

I must admit that I have not taken much interest in anyone
writing about me,but I guess there must be something there
for you to have been my club President for so many years.
So,I hope your writing will be successful,remember,save a
copy for me.

Your friend

Dino
Beverly Hills,
March 1995

CONTENTS

When You're Smiling

When I was asked in 2016 to write the foreword for the first edition of this exciting and unique recollection of Dean Martin, I felt honored, delighted and a little bit apprehensive.

What could I add that Bernard and Elliot hadn't already covered, each being not only huge fans and incredibly knowledgeable on the subject but also two people who have had a connection to Dean all their lives?

Then I remembered that in 2006 I had met with Elliot in a London restaurant to ask him if he would kindly come up with something for my tour brochure of my then-forthcoming UK (and subsequent US) tour of *That's Amore - A Celebration of Dean Martin & Friends*. Elliot titled his article 'Mark of Respect' which I guess summed up what I felt about Dean. So this is me returning the favor.

My own association with Dean Martin began in 2002. I was asked to audition for a touring show called *The Rat Pack - Live from Las Vegas*. To be perfectly honest, I was not sure I wanted to go on tour again as I had not long finished a 6-month run of another production. I had a vague idea of who the Rat Pack were, but there was to be no Peter Lawford or Joey Bishop in this show, just the triumphant trio of Frank, Dean and Sammy. In fact the full title of the show was *Frank, Dean and Sammy - The Rat Pack Live from Las Vegas* just in case anyone was in any doubt! The fact that all three artists had been dead sometime did not stop some people turning up to see who they thought were the real thing! I had also never heard of the show's producers who had made their name more through touring rock and roll shows - so I was pretty skeptical. My interest grew, however, when I googled Dean Martin and started listening to his studio albums and live show recordings.

I then knew I had to play this man.

I was offered the role and then the real research

began…every book and every album I could come across and, scouring a charity shop, I struck gold. 13 LP records including LIVE AT THE SUMMIT (for £30.00 I might add, so someone in the shop knew its worth!). The voice was so good, so distinctive, it would be easy to parody. Impersonators would do that - but I wanted to nail it properly, not overdo it. I listened and listened and listened. I am still listening!

Finding live footage on stage was more challenging. This was well before YouTube! My next door neighbor at the time had a friend who was a massive Dean Martin fan. He had a VHS copy of the concert from the Keele Theatre, St Louis recorded in 1965. This was filmed live and played on closed circuit across the US. It was Frank's idea. Johnny Carson hosted in absence of Joey Bishop, and it is a cracker. I played it non-stop. Dean stole the show. The camera loved him and he it. He knew where they all were, staring down its cold lens with calculation and insouciance. This was the guy, this is who men wanted to be or at least hang out with, and who women idolized. This was the guy who could tell Frank, 'No thanks pally, I'm not hanging out tonight. I shall be on the golf course at 6am!'   This was the guy who made it all look so easy because he had done it thousands of times before. He could play straight or be the funny guy. Years of being with Jerry told him that.

All I had to do now is bring this into the show. It would prove difficult because the script we had was challenging. But over time I changed it: the laughs came; the interaction seemed real and not forced; the camaraderie genuine; the band got in on the jokes; I tried new things each night and if the gag landed I gave it a mark out of ten. I wrote down hundreds of one liners he used (by this time I had amassed tapes of *The Dean Martin Show* and subsequently *The Dean Martin Celebrity Roasts*).

To cut a long story short, the tour was a huge success and we ended up transferring to London's West end for what was supposed to be a six-week run! We ended up doing nearly three years in four different theatres! They couldn't get enough of us.

I had already been toying with the idea of a solo Dean Martin show. I'd base this more on his TV specials with different guests and of course the glamour of his backing singers, the Golddiggers. Not a tribute, much more than that. Dean Martin had Ken Lane, his brilliant pianist, I had Barry Robinson, who shared my love for Dean and was fantastic to have on stage. We toured the UK. We played the London Palladium (in Dean's very footsteps). We had a great time. And two years later we toured the US! Me, a bloke from Swindon, Wiltshire, UK touring the US in a show I had conceived, playing one of the biggest stars to grace the planet! Heady stuff.

Well, here we are now and over a century ago, Dino Paul Crocetti was born in Steubenville, Ohio. He became Dean Martin and he could do everything. As his partner, director/producer and friend at NBC TV, Greg Garrison, said, 'Who else did it all? He played theatres, clubs, night clubs, he made million selling records, he was a super movie star, making straight appearances as well as comic, then he became perhaps the biggest star on TV the world has ever seen.' No wonder after 15 years I still find things to say and do.

That's a mark of respect.

I am so excited about this new edition of the book because I know Elliot had been dreaming of it for a long time, to bring his father's lifetime's work to completion. His parents, who both sadly passed away, would be so proud, his dad looking over his shoulder as he types away.

If you are a fan you will remember and celebrate Dean's work and life and if, like me, you enjoy reading biographies you will learn a great deal about a kind of artist, a kind of man, that we don't get too many of these days. And if you just happen to read this out of curiosity, well, you are in for a treat.

Thanks for letting me share a little bit of your dream, Elliot.

Always,

Mark Adams

ONE

C'est Magnifique

There is a comment written on a Dean Martin album sleeve that goes like this:

Turning an ear in the direction of the mellow Martin voice is like lifting your face to catch a breeze off the sea on a sweltering day; it beguiles and refreshes and relaxes you.

Everyone has their own idea of what Dean's voice does – no matter who they are. But there is much more to him than just his voice. He created himself, his own persona. And in the eyes of the public, that persona is uniquely Dean Martin. This is the public willing enough to support and acclaim any artist, but one equally cruel and critical as to quickly discredit them. It's a risk in show-business that what starts as a loving gathering of admirers can so easily turn the other cheek and destroy a career.

But let us not forget that the positive proof of success in Dean's business is not to receive acclaim just once or twice, but to maintain that success in order to stay at the top.

That takes some doing, especially with modern media. So often nowadays, celebrities are created from reality television and that, in many ways, perhaps waters down the skills of truly talented people out there. In Dean Martin's day that was never an issue – in fact, then, to succeed meant you had to *exceed*.

Of course, he had as many failures as successes with his share of great happiness and sadness along the way. That's the nature of life, and is not just restricted to the entertainment industry.

There has been much said about how glorious this person or that person is; who can do no wrong; who is perfection personified…all the false accolades that are bestowed upon such personalities as Dean Martin.

But when it all comes to the final reckoning, it's the genuine personality of Dean that shone through - in both his public and private lives.

All people have good and bad attributes that they present to the world, but in his case, he expressed sincerity and kindness in his work, allowing his personal feelings to take their place exactly as they should have done, correctly and diplomatically.

Dean Martin was an expressive, underrated, but sincere vocalist. He was sure there were better singers out there (he name-checked Gigli, Pavarotti and Caruso as those who could sing) and was also of the opinion that he himself didn't have the best singing voice there was.

But, sales of his recordings proved otherwise: he had the voice that sold and even today, years after his death, he still has.

Not every song met with resounding success, but Martin tasted a glorious cross-section that gave him the first-hand experience he needed to survive in the hard and fast business of entertaining the fickle public. He had consistency: he sang every song as if it had been written especially for him; in fact, you could never mistake that voice, or think him similar to anyone else. He behaved with cool professionalism on movie sets, cabaret stages, on radio, on television and in recording studios, as if he had done all of those things a million times before.

Yes, it is said that he was not the greatest in the world, but how many personalities had such a wide variety of talents - all packaged into one man?

Dean Martin was the ultimate personality, the total entertainer.

He worked with panache, and had talent and good looks that paid handsomely. That magnetic charm of his, coupled with his attitude to life, certainly attracted many to him.

Dean Martin was never a 'pop' star in the way we've come to understand the term; he didn't have that 'bobbysoxer' or 'swooning' type of adulation in his career, although he did have a large proportion of passionate admiration from millions of people around the world, almost since the day he started.

There has always been that certain amount of quiet sophistication, a gentle, if you like, support and appraisal from his global admirers. And while musical tastes and style have come and gone, returned, and gone yet again, Dean remained a popular choice throughout it all.

He sang just about every song that was offered to him in those early days, presenting them in his own inimitable style. He found his comedy style taking shape as he began a film career with Jerry Lewis. Once that partnership ended, Dean tried all types of parts and characters, choosing a different film company almost every time he made a movie.

Thus, he gained much more practical knowledge, confidence and training, experiencing the moods, methods and ideas of his peers, and the continuation of his regular cabaret and club appearances meant he still had that link with a live audience.

But there was only ever apple juice in that glass.

Dean preferred cabaret work above all else, Vegas being his main focus. The seats were always full and, long after he had left the stage as his theme 'Everybody Loves Somebody' played out, his audience clamored for more.

He had a high demand on television, his weekly series for NBC garnering viewing figures in their millions, with screenings (including syndication re-runs) virtually every week of the year.

With such saturation, it was very telling that Dean himself projected, in contrast, a laid-back air of sheer relaxation.

'The thing is not to try too hard,' he told me. 'If there is a chance you can be relaxed and assured in front of your audience, then they will come to accept you and the act you are delivering.'

The greatest proof of this was Dean's success; he was someone who made it by working hard while appearing to have a distinct devil-may-care attitude.

'If you are too firm and scripted, there's a danger that you may give off an air of insincerity. The result of that, then, is that perhaps your public will dismiss you for being just too serious. You've got to have fun - otherwise you might as well let them throw dirt on you.'

He was not known for hanging around for small talk after his work was completed. He rarely socialized with anyone he was working with, a stance which made getting to know Dean Martin virtually impossible.

'The real Dean Martin? Well, this is me just as you see me, I don't put on any act. I can't. This is the real person you see here.' Yet Dean remained, for his entire life, one of the most enigmatic characters imaginable. 'Look, I'm not trying to prove anything whatsoever with anyone. I'm singing, working, having a good time and getting paid well for it. Isn't that enough? I do the best I can, I can't do any more than that. I'd like to be remembered as a guy who did his best, pleased a damn lot of people and I hope that'll be what I'll always be remembered for. I sang some songs, acted here and there, but no way would I call myself exceptional. I just hope I did do my best for my audiences.'

Behind the façade, the public persona, he deplored changes of routine. He had long-term personal managers and staff with whom he kept a very close and exclusive bond. Rightly or wrongly, they shielded from him the burden of problems, of finance and business, allowing him the freedom to enjoy his work and his beloved golf, only matched by his adoration for watching television. It also, in some way, fueled his naivety.

His face was without expression if he was ever hurt or displeased with someone or something. If anyone gained Dean's confidence, it was never questioned, but should the reverse ever have occurred, it came swiftly. That said, he was not given to recrimination with anyone, any issues were dealt with quickly.

He gave the impression that he was aloof, cold and distant: but this is a distortion of the facts. Dean never confided in anyone or passed opinions on anyone and he flatly resented those who would attempt to spill out their troubles to him.

But where he became aware of a genuine difficulty, he would assist the person in the best way he knew, without any fuss and preferably without anyone ever knowing about it.

He rarely showed appreciation to associates, friends, or even family members. Away from the cameras he seldom shook hands (but when he did, his grip was tremendous), kissed on the cheek or patted on the back. But his loyalty is legendary and his working staff proved that by the long-serving devotion they showed over the years - and this is written from personal experience. The rewards that were not necessarily visible by working for him were truly gratifying and pleasing. When he did something for you, he never expected a thank you, rather he did not want to be thanked. Whether this was down to insecurity or embarrassment, only Dean knew.

But I do thank Dean. His legacy stands proud, even all these years later, amongst his peers, and that has to be the best tribute to anyone.

Having collected an almost diary-like mass of material on Dean's life since around 1952, many suggested over the years that I should write such a book on his life and career. I had always thought about it, wondering if I could do Dean justice. In 1994, with some trepidation, I finally decided that once I had received Dean's consent that I would try, but knew I, or he, didn't want a 'warts and all' sensationalist, scandal-filled exposé. There is enough of that in the tabloids already and Dean himself had been the target of much ridicule and scorn.

I simply wanted to tell his life story, directly and respectfully.

I was greatly privileged to be supported by this fine person and entertainer. I was immensely proud to call him my friend and this book is my way of saying thank you to him for all of that genuine time and friendship he gave me.

TWO

Arrivederci, Roma

The crossing was long, arduous, and the Atlantic a cruel mistress at the best of times, but the view from the steamships as they began their final stretch towards *L'isola delle lacrime* must have been as exhilarating as it was nerve-wracking.

L'isola delle lacrime: the place the Italians knew as the Island of Tears, and which was known to all as Ellis Island. But while this appeared to convey a sense of despair, for many Italian immigrants it was the beginning of a new life.

One immigrant in particular arrived in 1913, alone but for his professional status as a barber to bring him fortune. Having left Pescara (a fishing village on the north-east coast of Abruzzi, Italy) some weeks before to escape economic hardship, Gaetano Crocetti was just nineteen years of age. His elder brothers Archie and Joseph had already made the journey some years before.

The immigrant officials ordered Gaetano to stand in one line with other men while the women and children stood in another. Unnerving to him and the other new arrivals, many of whom could only speak Italian, it was this strict crowd control that had become a necessity in one of the world's busiest immigration stations.

The medical inspection followed, a harsh but certainly effective method by which to filter the sick, quarantine them, and return them to the immigration process once they were fit and well.

Crocetti had no such concerns. He passed the medical, and the US Public Health Service cleared him for the next stage of the process to become an American citizen, the immigration inspection itself.

This was a far more detailed procedure, almost an interrogation in some ways. Federal Law excluded convicted criminals and extreme radicalists and it was a requirement to understand the person's intention.

With this stage cleared, Gaetano was free to join his brothers in one of the nation's big steel towns, Steubenville. At that time, it was a thriving community and work was readily available.

Before the Great War, the US had molded itself into a land of freedom and happiness, and all who had passed through the conveyor belt on Ellis Island now looked for that large pot of gold at the end of the stars-and-stripes rainbow.

But Steubenville wasn't quite the land of plenty that Gaetano had hoped for. It wasn't by accident that it was nicknamed 'Little Chicago'. It was rife with gambling, prostitution and illicit liquor. Those in the mills worked hard and played harder; to survive, Gaetano had to adapt to this harsh way of living.

Yet his chosen trade meant he could position himself in the community as a reliable, much-needed figure. The barbershop that ultimately employed him, charging 25¢ for a haircut and shave, gave him the stability he needed.

Avoiding as much as he could the darker side of the town, one that stretched along the banks of the Ohio River, Gaetano, who by now was calling himself Guy in a bid to Americanize himself, met Angela Barra.

Although she was studying in the town's convent at the time of their first date, she had no strong allegiance to her faith that would mean she would ever enter a truly celibate life.

Guy's English was broken and he lacked the confidence to speak his adopted tongue fluently. Conversely, Angela could not speak a word of Italian, even though her parents had arrived on Ellis Island towards the end of the 19th century.

Irrespective of the language barrier, their love didn't so much bloom as explode and, besotted, they married soon after.

By 1914, and with Guy bringing home a respectable $30 a week, Angela gave birth to a son, William.

Life in the US for the Crocettis was comfortable, and both Guy and Angela had managed to accept and understand the American way of life, markedly different to that back in Pescara. Their home at 319 South Sixth Street was their place of solitude as the years went by; as their marriage strengthened, Angela became pregnant again.

But this time, it wasn't so straightforward.

On June 7th, 1917, Angela went into labor, prematurely and with some difficulty. The child was not expected to live and so was baptized almost immediately at St Anthony's church.

Whereas Bill had been given his moniker to reflect his parents' absorption into American society, his new baby brother Dino Paul was so-named to show pride in their Italian heritage.

THREE

I Got The Sun In the Mornin'

Growing up was tough for Dino, not because of any difficulties in his home life but because the poor neighborhood was challenging for kids and adults alike.

'I was pretty cocky and a mischievous kid. I felt I had to be,' he recalled.

As a result, times were hard, and not many of the family's possessions were new. Toys and even household items were sometimes hand-me-downs from friends or perhaps from another family they knew.

Further, Dino hated school. He simply couldn't see the point in it. He much preferred playing in the streets and on his bike. True, he could not hold a proper conversation and wasn't Grant Junior High's best student at reading or writing (whenever he ordained to turn up), but somehow - with a lot of assistance from his patient and attentive parents - he made it to Wells High School and, by the age of fourteen, had also attained a height of six feet with a fairly substantial frame. He wasn't your average-looking school boy and, together with dark wavy hair and a typical Roman nose, found that he was turning heads, too.

'I told my father one day that I wanted to leave school. He was pretty bewildered, even though he knew I didn't always go.'

Guy, naturally, wanted to know why, and asked if young Dino thought he knew more than the teachers. 'Yes,' came the determined response, and Guy begrudgingly agreed to pay for his son's initial enrolment at a barber's training school.

'I wasn't interested in spending the rest of my life cutting hair six days a week.'

So instead, after he had left his school in his Tenth Grade in June 1936, his Uncle Joseph gave him his very first job: as an assistant on his milk round.

Five weeks later, he'd had enough and tried his hand in a

soda store but boredom quickly set in again and he found a position as a gas station attendant. With more gasoline on the ground and over the vehicles than in them, he soon walked away.

Somewhat desperate, his brother William (everyone called him Bill) managed to wrangle him into the Weirton Steel Mill in West Virginia, quite a drive from Steubenville. Dino tried not to let Bill down and seemed to settle into a routine for a few months.

'A four-ton coil of hot steel narrowly missed me one day. I didn't know if it was me not paying attention or something the other guys had done by accident, but I got out of there like a shot and never went back.'

Now unemployed and with little opportunity to earn any income, he fooled around with his old school pals, playing pool, swimming in the Ohio river, with snatches of basketball whenever he had the chance.

But he was very restless, still wandering around town looking at the way the gamblers worked in the bars, and he fell in with a crowd that taught him the ways of pettiness. This society that he found alluring led him to the circle of amateur boxing, specifically under the tutelage of Tony Romano, a small-time time fight manager who convinced Dino there was good money in boxing. Persuaded, nineteen-year-old Dino became a prize-fighter with some enthusiasm, earning the name 'Kid Crochet' in the process. Winning twenty-four out of his thirty bouts as a welterweight, he'd worked himself up as a semi-professional for about ten to twenty dollars a match.

But a bent nose, wrecked hands (his manager knew nothing of properly binding his hands under the gloves) and the misconception that being a boxer would more easily win him girls, tired the restlessness within Dino once more.

He moved to a steady capacity as a delivery boy, but it was bootleg whisky he was carrying around town and occasionally to Canonsburg, Pennsylvania. Dino doesn't recall if his parents truly knew what it was he was doing.

'I prayed a lot in those days,' he said, supporting the family's

Catholic faith, 'and I'm sure they would have called in the priest had they found out, so I got myself a job as a clerk.'

But the Rex Cigar Store that employed him was a front for one of Steubenville's biggest gambling houses. It was considered almost routine then that a tobacco store would have a gambling concession and, aside from his normal capacity, Dino would go into the back rooms and watch the big players gamble. He'd stay around and play with the chips and the roulette wheel, learning very quickly how to deal and play cards with expertise. When the store realized that he was beating them at their own game, they made him a croupier.

If you ever saw Dino playing cards or dealing at the tables in Las Vegas or in a film you could see that precise expertise on display.

With his skill at the time, he was earning enough each week to enable him to help pay off his parents' extended mortgage and to get his brother into college. But still, he looked beyond what he had, still pining for something that was missing in his life, leaving him unfulfilled.

Dino used to sing on many an occasion (even during those rare times when he assisted his father in the barbershop), at home or wherever he could - even while at the cigar store.

'Several of my pals used to encourage me to sing almost anywhere and they even would persuade me to sing a song or two at parties. Damn it, it was terrifying but I got up there and did it.'

It was these tentative steps in the early 40s that made Dino realize singing was a way to express himself, backed by a small combo that always played at these places, usually at Reeds Mill Roadhouse or Walker's Nightclub.

With his pleasant baritone style, it wasn't long before a bandleader called Ernie McKay offered Dino the position as regular vocalist at Walker's. However, he was in no way impressed or attracted by this offer.

'Why would I be? I was already collecting a lot more that the $50 he was offering me.'

A combination of legitimate earnings plus those 'extras' he

was earning at Rex's cigar store meant he was fetching home in the region of $125 a week.

But his refusal only fueled a streak of depression.

For the first time, he'd realized what he wanted to do but saw no financial gain in it, instead living day-to-day in a job that was unfulfilling and directionless.

'I didn't want to talk to anyone or anybody. And before I knew it, no one wanted to talk to me. I hated it. It took me a while to start talking to my buddies again and they told me I'd been a fool to not accept McKay's offer. And what they'd been planning behind my back I wasn't happy about but I got around it and accepted it.'

Between them, his friends, namely Izzy McGregor, Dom Gilbertoni, Tony Tarantino and Harry Barbra, had been working out a deal in which they would support Dino's singing career, providing he would give them a cut from any future earnings.

'How could I turn that down? I went back to McKay and said yes. But he told me I needed a new name. Nobody could say Crocetti right so Ernie said I was now going to be Dino Martini. I wasn't happy with that but I guess he knew what he was doing.'

He stayed with McKay for six months on inland tours and it was on one of those stop-overs that Dino was spotted by another bandleader, Sammy Watkins, who offered him a cool $100 a week.

In a precursor of Dino's future management choices, he signed the contract without reading the small print (much to McKay's chagrin) and was now committed to a seven-year stretch with 10 per cent of his earnings to pay agent fees. Further, Watkins didn't like 'Dino Martini' and wanted a more American-sounding and easier to remember moniker. So, in a change that stayed with him for the rest of his life, 23-year old Dino Crocetti became, to the world, Dean Martin.

One of the Sammy Watkins Band appearances took them to the Hollenden Hotel in Cleveland and it was here that another chapter of Dean's life would begin.

'I just couldn't believe it. There was this girl in the audience. Man, her eyes just sparkled.'

Elizabeth Anne McDonald was staying at the hotel with her father and, intent on finding out who she was, Dean purposely kept bumping in to her: in the hotel lobby, down a corridor, in and out of the entrance, just anywhere he could catch a glimpse and even try and talk to her. But Elizabeth, or just Betty, was coy, annoyed and seemingly uninterested in this cocky Italian lounge singer.

'She told me to go away and that I was annoying her. I don't think she ever said she would tell her father! But I saw something behind her brashness and so I just asked her out on a date. She said yes.'

Dean and Betty saw much of themselves in each other. They both had a shy confidence about them and didn't hold back in telling people what they thought. She was a few years younger than him and was Irish-born to a liquor manufacturer in Morion, Pennsylvania, and had not travelled very much in her life up to that point, so a mere chance meeting at The Hollenden started off an intense romance.

They'd been dating for three months when Dean told Betty that the band was about to take to the road on a long tour on one-night appearances across the country. This seemed to point to their romance being doomed from quite early on.

Naturally needing the money, Dean had no choice but to prepare himself for working away from home, spending indefinite periods in hotel rooms, on the road, with late nights and all the unaccustomed routines that would come with his new and chosen career and lifestyle.

For Betty, she wanted perhaps more than Dean was able to give her, a settled home-life and stability. But she saw his passion when he was up on stage, and knew that she couldn't suppress him.

For these two lovers, parting seemed like the end of the world. Dean's work was inevitably to stand in their way, and he had chosen his future. However, he wanted Betty so very much, and there was only one solution, however drastic it proved to be.

They went back to Steubenville and Dean promptly showed Betty off to his stakeholder friends who had continually convinced him he was a better singer than he thought he was. With their approval of the dark, Irish girl on his arm, he went home to tell his parents he was getting married.

Mama and Papa Crocetti fully approved of her.

With only a handful of days left before the band started their tour, Dean had another problem: the Catholic Church insisted on the wedding bands being posted for at least six weeks before the ceremony. But luck was on their side and Betty's own priest gave special dispensation for the couple to have an immediate ceremony. The families, friends and the complete Sam Watkins Band all gathered together for the joining of husband and wife the very next day, on October 2nd, 1940 at St. Ann's Church in the McDonalds' home town of Cleveland.

Dean's mother made the bride's dress, and the reception was a fairly grand affair for those days, considering neither party were high earners.

While desperately in love, Betty was not sure of the future herself. Would her new husband be a success? Would he really want to stay in this business? She could obviously not see the course they were both to take but she saw he was happy and accepted the life she had chosen as a band-wife, following Dean around the country, their first stop being Louisville, Kentucky. His attention to the band, however, more often than not overrode his matrimonial responsibilities and he would often stay behind after shows playing cards in his dressing room. Nevertheless, Betty announced to Dean one evening late October 1941 that she was pregnant. Her news didn't make him change his approach and she began to feel somewhat isolated, and that there was only one person truly in the marriage.

Craig was born on June 29th, 1942, but from then on things became increasingly difficult for Betty: Dean was always away on tour, and the little home they'd set up in Cleveland was mostly absent of a father. He was travelling frequently now and even if he was able to go home after a night's performance, he would normally roll in in the small hours, the allure of card-playing never leaving him. Gambling and drinking seemed much more preferable – and fun – than being the family man.

FOUR

Just In Time

One night in 1943, Dean was playing cards with Merle Jacobs, the MCA agent who always organized the band's bookings. He suggested that Dean went out on his own: he was convinced that the days of the Italian-American crooner were not yet at their peak.

'After all, that skinny kid from Hoboken had just made it at the Riobamba so perhaps Merle was on to something,' Dean told me. As a result of 'that skinny kid''s success, agents and managers were all scurrying around looking anywhere for Italian 'baritones', ballad singers who could throw a good tune. Merle told Dean he was excellent material for nightclubs. Dean was convinced, and Merle suggested he tried something in the New York area; he wanted to get known and, after all, if he made it there, he could make it anywhere.

Like most young male singers of that period, he could carry a tune reasonably well and did imitations of Bing Crosby and other popular radio singers, but at the same time developed a pleasant and easy-going style of his own.

Anxiety almost getting the better of him, he did nevertheless go to Club Riobamba at 151, East 57th Street, New York City, taking the stage not long after the same skinny kid had finished his set. The kid was, of course, Frank Sinatra.

That first evening was indelibly engraved on Dean's mind: 'I still remember what I was wearing: a light blue dinner jacket and a maroon tie. Damn, I was so nervous that I imagined the audience thought I was singing a rhumba and had castanets hidden in my knees.' To make things worse, it was celebrity night and the audience was almost entirely composed of Hollywood stars. 'Wherever I looked I saw these famous people looking right back at me. I felt like a fraud.'

Unbeknownst to him, however, a small-time performer was sitting at the bar to avoid the cover charges on the tables. There to watch Sinatra, he was known for miming along to records, an act that didn't seem to show any particular signs of remuneration or recognition. Jerry Lewis was his name and he'd missed Sinatra's performance, not aware that the running order had changed. He didn't ask for his money back.

Instead, he watched, entranced by the sight of this unknown who could sing to an audience so easily and with what seemed such confidence.

Then, sometime later, whilst appearing at Loew's Theatre (where Jerry was also on the bill), Dean was seen to be clutching something in his hand. Curious, Jerry, who had already finished his act and wanted to watch this new singer again, wondered what it was. He later found out that it was a little white crucifix.

In the next few months, Dean and Jerry occasionally crossed paths on their way to dressing rooms or exiting theatres. Jerry was quite taken with this laid-back, easy-going Italian, and Dean often found messages from Lewis scrawled on various dressing-room walls, mirrors, or even on make-up dressers.

'Hi, Dean, I was here, hope you do well,' he would write from time to time. Dean would ignore nearly every one.

During Dean's time at the Club Riobamba, Irving Zussman, a public relations man, spoke to him at length and suggested he stay in the New York area for work, meaning he would receive a steady $400 a week, allowing him to move his wife and son into rented accommodation at the London Terrace apartments, some of the finest buildings in Lower Manhattan.

The reviews in the New York press of Dean's Riobamba appearances were abominable. One reported that he wore an ill-fitting tuxedo, had a reasonably fair voice but had a lot to learn, and would seem to be lost without a microphone - and this was one of the kindest.

His audiences dwindled and, after a few weeks, Dean found himself out of work, debts growing, and Betty pregnant for a second time.

They moved to cheaper accommodation but he owed the London Terrace so much in back rent that they claimed a minimum of $30 a week until it was cleared.

Dean sent Betty and Craig to her parents in Pennsylvania to have their second baby. When Claudia was born, her father was appearing in Montreal and unable to get home. He was singing in second-rate clubs (also on the East Coast) and worked his way around numerous venues for months whilst Betty stayed with her parents.

With less than $200 a week coming in now, he was seriously in debt to MCA and everyone else with his cards, gambling and the occasional gratification with women, in no way allowing him to live any sort of reasonable life. He was beginning to wonder if this was all worth the trouble and stress. It still didn't stop him.

Lou Perry, an independent agent, saw Dean at the Riobamba and was sure that this young man had a bright future. A fellow Italian, Dean said that Lou '...was the only guy who seemed to have this idea about me or any faith in me at all. I was spending more money than I was making so why the hell he was interested I never knew.'

Dean was tied by contract to MCA but Lou Perry found out that they were only too pleased to dispose of this person from their roster; he was a chain around their neck and they were more than willing to sell Dean to the highest bidder.

Lou's faith was indeed so strong that decided he would buy out Dean's contract, and paid off his debts to clear him completely from MCA.

But Dean had no bookings anywhere, was hopelessly in debt with so many people (including his friends back in Steubenville) and had nowhere to live. Further, his devotion to Betty, Craig and Claudia was far from perfect.

Lou lived in the Bryant Hotel on the corner of 54th Street & Broadway, a low-class hovel of a building catering for the lower-bracket performers in show business. Perry's part of the building was one room with just a double bed and a table, the full sum total of Lou's belongings, but he still took pity on Dean and invited him to share the room. Dean at least now had a roof over his head.

Every so often, devoted Betty would come and see her

husband and share some time with him. Lou would discreetly disappear for a while, allowing them to spend a few hours together, but other than the occasional visit, she would see little of her husband.

She was living a desperately sad life, hardly ever seeing Dean, and managing to survive mainly because she happened to be at her parents' home. Her husband only managed to send sporadic amounts by borrowing money from Lou, who was also paying for all of Dean's food, laundry and anything else needed for his day-to-day existence.

But deep down, Lou believed there was talent there, that Dean had that something, but needed that stroke of luck to get him going. He stood by Dean, willing to make sacrifices.

'I didn't get what he saw. I was a bum.'

One thing Lou thought could improve this young man's looks even more was an operation on his nose. Dean was a reasonably handsome guy, but his nose was rather large and it had seen some action back when he was Kid Crochet. Lou thought the idea of a new nose could maybe work to his advantage, so he managed to borrow enough dollars for a plastic surgeon.

The operation in New York was successful and both Dean and Lou were more than pleased with the result, the young singer feeling a bit more confident now that perhaps his future may turn to better things.

'I kind of hoped this surgery was a turning point. I guess it was.'

Meanwhile, back in her uneventful life, Betty was suffering in the atmosphere of her parents' home, and becoming increasingly upset when her parents and friends told her she was a fool. That her husband didn't care that much for her was clear; he rarely supported her in a proper manner.

Angela and Guy Crocetti even offered their home for Betty, and upset, frustrated and with financial problems mounting up, she took the decision to move over to Steubenville for a change of atmosphere, moving in with her parents-in-law.

She demanded Dean make more effort with her and the

children, but he wasn't interested. He had enveloped himself in work and had found the attention from female followers to be rewarding. He wasn't faithful to Betty and his gambling never wavered.

In his head, he simply didn't have time to be a husband and a father.

Then he got drafted for military service.

He was stationed at Akron in Ohio in training for fourteen months, and hated every minute of it until the army doctors discovered he had developed a hernia. He did not actually leave the base during his tenure so never saw active service as such. Instead, he came out rather pleased with his invalidity and went home at last to his family.

Perhaps it was due to a shortage of artists because of America's part in WWII, or just sheer luck, but by 1945 he had put in so many appearances locally and places further afield such as Chicago, New Jersey and the like, that he never brought in less than $250 a week. He peaked at $1000 a week.

Perhaps Lou's faith in him was not unfounded after all.

This was way above anything New York had given him overall, but he was still in debt, with hordes of people chasing him. Family life was not at its best either, letting Betty have money as and when he could spare any to send back home – his situation had improved but the way he lived his life hadn't altered one iota.

Dean wore a camel-hair coat in those days, and it proved to be something of a beacon, certainly as far as one particular person was concerned.

He was leaving the Belmont Plaza one lunchtime and spoke a few words as usual with the doorman. Walking nearby was 19-year old Jerry Lewis.

Jerry, of course, remembered Dean from the Riobamba. Dean didn't even notice Jerry was there at the Plaza, and Jerry never got the chance to say anything.

That camel-hair coat, or rather the man inside it, was the path to Jerry's new world – but neither of them knew it.

On a cold March morning sometime later, Dean and Lou

were walking down Broadway. Lou, knowing, of course, most of the talent in the area, spotted singer Sonny King on the other sidewalk. As they crossed 49th Street, Lou called out to Sonny, beckoning him over. But Sonny wasn't alone. Lou introduced Dean to the singer, then turned to Sonny's companion.

'Jerry Lewis, meet Dean Martin. Dean, meet Jerry.'

FIVE

Never Before

Dean felt Jerry was a bright little kid, but hadn't thought much more about him since their occasional brushes past each other over the last few months. Other than those notes that Jerry had left Dean here and there, neither of them had had time to really talk to each other, and Dean had been somewhat dismissive before: they moved in different circles, and their acts were miles apart.

Sonny King suggested they all get together for a drink one evening.

It was Dean who did most of the talking, spilling out much of his past history for what it was worth, all the while Jerry hanging on to his every word, enthralled by his new-found friend's exploits.

These were strange times: both men were only just starting out and getting to know who they were themselves, let alone exposing their respective talents to the world.

Yet here they were, in Sonny's rooms, performing for each other. Sonny and Lou had both thought each of their acts was good in his own right, although all four of them knew there was one hell of a way to go before any substantial sort of success would be realized.

Jerry had more or less been performing since he was six so it was natural for him to have ambitions of becoming a star, but thirteen years later, Joseph Levitch was still struggling to be as internationally famous as Jerry Lewis.

He was born March 15, 1927 in Newark, New Jersey, the son of show people who had hoped he wouldn't follow their profession. As a child, Jerry was always alone: his parents were forever moving from place to place in show business.

In 1944, he married Patti Calonica, who had taken the professional surname of Palmer when appearing with the Jimmy Dorsey orchestra. Jerry's determined campaign for

Patti's hand reached a successful climax when she discovered a pair of tiny baby shoes hanging from her dressing-room light. There was a note attached: *What do you say we get married and fill these?*

As a boy, Dean had also had big ambitions of getting somewhere and being somebody, but after a routine life of playing around with his school buddies, owning his first bike (even if it was second-hand) and a brief period as a Boy Scout for Steubenville Troop Ten (where he was the troop drummer) he still wondered, even now, what would become of his dreams.

'I liked playing cowboys when I was a kid. I loved playing the drums – but I was never gonna be a Buddy Rich – and I loved to sing. Sure, I'd spin Russ Columbo and Bing Crosby records on my wind-up player and sing along with them but, man, I still wish I could sing like Bing.'

Dean found singing an easy way to express himself and Lou still had that faith in him, so much so that he secured a brief recording contract with Diamond Records.

Although Dean's first recorded performance was in Chicago, August 1944, with the Jerry Sears orchestra on a radio show, 'All of Me' became his debut commercial 78rpm single.

'I think we sold about eight copies! I'm sure they put the hole in the side of the disc instead of in the middle!' he later joked, but you could already hear the strength he had as a recording artist. Accompanied by Nat Brandywine and his Orchestra, Dean's tonal approach was pitched lower than his later output, but listening to those early recordings, they have that clearly definable and very recognizable Dean Martin sound.

The original issue of 'All of Me' (recorded July 15th, 1946) is now of course an extremely rare collector's item.

Metro-Goldwyn-Mayer and Columbia Pictures both showed some interest in this new singer, with a view to him appearing in musicals. This genre was a great money-spinner at that time and guaranteed international exposure for the artists once those films had been seen around the world.

But both companies rejected him: it seemed that he did not have the correct phrasing and speed when he read the scripts given him and, in fact, some later reports stated he was almost illiterate and just could about hold a conversation.

Lou managed to book him into the Glass Hat in the Belmont Plaza, where Jerry was appearing on the bill. He was presenting his usual mime act with records and still remained unsuccessful.

Dean and Jerry's paths didn't cross that much during the few weeks Dean was booked there and, once his tenure had finished, he was out of work once more. Meanwhile, Jerry had moved on to the 500 Club in Atlantic City, continuing his act.

But Jerry was unhappy with the faltering start of his career and was desperate to improve.

He'd been corresponding with Dean by postcard and, when Paul 'Skinny' D'Amato (the club's owner, so-named because of his stick-thin silhouette that made even Jerry look overweight) threatened to end Lewis' run, Jerry immediately thought of Dean.

He suggested to Abner J. Greshler (his own agent) if Dean could be booked in there for work, thinking that somehow, they could support each other's solo acts.

Abbey agreed and Dean arrived July 25th, 1946 in Atlantic City.

But Skinny thought Dean was terrible on his own, almost as bad as Jerry was, and suggested they either do something together or they'd be out on the street.

Dean and Jerry went to their dressing room (a nail on the wall!) and tried to think about what could be done.

Jerry had always been highly creative and so it's no surprise that it was he who came up with the initial, albeit crude, idea of Dean simply starting to sing while Jerry would follow and make a 'lot of noise' as he put it.

'Jerry put on this busboy's jacket and out he came. He'd juggle, run around off-stage, throw dishes, drop trays while I sang. We'd just create chaos.'

Amongst the still and cautious audiences was Sophie Tucker,

a Ukrainian-born American singer/comedian otherwise known by the nickname 'The Last of the Red-Hot Mamas', and upon her laughing out loud, this was the cue for the rest of the public to laugh at this pair of lunatics with their act.

And laugh they did: Jerry went mad turning over customers' empty (and full) plates; switching off all the lights so that the waiters dropped even more trays; squirting soda down the girls' blouses; cutting off the men's ties – and ended up getting most of them to join up together to make a long conga line.

With a look of horror and shock on Skinny's face, everyone loved them and patrons were queueing up right around the block every night, waiting to see this madcap pair everyone was raving about.

Skinny made the pair do their act six times a night, upped their salary to $750 a week and kept them there for six weeks.

Dean and Jerry would come up with inventive ways to bring more people to see them: Jerry made out to be drowning off shore one afternoon, and Dean rushed to his 'rescue'. With crowds gathered, including the lifeguard, they'd both jump and declare to everyone that they were at the 500 Club that night!

They had blasted themselves on to the scene and it seemed that nothing could stop them.

SIX

Hanging Around With You

With World War II over, people were looking for some pleasure and difference in their lives and live entertainment was, whilst a luxury, certainly a prime objective.

Martin and Lewis perfectly filled the bill; they arrived just at the right time and were able to realize those dreams for their audiences. But there was a problem: Dean was tied to his contract with Lou Perry for another couple of years yet, so they could not call themselves a team or even a working partnership.

They were in the Havana Madrid on $1,500 a week, split evenly. Following their raging success in Atlantic City, Abbey got them into Latin Casino in Philadelphia. But Dean was billed on the top spot with Jerry as the extra attraction, most likely Lou's doing, something that Abbey was not happy about.

When I asked him what happened with Lou, Dean wouldn't be drawn on the subject but clearly some behind-the-scenes wrangling meant that Abbey Greshler was, before long, in full charge of the act, with a $4,000 pay-off to Lou.

'Martin and Lewis' was born.

All the help and assistance Lou had given Dean in the formative years had kept him from many debtors, but now it was big money coming in and things were going to be so different from now on.

Dean had become a father for the fourth time (their third child, Gail, had been born on April 11th, 1946). Deana had arrived August 27th, 1948 and, although he saw Betty as often as he could, things were still far from pleasant in their family. He was spending almost ninety percent of his time away from home and although the family was better-supplied with money now that Dean was fast approaching the big time, this did not compensate for his lack of devotion.

Work came thick and fast, including radio shows —which

gave them an even wider audience --and Dean found that as well as the public liking him for his comedy, he particularly noticed the applause he received when he did his uninterrupted solo songs.

His first love was singing, and from time-to-time, he privately considered whether he would ever make it to a recording studio again.

'Those previous early attempts of mine had proved totally useless and I really thought that they were most likely lost in some vault somewhere.'

He organized the move for Betty and the children to New York, enabled by a much-improved income (at one time $15,000 a week, the radio contract giving Dean his half-share of the £30,000 Martin and Lewis were earning). Television also beckoned and their debut on Ed Sullivan's *Toast of The Town* on June 20th, 1948 was followed by their appearance at the Copacabana which sealed their success: two or three lines of people wrapped twice around the block, absolutely desperate to see these two talented and marvelous entertainers with a brilliant new, outrageous approach.

"Variety", the trade tabloid, gave them accolades and sometimes gave Dean a better review of his tonsils than they did of the team. Chesterfield-sponsored radio shows ran for ten weeks, and more TV spots followed – including the famed 7pm Sunday night 'Colgate Comedy Hour'. Every show caused havoc and jammed telephone switchboards all over the country.

Even in those early days, Abbey was also convinced, just like Lou Perry before him, that Dean could become great on his own, but everyone demanded the double act: they wanted the singer, yes, but they also wanted the comedy act.

With Betty and the children now in a ten-room rented apartment, things were really looking up in many ways; she had become great friends with Jerry and his new wife Patti. The four would frequently spend time together and go out dining Italian.

But while on the road, Dean was not too hesitant in dating

any girl his brown eyes noticed wherever and whenever he wanted.

He naturally left a trail of broken hearts in various places, with one instance of a certain Miriam Davelle who had followed him around as far as California. She later committed suicide, although no explanation was ever found suggesting any affair or connection with him at all, other than media gossip.

Nevertheless, Dean's libido never wavered and Jerry, disapproving, would on occasion mention his partner's flirtations to Patti.

Money seemed little object now and he had already moved his parents over to Long Beach in California and wanted to do the same with Betty. He felt that a move to California would be ideal for his career and had never really liked the East, particularly New York.

It was now 1948.

While working at Slapsie Maxie's in Hollywood, both Jerry and Dean began talking to one of the owners, Mack Gray, Dean pointedly mentioning his Diamond recordings. That September, Gray secured him a new recording contract with Capitol.

Martin and Lewis were highly-acclaimed, and considered at the top of their game now, and being based in Hollywood meant they attracted people like Cary Grant, Edward G. Robinson, Bette Davis and Darryl F Zanuck. They also had renowned brothers Dick and Joe Stabile and their orchestra backing them.

But amidst all the glitz and glamour, Dean's marriage was, unsurprisingly, in trouble. His affairs with other women was becoming out of hand, although one in particular had caught his heart.

'She'd won the title of 'Queen of the Orange Bowl' and I presented her with a huge bouquet of flowers on that New Year's Eve [1948]. I fell in love with her there and then.'

Nineteen-year old Jeanne Biegger was an art teacher at Miami University and Dean spent as much time as he could with her, incredibly avoiding Hollywood gossip columns. But Patti and Jerry knew, and had decided to keep this romance as far from Betty as they could.

Joseph Hazen (business partner to Hal Wallis, who had produced *Casablanca, Now, Voyager,* and *The Maltese Falcon* among others) had seen the Martin and Lewis act and signed the pair to a five-year contract for seven films at $100,000 a picture. Further, both Hazen and Wallis agreed to allow them to freelance one picture a year for their own company, York Productions, that Dean and Jerry had set up a few weeks back. This meant they were able to make their own films whenever they wished, agreeing that distribution would be through Paramount Pictures. Such was the faith in this double-act.

Yet Hal Wallis admitted that he had only seen Dean and Jerry live and not limited by a script. He'd recently bought the rights from CBS Radio to the very successful comedy series *My Friend Irma* and, after much discussion and screen-tests (nine on Jerry's part, mainly because the original radio stories didn't lend themselves to the physical comedy Jerry did), roles were penciled in for both stars.

Released in 1949 and directed by George Marshall, who'd cut his teeth on silent movies, *My Friend Irma* tells the story of Irma (Marie Wilson) and Jane (Diana Lynn), two working girls who room together in Mrs O'Reilly's apartment house. Ambitious Jane wants to marry a millionaire and lands a job as a secretary to one, Richard Rhinelander (Don DeFore), who falls for her. Irma loves Al (John Lund), an unemployed dreamer who wants to get rich quick and easy (via Rhinelander). Al meets two talented performers, Steve (Dean) and Seymour (Jerry) and promotes them to Broadway. Meanwhile, Irma, an incessant bungler, tries to help everyone. Filmed on a budget of $500,000, it made over $3 million. Martin and Lewis' film career had begun in earnest.

Jerry was originally cast as Al, a role inhabited by English actor John Brown for the radio series, but it soon became clear that he wasn't right for the part. Lund stepped in and took over while Jerry, concerned that he would be dropped from production altogether, suggested he be the sidekick to Dean's character. Seymour was written specially for him and so cemented Martin and Lewis' film partnership style from the very outset.

When Jerry went to Paramount's wardrobe department, the studio dresser, following the production team's guidance, found the oldest looking suit on the rack. As Jerry slipped it onto his slight frame, he noticed the name written on the label: Jack Benny, 1937. Jack had the suit made for him when he was working on Paramount's *College Holiday*.

Received by fans and critics alike, gossip columnist Walter Winchell considered Martin and Lewis to be the best two-man comedy team since the vaudeville/Broadway pairing of Gallagher and Shean, nearly thirty years before.

For Dean, things had finally crumbled at home. He had no hate for Betty but had fallen out of love with her. His infidelity had fueled that, but he admitted that he'd fallen so hopelessly in love with Jeanne that he was prepared to make the break from his wife forever. His unhappiness in his private life spilled out into his working relationship with Jerry, and already arguments were brewing.

Usual US marriage laws in the 1940s stated that persons had to wait one year for a divorce to become final before any further marriage can take place, but Jeanne and Dean were so impatient that they actually asked Elizabeth if she would mind going to Nevada for a special 'quickie' divorce. After eventual consultation with her lawyer, Betty agreed and left for Las Vegas, the four children in care of Dean's parents.

Angela and Guy were deeply upset by the decision and manner of their youngest son. Their disappointment plain, string-willed Dean had, nevertheless, made up his mind – that was that, no discussion.

Betty and Dean were divorced August 24th and just over a week later, on September 1st, 1949, Jeanne Biegger legally bound herself to Dean at Herman Hover's Beverly Hills home. Jerry was best man. (Hover was the owner of Giro's, a venue where Dean and Jerry had appeared countless times with great success.)

The newlyweds moved into a large house on the corner of Lomitas and Alpine Drive in Beverly Hills – but there was no honeymoon. Dean's time with his new wife was spent on a mad, rushed tour around the country promoting *My Friend Irma*.

Was this already a case of history repeating itself, with Dean focusing so much time on his career?

Although his first-ever Capitol release, "The Money Song", was with Jerry, Dean managed to record a few songs...which one could say more 'escaped' than were released: not exactly gems for him to be enthralled about, but singles that certainly increased his bank balance.

Every little helped, of course, because payments now had to be made regularly to Betty in addition to the payments towards the debts that had occurred in the earlier years of his career.

Now in the millionaire class, Dean and Jerry had a good footing in order to gain more confidence, and while the pair were carrying on their publicity for *My Friend Irma*, Paramount were working on their next film appearance.

Abbey was also pushing hard at NBC Television for them to appear on the network, because although Martin and Lewis were box-office smashes nationwide, broadcasting had not really boosted them nationally and he felt the time was now ripe for them to be presented across all states; the films and records would do their own thing around the world, but this fairly new medium of television reached people in their homes.

True, their debut had caused a stir, but Abbey wanted regular appearances, as many as possible, to promote hard the image of these two talented men.

Paramount moved forward to *make My Friend Irma Goes West* in 1950, with Dean's Capitol contract letting him have most of the songs he would sing in future films issued on that label as a matter of course. This was a good way for Dean to have a double-dose of remuneration, something he was to continue to do for almost his entire film career.

This sequel again starred Marie Wilson, Diana Lynn with John Lund, and listed Martin and Lewis as supporting cast with guest star Corrine Calvet. Hal Walker directed this time, and it followed much of the same storyline as the previous film with the luckless Irma helping those around her. A Hollywood film tycoon signs up Steve and Seymour, but turns out to be a racketeer.

Both films had that scatty comedy approach, where the established stars were somewhat overshadowed by the new comedy team; indeed, you just watched for those first moments when Dean and Jerry appeared on the screen.

Dean and Jerry continued to make various appearances and publicity tours to build up their very popular image even more. Dean always went along with the tremendous amount of practical jokes and antics that his partner Jerry got up to at different times and places. Their regular orchestra leader Dick Stabile was their favorite target and over a short period he had lost eight tuxedos, which were quite literally destroyed during part of the nightclub act. His shoes, he found very often glued to the ceiling in the dressing room. Jerry was the main instigator of these drastic ideas, but Dean was just as bad (or good, depending on the mood of the victim and the situation), such as the instance when they were in an office on Broadway and yelled out the window to the crowds below that they were being murdered. Naturally, the police arrived and had to smash the door down, only to find Dean and Jerry sitting reading magazines.

That was the happy, odd madness of Martin and Lewis, America's favorite pair. No one was safe from their pranks (which all helped with publicity as well, of course) not even the Paramount top executives, even practicing jokes on each other.

This attitude, mixed with their presentation, was what made the team tick; it was totally unique. No one could come anywhere near the art and finesse that was Dean and Jerry. It was all a part of a pleasant history that happened in my own lifetime and I am so glad to have been there at the start, watching Dean's fledgling career with adoration.

With Dean now recording such songs as "I'll Always Love You", "Rock-A-Bye Your Baby'"and others, he was beginning to be noticed by the record-buying public. His initial attempts at Capitol were marred by the musicians' strike in 1948, where he travelled with Jerry to Mexico to lay down the tracks.

But his recordings after that were all recorded at the Capitol Tower in Hollywood and Vine, a magnificent and unique structure on the Californian skyline that looked like a pile of discs on top of each other.

York Productions commenced operations with *At War With the Army* partly financed through Screen Associates, organized by Abbey. Dean and Jerry's natural top billing allowed them more screen time. Released in January 1951, as song-and-dance pals prior to drafting, Puccinelli (Dean) and Korwin (Jerry) clash when they become Sergeant and Private respectively. A slim story but nevertheless one that allowed Dean to showcase his singing talents. Dick Stabile had a part in this film as Pokey, with Hal Walker directing plus Mack David and Jerry Livingston writing the songs. Dean's girlfriend in this little romp was Polly Bergen, who would also make a name for herself later.

The Stooge went into production just prior to *At War With the Army* but stayed on the Paramount shelf for some time. Directed by Norman Taurog, Jerry played Ted, the stooge to Dean's conceited variety singer, Bill, and in a plotline that would repeat itself over most of their pictures together, the two conflicting characters would reconcile at the finale. Polly Bergen would return to accompany them.

And Dean was neglecting Jeanne.

Touring, filming, recording, or playing golf (a pastime he had been introduced to by Lou Perry and which easily countered his hatred of confined spaces, having been stuck in an elevator or two in his time - giving rise to his claustrophobia), Dean left her alone many times in the first phase of their marriage. Further, he had begun to detest parties and meeting people, and had no real friends. Jeanne was also being snubbed by Patti Lewis, who had seen what Betty had gone through.

But Jerry told Patti that Dean was his best friend and that he loved him, so Patti eventually came around to Jerry's way of thinking and relented in her animosity towards Jeanne.

But Dean was so very much a loner. He worked the way he wanted to, but any spare time he did have, he spent watching television at home (or, of course, playing golf). He just didn't want to be involved with any problems that arose with arranging recording dates or his next call time on a film set – he just wanted to know where and when to turn up. Even domestic chores disinterested him.

SEVEN

Give Me A Sign

In those days, even the great powerhouse film-makers Metro-Goldwyn-Mayer showed an interest in Dean for their musicals, but he never even got the opportunity for screen tests, the reason being given that there were '…too many other Italian crooners about…'

By 1951, Dean himself was earning around $80,000 a year, but still had to pay out approximately half of that amount to Betty. Troubles surmounted when Dean and Jerry were reminded by the Inland Revenue that they owed five years' back-taxes, which came as a diabolical shock to both partners as they both understood that Abner Greshler had been dealing with their finances and tax payments.

Dean was worse off than Jerry. He'd already filed for bankruptcy in January 1949 and, with his success, all of his previous associates had suddenly re-appeared, suing him for back payments never received, or in relation to contracts that Dean had signed over the last handful of years without bothering to look at the large print, let alone the small wording.

Sam Watkins, Xavier Cugat, Lou Costello and numerous others all had debts owing to them from Dean, some going back to his cigar store days. He had signed, too, individual contracts with three different record companies (prior to Capitol Records) so that he could have a cash advance each time. He would record a few songs (sometimes just two) for one label, then go on to another company and possibly do the same thing again and not bother to keep track of what he had recorded and where. Some of these early efforts have now been lost in the mists of time. And while some have appeared since, Dean himself had no idea what some of the songs were, or where or when he even recorded them.

But these debts had to be paid somehow, some of it jointly by Dean and Jerry, but some of it was 'worked off', as in one case when Dean had delivery of a brand-new Cadillac and it was claimed back; only for the fact that Harold Kopler gave Dean $6,000 on the understanding that he and Jerry play his Chase Club in St. Louis (which they gladly did!).

In the midst of all the many commitments, Jeanne announced that she was pregnant and that the baby would be due later that year. Dean had already arranged that his four children with Betty would move in to his home, to be looked after by Jeanne. He had claimed that his former wife was not capable of looking after their children in a proper and reasonable way, and a fairly strict discipline was in order from Jeanne; she knew she had to be firm with the four children already growing up, and with her first due soon.

Dean, naturally, as was normal for him, left all the details of day-to-day routines to his wife, whilst he carried on with his career.

Jerry became very concerned with their business affairs. *At War With the Army* had earned them nothing, and any fees from stage appearances and record sales were being swallowed up with debt. Together with Dean, Jerry came to a decision: they both agreed once and for all to be rid of Abner J. Greshler.

No one ever really knew why Abbey had behaved this way to them. Greed, perhaps?

But whatever, there was no need to cause themselves any more worry or concern over this matter. They had been together now for over five years and the work could only be called magnificent for them both, with much more than they could ever hope to accomplish in their lifetimes.

Television was now beginning to attract the pair, too. They had felt previously that the time was not right, but after several talks with NBC, they appeared as guests on various shows, amongst them the famous and renowned *Milton Berle Show*, plus numerous guest spots elsewhere. They even headlined their own *Martin and Lewis Show*.

But within himself, even after several years working with his very talented partner, Dean wanted out, to be on his own.

He frequently became frustrated and annoyed with Jerry taking much more interest in the behind-the-scenes work that went on when making a film or television show. That was Jerry's ambition--he wanted to get more involved with the production side of their partnership and much time was spent behind the camera, sometimes suggesting major changes in the making of their films with the producer and directors.

'I was hanging around for the next shot but Jerry was there telling everyone else how to do it. Even my parts were getting less and less important than Jerry's.'

Jerry could see Dean's point of view, but he still insisted on being behind the camera, and wanted more time in working behind the scenes as well as being in the picture with his partner.

There was increased annoyance and more frustration from Dean on the set of *That's My Boy*, their fifth film together, in August 1951. With a bad atmosphere on set, the pair argued frequently and rarely saw eye-to-eye with the numerous suggestions that Jerry made.

Sadly, the truth of the matter was that Dean wanted to go solo; he wanted to be able to do his own things when he sang and made films and he could see nothing here that would improve that situation for him personally.

Today's top-line comedians: funnier than ever! ran the original press release for the movie, giving no hints of the friction that was gaining momentum. Hal Walker returned for directing duties, guiding Dean and Jerry against the odds to tell the tale of an ace football player (Eddie Mayehoff) who is disappointed with his hopeless son, Junior, played by Jerry. Dean would play the crooning football coach who would turn Junior's life around.

Their best yet! played to packed houses all over the States but Dean wasn't feeling it. The press remarked again that he was 'a likeable fella with a fairly pleasant voice' whilst Jerry got rave reviews for his comedy antics.

Nevertheless, at the same time and in contradiction to his own frustrations, he was content to let Jerry do all the arrangements and organization for them both, while he carried on with his work and playing golf as much as he could: a trait Dean had had in the early part of his career and which he carried on until he retired.

He wanted to plan his future, but let the others carry it out for him, as long as it went the way he wanted it.

The Martin and Lewis Show on NBC was doing well, as were their films, but Dean's recording output was not yet making many people sit up and take note. True, as they all said, he did have a likeable and pleasing sound, but that did not see too much of an income from Capitol. Dean, though, was using the expertise and facilities of musicians such as Lou Busch, Paul Weston and Frank DeVol whenever Dick Stabile was not available.

It was the later recordings that were to regularly use Dick's accompaniments for the bulk of Dean's output, more or less until 1959, when Gus Levene and Nelson Riddle were to complete his repertoire for Capitol until he left the label in 1960.

Meanwhile, Jeanne and Dean's first baby, Dean Paul Jr, came along on November 17th, 1951.

At Sea With the Navy (an intended follow-up to At War With the Army), was released in 1952 but not before it was retitled *Sailor Beware*. The film itself once again showed the cream of the partnership against the backdrop of the US Navy, with Jerry's character having a peculiar allergy to cosmetics and Dean's suffering from a weak knee. *Start nineteen-fifty-two the Right Way…the Martin and Lewis Way!* screamed the publicity slogan, and it seemed that indeed the Martin and Lewis machine had no intention of letting up.

Jumping Jacks came off the production schedules next, in July 1952, featuring Robert Strauss again, and Mona Freeman. The movie had Jerry, as Hap Smith, sneaking onto an army base to help his Corporal pal Chick Allen (Dean) provide some entertainment for the troops.

One of the stuntmen on this production needed an expensive operation following an accident, which Dean and Jerry paid for in full, something this pair were to do for many years hence.

Not so hilarious was the Martin household.

With baby Dean Jr, Jeanne was well involved with domestic chores and family organization. Although the Martins were now in a nice position to be able to afford staff at home to cope with the many and varied situations in running a family home, Jeanne liked to be directly involved with what was going on, the stark opposite to her husband.

Jeanne managed well, even though Dean Snr was still noticeably absent.

The other marriage in Dean's life, that of Martin and Lewis, was ever more fractious and rocky: Jerry would involve himself deeper and deeper in production while Dean, admittedly working harder than ever too, would simply get out as soon as shooting was finished for the day.

Those arguments that had only happened occasionally, became more frequent, but Dean and Jerry maintained a pleasant facade to the ever-clamoring public: Dean was the handsome man who always got the girl while was Jerry the clown who always seemed to create havoc in whatever he did. They'd done a mere ten-minute segment in the 1952 Columbia feature *Hollywood At Play* plus a cameo in the Bing Crosby/Bob Hope film *Road To Bali* and many more special appearances, and *The Stooge* was finally released in February 1953.

Jerry was making a handful of recordings, with moderate success, but then his recordings were only in small quantities, even when he did the occasional duet with his partner.

Dean, on the other hand, was now beginning to see his recordings sell in large numbers for Capitol. This was exactly what he had always wanted: that he could perhaps make a career of singing at last, his original ambition many years back in Steubenville when he was a teenager.

The record executives knew that they had a popular singer on their books and he recorded many, many songs for them, not all great, but providing Dean with more and more valuable time in the studio, as well having film-acting experience alongside Jerry.

Even in those days, Dean cracked jokes whilst recording and it was always a popular event when word got out that he was at Capitol in Hollywood. He took his work very seriously but, at the same time, put in those light-hearted quips which always made him very popular with the musicians, technicians and anyone else who was lucky enough to have been there in those studios at that time. Some of those instances have since been made available on such commercial releases as the remastered "A Winter Romance" and the 2012 concept album "Forever Cool".

It was this unique and pleasing attitude that made Dean Martin popular with everyone he ever worked with and, while this was prevalent at his work, his home life was continually at odds.

A lot of the friction between Dean and Jerry, and the problems that arose as a result, spilled over when he got home to Jeanne. Many times, he took it out on her with arguments and experienced fits of depression, where he would go to a room in the house to be by himself, and would not speak to anyone for hours. At this particular time, Jeanne and Dean separated; she went home to her mother and Dean spent some of this time to try to get something cleared if he could with Jerry. Although they spoke about these problems, and Jerry was upset that his friend had split with his wife, nothing came of their differences. A few days later, husband and wife were both back home, having settled their problems for the time being.

EIGHT

Don't Fence Me In

On March 3rd, 1954, Dean and Jerry came perilously close to a parting of the ways.

The volcano of tensions that had been angrily bubbling away finally erupted into a crisis at the winter headquarters of the Clyde Beatty circus in Phoenix, Arizona. Here, the top comedy team of their generation had been on a 2-month location shoot for *3 Ring Circus*.

'I was sick and tired of playing stooge to that crazy mixed-up character,' Dean said.

Conversely, Jerry said at the time that he was '...fed up of [Dean's] sensitivity. Everything I do is wrong! Anything that happens that he doesn't like, he blames me. He hates me. He's got a chip on his shoulder.'

For nine days, both men sulked, refusing point-blank to talk to each other until March 12th when a truce conference was set up in the Beverly Hills office of MCA. Tempers were somewhat soothed and a statement was issued that they intended to remain in partnership. Then, when Dean wasn't invited to Jerry's birthday party, whispers started expanding across Hollywood. Experts and critics gave them anywhere from three months to a year before Martin and Lewis would dissolve for good.

I asked Dean if he had felt at the time that the partnership really was washed up.

'If people would only have left us alone back in those days, then maybe Jerry and I wouldn't have had any trouble. Sure, we had a blow-up in Phoenix and I guess you'd say it was kind of tough but we'd had them before. I fuckin' hated the trip to London, too, when we did the Palladium. I don't know if it was because of what was going on. Do you know any two people who didn't sometimes have their arguments or fall out? It was like I was married to the kid.

'If Jerry and I had been in the hardware business or running a hamburger-and-root-beer joint on Ventura Boulevard, nobody would have had any interest in our spats. But because we were who we were, I guess it was big news.

'I felt then that individually, going it alone, we would never be as great as we were together. When we shook hands on our partnership, I said in my heart that it was forever, until death do us part. I really believed that. I was pretty stupid.'

And then Dean spoke at great length about Jerry's talent and it was clear to me all these years later that he still saw that spark in him.

'Jerry is more than a wild crazy guy. Like any comedian he can project sadness and pathos. There's nobody living who can play a scene like he does. What I learnt about acting and timing and how to make an audience break up...it's all from being with Jerry. Yeah, sometimes he made a mistake. I guess he probably still does. Hell, I know I do. But I just wanted all these people to leave us alone, to allow us to keep going. I can't imagine though ever working with him again. He was hard work, y'know?'

Jerry's feelings towards Dean not long after the truce said much about his relationship with the Italian, saying, 'The closer you are to a person, the deeper the feelings, and if they are hard feelings, they hit twice as hard. If you're emotional like Dino and I are, well, you can't help flipping your lid sometimes. Instead of us settling arguments in private, we yell at each other in public and then everyone says we're gonna bust up – but never in a million years! We're a real partnership: people have the idea I'm the clown and Dino's the straight-man but it's wrong. He has the same amount of jokes that I do, it's just a different style of putting them over. But we're both essential to each other's success.

'Outside of my wonderful wife, Dino is the closest friend I have. When I was young I was a lonely, unhappy kid and didn't have any brothers or sisters or any friends until I met him. Now to me, he's the best man in all the world – that's why our act is good – only because of the friendship between us. You think I'm crazy enough to throw this partnership out of the window?'

For years, Dean's recording career had never properly made its mark, then suddenly, with "That's Amore" from 1953's *The Caddy*, he had a two-million copies seller on his hands (in fact, it became a requisite part of his subsequent live stage acts even though, ironically, Dean became to detest the song).

'I didn't even like it the *first* time I read it. The lyrics were nonsense. I suggested they give it to the kid. But it became big and I've been stuck with it ever since, so what do I know?'

At once, movie studios and recording executives began to sing a siren call in his ears. *You could be as great as Bing [Crosby] if Jerry wasn't holding you down*, they said. *Get rid of this ball and chain and you'll be playing romantic leads in pictures; you'll have more hits; you'll be your own star. Why let Lewis plan your career for you?*

Ordinarily, these arguably malicious remarks would have fallen on deaf ears. But by the time of the rift, the seeds dropped into fertile soil: in *3 Ring Circus*, Dean's part was so small as to be almost invisible. He came on set to sing a few songs, and that was it. He had virtually no part in the story and for the first two weeks on location he had nothing to do; he saw a local magazine that ran a feature of *Living It Up*, displaying a publicity still of co-star Sheree North between Dean and Jerry – except the editors had cropped Dean out of the photograph. He strolled one afternoon into Jerry's trailer and found professional photographers taking pictures of his partner.

'I was the fifth wheel. If I wasn't important to the act any more, I just wish Jerry had had the guts to let me know. 'Say the word' I used to say to him. I wanted it to be over but dammit, I kept going.'

In fairness, the truce did turn things around, albeit temporarily.

Jerry approached Hal Wallis and insisted he would not continue making pictures unless Dean's part was expanded to equal stature with his, a demand Wallis met. Yet Lewis had an almost maniacal compulsion to work, pushing out three movies a year, doing regular television, constant engagements in night clubs and personal appearances as far as Europe. This desire clashed head-on with Dean's easy-going, shrug-of-the-shoulder attitude. He deliberately left all the decisions to Jerry, content to make one movie a year and record some records. This of course meant that whenever Jerry made, in Dean's eyes, a bad decision, Dean found himself forced to go along with it. Therein was the paradox: Dean's continued unhappiness in the situation he was in fueled by a level of his somewhat laissez-faire outlook.

When I examined their relationship myself in 1957, I considered that they'd probably attempt a trial separation. If Dean and Jerry could prove to themselves that they could stand alone in show-business, I doubted that they would ever reunite. But I knew that they were magnetically together in more ways than one and that any break-up would not be easy. The balance was skewed for the remainder of their pictures together. Yet *Living It Up* and *You're Never Too Young* included ballads that were to become typical of Dean's ultimate style: "How Do You Speak To An Angel?", "I Know Your Mother Loves You" and "Simpatico".

But in all honesty, and Dean admitted to me the same, everyone went to see Lewis and Martin, not Martin and Lewis. Who really went just to see Dean sing? (Apart from me, that is.)

Yet as a set of films, the Martin and Lewis canon had their ups and downs, as do all modern franchise equivalents. They included *Scared Stiff* (channeling Abbott and Costello's Universal Monsters comedies while actually being a remake of an old Bob Hope picture *The Ghost Breakers*), *Money From Home*, *You're Never Too Young*, 19-year old Shirley MacLaine's film debut in *Artists and Models*, *Pardners*, and finally *Hollywood or Bust* in 1956, arguably their finest hour.

'The best thing I ever did was to join up with Jerry,' Dean said. 'The other great thing was to split from him. That gave me the chance to show the world what I could do by myself.'

'Dean was my catcher,' stated Jerry, 'the greatest straight man in all of the history of show-business. His sense of timing is flawless, so infinite and fragile, yet he always looks as if he does nothing at all.'

Such beautiful words and expressions, but nevertheless most sincerely meant by both artists. They had had their time together and had been more than successful; but time told them both that they had to go it alone. When it was finally announced that Martin and Lewis were to split, it shocked the entertainment world.

Drastic meetings were held at Paramount with Hal Wallis and his executives to inform Dean and Jerry that because of contracts binding in law, there was no way the partnership could split.

At this particular juncture, Jerry was willing to negotiate something that would please the board and mainly his partner Dean. However, Dean was not interested; he had had enough of this partnership and was weighing up his singing career (which seemed to be doing fairly well at Capitol). Now that he had spent over ten years in films, radio, and live appearances with Jerry, he finally wanted a solo career and was willing to step out alone. While he was not so sure about this comparatively new medium called television, he felt secure that his voice could maybe carry him on to more lucrative pastures new if he had the chance.

When Dean had previously signed with Jerry for a five-year contract for NBC TV, they did not consider the eventual possibilities - but now it was getting bigger. As important artists in their own right, NBC eventually adjusted Dean and Jerry's contract so that they could appear as solo artists.

But even though he wanted and yearned for the split for so many years, once it had actually happened, Dean felt empty. Yes, he knew deep inside that he could do more in this business but he couldn't deal with conflict and was unsure what he thought he could do and what he wanted to do.

Quietly, he was convinced that he could make it out on his own as a solo artist but, sadly, everyone else thought differently.

Critics as well as company executives were unconvinced when the split finally occurred that Dean Martin would be any sort of success without Jerry Lewis.

He was sick and tired of the whole affair and wanted out, recklessly threatening to walk out of everything, disregarding his legal liabilities.

Jerry was broken up: he had pleaded with his partner and Paramount to get their problems sorted out before they had even started making *Artists and Models*, but the bitter arguments raged back and forth, Dean wanting out at any cost.

He hammered at the situation, so annoyed and depressed now that he just could not be persuaded to listen to all the discussions taking place. At times, he was not even present at Paramount when talks took place about his own future.

Again, he had not looked too closely at the contract when he had signed with Paramount, which had tied him and his partner together far more than perhaps either had realized at the time.

Both men had been in the business for some years now and they wanted changes in their careers that the other simply couldn't accommodate: Jerry was always lining up the cameras, the shots, the positions, sometimes taking over from the producers and directors, taking this extra time to get involved behind the camera.

Many times, Dean had asked Jerry to let him know when he would start work on this picture instead of Dean waiting around. He would often and furiously walk off the set, until Jerry was ready.

Their films, however, continued to attract large audiences. I can remember queues outside the Croydon cinemas in South London each time a Martin and Lewis film was showing there in my youth: buildings like the famed Davis Theatre (a beautiful building, sadly, like the way of many, now demolished); the Granada Thornton Heath and the ABC Savoy in Broad Green.

Cinemas globally enjoyed similar success. Dean and Jerry were a good box-office attraction everywhere and the films returned to cinemas time and again.

Meanwhile, Dean's recording career was steadily creating a gentle stir here and there. Songs like "There's My Lover", "When You're Smiling", and "What Could Be More Beautiful" had reasonable sales, and his name was popular among record-buyers everywhere.

His grand success with "That's Amore" made Dean even more determined, and the sweet, sweet "Memories Are Made of This" sealed the decision he was to make.

This increased financial success now helped Dean to clear some of the debts that still hung around: he was getting near the end of those past nightmares and gaining more confidence.

Dean was still paying Betty $1,000 a month and, declaring that she 'was an unfit mother and not caring for them in a satisfactory way', he now filed a suit against her for the legal custody of their four children. Elizabeth did not contest at all this claim by her former husband and on December 10th, 1957, the courts granted the official custody to Jeanne and Dean.

With all children now residing with him, Jeanne and their three own children, the Martin family needed extra space and he bought a $250,000 home in Mountain Drive, Beverly Hills. This was an English-style mansion containing a tennis court, swimming pool (Dean had always been an excellent swimmer), and hosts of other features for the good life with his wife Jeanne and their children.

With one legal affair dealt with in his personal life, Dean now faced another great upheaval and this, too, was soon to become legal and final.

NINE

Get On With Your Livin'

On Monday, June 19th, 1956, Martin and Lewis officially separated.

They still had a few joint commitments to complete, with their final appearance together as a team July 24th of that year. The end of a decade and more, with all of its publicity, promotions and merchandise (including comic strip adventures in books and magazines), was placed in the history of our times.

Dean was out on his own with an uncertain future and one of the first solo appearances was in May 1957, in the 24-hour 'City of Hope' telethon in New York. While he'd decided to sell his interests in York Pictures Corporation and Hal Wallis had eventually settled all of the legal entanglements concerning the Martin and Lewis team, Dean was still committed to remain under contract. This ensured that Wallis could get at least another four films each from the estranged pair, twice the number of pictures had Martin and Lewis actually stayed together.

Dean would eventually make *Career* (1959), *All In A Night's Work* (1961), *Who's Got the Action?* (1962) *and Who's Been Sleeping In My Bed?* (1963) to clear his fixed contract but was free to work with other studios too.

Prolific Hungarian-born film producer Joe Pasternak, who in 1945 had made *Anchors Aweigh* with Frank Sinatra and Gene Kelly, approached Dean with the view of casting him in a new picture that told the story of millionaire playboy Ray Hunter who travels to Rome to acquire a hotel. Although not the most complex of plots, 1957's *Ten Thousand Bedrooms* at least gave Dean his own screen-time and finally a shot at solo stardom, but still no strength in a meaty character part. His career needed a strong and substantial role to prove his point but absolutely nothing was forthcoming.

His recordings for Capitol were not too healthy either, having recorded insubstantial songs like "Give Me A Sign" and "Bamboozled". They sold in reasonable quantities overall, but there were no other golden efforts.

'I didn't know what was going to happen to me. I couldn't imagine myself working in an ordinary job again. I'd come this far.' His management was desperately searching for suitable roles but it was proving unceasingly difficult. 'It was smothered with ballad singers, why should the world want another Italian?'

Because of his years with Jerry, Dean was already labelled as a light-hearted singer and comedian, nothing special, and with not much else to offer.

That was the general consensus in the late 1950s: Martin and Lewis had broken up with and everyone assuming that Jerry would succeed over Dean.

It did seem that in those initial months, Jerry was going from strength to strength while Dean was floundering. They had both attended Judy Garland's first live recording at the Cocoanut Grove in the autumn of 1958 but remained on opposite sides of the venue, Dean keeping himself to himself more than ever.

After the embarrassing flop of *Ten Thousand Bedrooms*, everything seemed to be the absolute pits: he had recorded the songs from the film for an EP album by Capitol but sales across the world reflected the film's failure as it went around the cinema circuits.

At the beginning of 1957, Dean had recorded a batch of good solid standards, compiled as PRETTY BABY, earning him roughly $250,000 and allowing him to clear more debts. Today, it's a great example of early Dean, and quite an enchanting album. In 1996, I approached EMI, suggesting a 'two on one' CD release coupling PRETTY BABY with 1960's THIS TIME I'M SWINGIN'. It was a sales success and the format instigated similar highly-successful releases for other artists by EMI.

But the vocal stance Dean took on PRETTY BABY simply

echoed the roles he'd been playing since he started his film career: that of a romantic, light-hearted balladeer. It was a contrast to the Dixie-driven SWINGIN' DOWN YONDER from 1954, his first full-length album.

Consulting with his management, Dean decided not to have the lead role in his next few films (if any ever came along that is, and overall this decision was something that marred his movie career as a whole) but meanwhile, he carried on with live appearances here and there.

While performing at the Twin Coaches in Pittsburgh, Dean took a telephone call from his agent asking if he would like a part in a war film with Montgomery Clift and Marlon Brando.

'Was he crazy? Brando and Clift? Man, those guys were huge. I said I'd do it for nothing!'

In fact, his salary was considerably less than his two co-stars, yet third billing beneath them meant his $35,000 pay check was something he could easily swallow.

Part of the filming would take the crew to France, and Dean had to admit he was not too happy. Travelling was not one of Dean's favorite pastimes and he'd previously had to accept so much moving around with Jerry in the past. But this time there was no Jerry in his ear: this was his career and he knew he would have to disregard this fear as best he could. The seven weeks he spent in Paris he despised, but got on well with Brando and Clift for the brief occasions he was required to film at the same time as the former. Jeanne stayed with him for part of the time, easing his anxiety.

Directed by Edward Dmytryk in CinemaScope for 20th Century Fox, *Young Lions* was an outstanding war film for 1958, gaining the *Picturegoer* seal of merit but Dean remarked he was 'the ham between Brando and Cliff', perhaps recalling his earlier roles!

Dean was never a big reader but did complete the original Irwin Shaw novel prior to filming, convincing himself that this was one of the biggest gambles of his career, sharing screen time with two heavyweights of Hollywood.

Yet it paid off handsomely when the acclaim he received for his performance made some critics even remark that he 'outshone Brando and Clift' giving Dean a terrific boost of confidence that he'd never had before and for the first time, he actually sat down and thought about acting seriously.

Bold! Outspoken! Frank! Sinatra!
So proclaimed the advertising slogans for Dean's next film, another military effort and another where he didn't get top-billing. That, of course, went to Frank Sinatra.

They'd met before, crossing paths at various venues around the US but the opportunity to work together had yet to present itself. That took place when Vincente Minnelli was looking for two strong personalities for his adaptation of the best-selling James Jones novel that told the story of an ex-serviceman who returns to his home town, only to trigger a series of tragedies. Cast as Dave Hirsh, the protagonist, Dean would share scenes with Frank who would play Alabama Dillert, a playboy-type drinker and gambler.

But it soon became clear to Minnelli (best known for *Gigi* and *An American In Paris* as well as being Judy Garland's second husband and father to Liza) that Dean would be better suited as Dillert and be stronger at supporting Sinatra than the other way around.

Some Came Running became Dean's third solo film, reuniting him with Shirley MacLaine and shot in CinemaScope, the comparatively new wide-screen look to many films since its inception with the Richard Burton vehicle *The Robe* in 1953.

Dean gave a demanding and full characterization of a strong part, playing it to perfection (and never once removing his hat!), as did Frank, who was pleased to finally be working with Dean. It goes without saying that it was a blossoming friendship for the two men in both their personal and professional lives.

Shortly after the film wrapped, Shirley was dining with Dean and his family at his home when a fishbone caught in her throat. Somewhat in a panic, it was Dean who removed the offending item and today, Shirley still remembers the day he saved her life.

Released in 1959, Dean had superb notices on his performance in *Some Came Running*, with columns reporting that he out-acted most of the cast, cementing his abilities in the critics' eyes.

His recording career was building, too, with hits such as "Volare" and "Return to Me" forcing those people with influence to take another hard look at his output and hopefully, help realize his potential.

This was endorsed further when Frank conducted the orchestra on Dean's new album SLEEP WARM, a lush and dreamy album and a good seller for them both, with Dean's voice in excellent form.

During the hazy summer over a period of three days (29th July/4th and 6th August 1959) Dean recorded a dozen songs at the Capitol studios in stark contrast to the season: a batch of winter and Christmas songs to make up his first-ever collection of seasonal Yuletide music. With fine arrangements by Gus Levene, A WINTER ROMANCE was Dean's most successful album at that time and his clout in the industry, coupled with his friendship with Frank, was gaining momentum.

He had also set up his own production company, Deanric, to allow better control over his projects, and his agent, Herman Citron, was now able to pick and choose on behalf of his artist, the most promising selections for his future.

Fellow performers were also noticing what an impact Dean was having: Bing Crosby said that he was 'a charmer and a friend, despite his pranks. I reckon he's wittier off-stage than most professional comics, sings a pretty good song, too '

A compliment indeed from a master of song who had certainly been around!

An actor Dean had greatly admired for many years was John Wayne and, when he was offered the part of Dude, a no-good down and out drunk in *Rio Bravo*, alongside Wayne's Sherriff Chance (not to mention a supporting cast of Angie Dickinson,

Ricky Nelson, Walter Brennan, and renowned filmmaker Howard Hawks) he jumped at this golden opportunity.

Hailed as the greatest Western since George Stevens' Shane, *Rio Bravo* became an instant classic. Crisp, witty, fast-paced and straight from the shoulder, this glorious drama budgeted at $3million contained all the highest traditions of the Western genre.

It also gave rise to a number of interesting facts and events: Wayne hadn't picked up a rifle since appearing in *Stagecoach* in 1939; Angie Dickinson's legs were voted the prettiest and longest in Hollywood; Ricky Nelson's duet with Dean was wonderfully understated; Walter Brennan drove a nail into one of his shoes so that he jolted himself into the limp he portrayed throughout his scenes, and Wayne gave Nelson the hat he'd worn in *Stagecoach*.

There's a scene where Dean, as Dude, pours his drink back into the bottle without spilling a drop. Horror maestro John Carpenter, in an interview in 1994, classified it as being his very favorite film sequence of all time.

With his first solo western, Dean finally got the recognition that he deserved. While John Wayne had always pulled in the crowds for most films he made, for this film in particular, Dean had a much bigger audience. He received very impressive reviews for his part and had thoroughly enjoyed making the film, even managing to sing some songs on screen and giving Ricky Nelson some 'insider' tips on singing (even though Nelson was already a successful singer in his own right, having been in the business since a child with his parents).

With this sort of success and acclaim, Dean was now able to add more strings to his bow: he agreed to appear on stage at the prestigious Sands Hotel, Las Vegas, creating his own unique act and an association with the venue that was to become so very famous for him in years to come.

He had that flair for working very hard and making it look as if he did nothing, but he was determined to gain more and more experience and confidence in all chapters of the business.

When he sauntered on stage for the 1959 Academy Awards in his rubber-soled shoes with blue slacks, a pork-pie hat and a dark red shirt, he was effortless in his delivery and quips – but he'd been spotted in the wings learning his lines and timings to the second. He always knew his cues --and those of others-- and was ever the professional.

Dean returned to Paramount for *Career*, a film that was promoted as *The Most Scorching Drama of Young People to Ignite The Screen In Years!* It was a tough drama exposing the behind-the-scenes of show-business: the tricks, the dirt and the deceptions. It was a fascinating story of an incurably dedicated actor played by Anthony Franciosa clashing with a ruthless director (Dean Martin). Shirley MacLaine co-starred and Joseph Anthony directed for producer Hal Wallis.

'I love this acting stuff,' said Dean at the time. 'At last I am getting interesting roles. The one I have here is the most colorful and exciting one I have done...such a change from my past characters.'

Dean recorded the title song for Capitol on 31 August 1959, released as a single titled "(Love Is A) Career".

Yet, while he was sky-rocketing, it was Jeanne and the children who still suffered. Dean was rarely at home: if he wasn't on set he was on stage or recording. To compound Jeanne's frustration, he was often seen in public with Anne Francis (a New York-born actress with the sci-fi classic *Forbidden Planet* on her résumé) and the subject of divorce was raised.

With tempers at home temporarily subdued, Dean changed management, with Eddie Traubner stepping into the fray.

In 1960, Dean completed his first film for Columbia Pictures. *Who Was That Lady?* was his return to comedy since the final Martin and Lewis picture, *Hollywood Or Bust* four years before. Headlined by Tony Curtis (still no top-billing for Dean), their mutual co-star was Janet Leigh, Curtis' then-wife who had recently performed together with Kirk Douglas in *The Vikings*. While Curtis had been seen in arguably his most memorable role in *Some Like It Hot* in 1959 with Marilyn Monroe, Leigh's next movie after *Who Was That Lady?* would become the one that she became most associated with: *Psycho.*

The high-tension drama of Hitchcock's untouchable *Psycho,* however, was miles away from *Who Was That Lady?* in which she played Ann Wilson, catching her husband David (Curtis) kissing another woman. In a convoluted series of events in which David, and Dean's character Michael, convince Ann she didn't really see what she saw, Martin and Curtis bounce off each other perfectly, leaving poor Janet flummoxed at their respective characters' every move! It's one of my son's overall favorite movies and his 'go to' Dean Martin film!

Following his success for Vincente Minnelli in *Some Came Running,* the director cast him again as the male lead, this time in an adaptation of *Bells Are Ringing,* a hugely successful Broadway show starring the talented and vivacious Judy Holliday. MGM produced the screen version and Holliday reprised her stage role.

Capitol Records purchased the soundtrack from MGM, including the song "My Guiding Star" which was made for the film but not included in the final cut. "Long Before I Knew You" was the other song recorded but not included and it seems to have been lost in the transition of ownership. One of the highlights of the film was the duet between Judy and Dean singing "Just in Time". Dean recorded his own solo version of the same song less than ten days later on May 17th, 1960. He added a new batch of songs to his catalog too, a policy which was to continue to naturally build up his prestige as a singer as well as an actor.

One Cup Of Happiness

Dean seemed much happier of late. Most of his financial debts had been paid off, and he felt assured about his rosy future, now being able to consider what he wanted to do next, as opposed to having been told what to do for most of his career so far.

'I felt I had this freedom I'd never had before. I always hated being ordered around and having the chance to choose what I wanted was a long time coming,' he told me.

His own satisfaction with his role in *Bells Are Ringing* showed throughout his performances in this Arthur Freed production and he loved working with his leading lady, even though her illness held up a lot of the filming. But Dean was patient and only worked when she was ready, and he relished every moment.

For the "Hello" sequence, the film crew used 350 extras, 50 bit players, 70 taxicabs, 100 cars and 2,000 feet of the MGM lot for filming!

Sadly, it proved to be her last film. Judy succumbed to breast cancer and died five years later in 1965.

'She was a gorgeous girl. It was heaven working with her,' Dean said. 'I still miss her.'

On the very day of completion, Dean had to leave immediately for solo appearances at the Sands Hotel and, owing to excessive commitments, he had to refuse a part in the Sophia Loren/Clark Gable production *It Started In Naples*. Excessive commitments was perhaps an understatement!

Dean had so many offers coming in that his management had a hard time deciding what would be best for him. He himself wanted variety, in his film work particularly, but had no wish to be tied down to one studio. Many were offering incredible sums to get him to sign an exclusive contract, but he refused them all.

Instead, he decided that an assortment of film roles for a

variety of studios would suit him better; each company had their own routine and method of film production and, with his own production companies, he could ensure good financial deals and top status with each and every project.

Thus it was that the man progressed; he was very sure of what he wanted and, determined, he now had the finance and the power like he had never had before. Things were looking very good and there was so much more he knew he could achieve. His friendship with Frank had widened his appeal and they were often seen together along with Sammy Davis Jr, Peter Lawford and Joey Bishop. Dean wanted total security and independence for himself and his family.

It was going his way – and the way was his!

With *Bells Are Ringing* less than a month into its journey around the cinema circuits, Dorchester Productions signed him for the Warner Bros film *Ocean's 11*. Dorchester was Frank's company and the story concerned the robbing of five Las Vegas casinos simultaneously at precisely 1 minute 38 seconds past midnight, when everyone was celebrating the New Year.

This was the first gathering of the Rat Pack for a film, the title the media attributed to Frank Sinatra and his friends when they worked and played together. It was a label they never acknowledged, liked or used themselves.

Frank had gathered together his Clan: Dean, Sammy, Peter, Joey, Angie Dickinson and Richard Conte plus guest stars George Raft, Red Skelton, Cesar Romero, Akim Tamiroff, Henry Silva, Patrice Wymore and Ilka Chase, together with the splendid musical works of Nelson Riddle.

With all of these celebrities, the film could not help being a huge box-office success; it was the epitome of cool, encapsulating the Clan's image. In fact, its success at defining the Rat Pack is still maintained to this very day. In 2001, Warner Bros green-lit the remake, *Ocean's Eleven*, directed by Steven Soderbergh, featuring its own contemporary ensemble cast including George Clooney as Danny Ocean with Brad Pitt, Matt Damon, Don Cheadle, Andy García and Julia Roberts.

Two sequels of the remake followed, *Ocean's Twelve* and *Ocean's Thirteen*. A fourth all-female variation, *Ocean's 8*, starring Sandra Bullock as Debbie Ocean, the younger sister of Clooney's Danny, was released in 2018.

A regular remark of Dean's became the title of one of his very popular single record releases: "Ain't That a Kick in The Head". Some American radio stations actually banned its release, due to the suggestive lyrics by Sammy Cahn and Jimmy Van Heusen. Dean recorded it on 10th May 1960 especially for inclusion in *Ocean's 11* and was one of thirteen in a session for Capitol. The other tracks formed the superb collection THIS TIME I'M SWINGIN', all arranged and conducted by Nelson Riddle.

Dean didn't return to Capitol until mid-December, and with 1961 almost upon him, he was nearing the end of his contract with them. Rumors were strong that he may join Frank on his pal's newly-formed company Reprise.

After a handful of years out on his own now, Dean Martin had certainly proved his capabilities without any doubt.

It was only a few years earlier, that I myself had discovered Dean Martin as an entertainer. During the autumn of 1953, I had gone to my local cinema to see a film entitled *The Caddy*, not ever having heard of Martin and Lewis at all, and not sure what the film would be all about. Thinking that this was just another average disposable, forgettable comedy, when I heard and saw this Dean Martin fella sing "You're the Right One" in the film, I can only say I was - for want of a different word - *shocked* by the sound of his voice.

It just got me. I was just a teenager and this was the first time that any singing voice, male or female, had ever affected me this way!

From that time on, amidst my various activities, I eagerly went to see any Dean Martin film that came along. In those days, with an abundance of cinemas all over the place, it was so easy to catch up on a film or two that you may have missed the first time around – and I always went again and again!

Whether or not any of my girlfriends ever became staunch admirers of Dean's work after being taken to see his films I shall never know, but I paid my dues at the box office and in I went!

So began my almost demented desire to find out more about Dean Martin.

My collection of 10' 78s (and very fragile!) shellac singles were quickly starting to take up more and more space in the cupboard at home and I began to collect what I could on this actor and singer from America, articles, cuttings, photos…anything.

The man himself, meanwhile, was working harder and harder, and with the numerous offers of film work, plus his appearances, he had made a strong name for himself in show business.

With my continuing interest, I was somewhat surprised to eventually discover that what had been then the world's only Dean Martin appreciation society had closed down some time before.

After some thoughts and considerations, I made up my mind at some point in 1959 to contact Dean for permission to set up one myself. Although my dear parents thought I had perhaps cracked up with such a crazy and useless idea, I did write to Dean. Over a period of around eighteen months, across what must have been about ten letters merely and politely asking for his permission, I received absolutely no response at all. Without actually saying 'we told you so!', my parents were now convinced that I had finally gone mad and had wasted my time by sending all these letters.

In October 1960, I received a letter dated the 14th, signed by a Mrs Lois F Greene, secretary to Dean Martin. It was a small letterhead, with no address embossed on it – but at an angle in black italicized print in the top left corner, was the single name 'Dino'.

In the letter, she addressed me as Mr Thorpe and apologized for the delay in answering my letter sent in October to Mr Dean Martin. She continued by saying that Mr Martin had been preparing for a new picture and recording, so had been difficult to reach. She said that the day before she wrote the letter, he had some free time and she was able to get his 'most pleased consent' of my plan of a fan club in Great Britain. She trusted that she would be hearing from me for any aid that she could give me from her side.

I was stunned!

Less than a week later, another letter arrived, on the same clear and simple letterhead.

Except this time, the typed (albeit brief) letter dated 21st December 1960 began Dear Bernard... It referenced the previous letter and said that personal authorization for such a project was given because I had been so 'damned insistent'. Regular contact, the letter said, would be welcomed. The letter was hand-signed...

Dino.

I was 22-years old and Dean Martin had personally given me his permission to set up what I called initially, Dino's Fan Club, but Dean soon requested the revision to the International Dean Martin Club (Dean didn't like the term 'fan club' and told me to stop using the phrase).

I commenced our operations straight away, writing to Capitol in Hollywood and London, and to every film company both here and America. I asked his management for as much publicity material as they were willing to send me. I expected this to be a few photos and not much else, but within weeks, along came batches of varying (signed) photos and boxes of his then-latest vinyl LP THIS TIME I'M SWINGIN'. Lois was so very helpful in arranging regular supplies and we were able to quickly advertise the album's availability from us which helped to attract subscriptions. Dino had also signed a few copies of that as well which we were able to give away as competition prizes. Not long after, copies of the soundtrack to BELLS ARE RINGING arrived and we were able to sell these prior to their official UK released in October (they had already hit the US shelves in July). Everyone was forthcoming with so much information and I was overwhelmed with the support, especially given the fact that appreciation societies were relatively rare and occasionally given bad press because of the unprofessional approaches that sometimes came hand in hand with 'fans' managing such groups.

Warner Bros wrote to us, too, asking if we would find some advertising material useful for their new motion picture *Ocean's 11*. Useful was something of an understatement! This was Dean's big film for 1960 and Warner Bros. was amazing at supporting us supporting them - as if a giant such as Warner Bros. needed us anyway!

It was these initial dealings with my new Hollywood contacts that showed me the entertainment business wasn't always closed doors and hierarchical boardrooms. I do wonder if the fact that I was representing Dean Martin lent some weight to us receiving such attention. He himself was highly respected in the industry and wielded a lot of influence. We issued our very first newsletter in November 1960[1]. It was, admittedly, a very basic one-sheet typed bulletin and we followed with similar issues for Christmas, then, for 1961, May, August and December. Our first specially printed issues, headed *A Letter from Dino* commenced monthly from January 1962, complete with an authorized photo of Dean, as the club's Honorary President, at the top of the first page. In those early days, that was as about as 'illustrated' as we could get for our newsletters.

Yet I knew from the off that we had to be respectful and professional in all our dealings. We were, after all, representing Dean Martin.

Representing Dean Martin!

Even now after all these years and after everything we did for Dean, that still sounds surreal!

With our initial membership fee at four shillings (equivalent to 48p then or approximately £6.00 today), we were off!

---

[1] *See* The Dean Martin Association Journals, Volume 1: 1955-1967 *[DMA Books, 2023]*

In a matter of a few years, Dean Martin had proven himself in great demand - exactly the opposite of the critics' predictions after his split with Jerry. He had ensured that he would not tie himself down to one studio.

'It gave me complete freedom to portray different characters, as well as working with all those people through whom I could gain experience. I knew I would never be a great actor. I just wanted to be a good actor.'

Demand for Dean was great and, after wrapping *All In A Night's Work* for Paramount (again with Shirley MacLaine, and the first solo film in which he received top billing), he did a cameo for Columbia Pictures' epic production *Pepe*, starring the comedian Cantinflas. It told the simple story of a kind-hearted ranch-hand who, because of his love for a horse, found himself going on an adventure in the outside world where his path kept crossing with show-business personalities.

The promotional work for *All in a Night's Work* included Dean's recording of the title theme. As part of the four-picture deal with Hal Wallis, the producer had decided that this part was made for Dean as a playboy and working with Shirley again was just a dream for him. Paramount delayed the start of this film because they required Dean for it and no one else and at this time, he had already arranged enough work to clear him for the next three years - and demand for his talent was increasing all the time.

Joseph Anthony, who had directed Dean in *Career*, occupied the director's chair for this comedy, but this was the first time he'd tackled this genre. Comedy was new to him, but he found working with Dean to be rewarding, appreciating his star's natural and laid-back approach.

My wife Irene and I attended the film's UK gala premiere (at Paramount's invitation) on Thursday 11th May 1961 at the Plaza Theatre, Piccadilly Circus, London. It would be the first of many such opportunities my association with Dean would provide.

My family and friends, however, still considered me foolish to bother with this work for Dean, for some American celebrity who did not really need me, nor would ever take any notice at all or make contact. But the whole experience was so different and nothing like I honestly expected.

It was one evening in the summer of 1961, I think it was June, when our home telephone rang. I answered, wondering who would be calling at such a relatively late hour.

'Hello?' I said, hearing a couple of clicks and a pause. Then:

'Hey, Bernard,' a smooth voice said, with the emphasis on the *nard*. 'Dino.'

I nearly fell over.

He asked me how I was, how my family was, how the club was. I have always prided myself in the fact I rarely become tongue-tied but this call, completely out of the blue, knocked me for six. But I swallowed my overwhelming sense of excitement and chatted with Dean as if it was the most natural thing in the world. As I told him what the club was doing, he responded positively and said that he was hoping to make a picture with Lana [Turner] at some point and he hoped I'd like it. I said we'd seen *All in A Night's Work* and he replied, saying he'd been happy with this film and recalled the incident when mayonnaise was applied to his face to encourage the dog, Jasper, to lick him and make a fuss of him on camera!

As the conversation ended (it could only have been five or ten minutes), he said I could call if I ever needed anything. I thanked him. He never responded but just said goodbye.

When I had the idea to set up a club for him, I don't think I really, truly expected anything more than a couple of letters, if that.

But I'd just spoken to Dean Martin.

ELEVEN

Shoulder To Shoulder

I wondered if he'd made the call himself to 'check me out' so to speak, to see if I was really determined to make this work. I'd like to think I'd impressed him because his office sent more and more updates on his work and words of encouragement in what we were doing.

But our society was just finding its feet. We'd had a bad start with membership and, even though we were advertising as much as was financially possible, things did not take off too well until 1962.

There was a very gradual intake of members – painfully slow if I'm honest – but we kept our determination to establish the organization for Dean, and, with his support, and photographs and various other items that we regularly received from his office, things were slowly but surely trundling along!

Meanwhile, Dean was earning approximately $300,000 a picture, $50,000 a week in cabaret, similar for television appearances and on top of all that, other payments from his company stocks and shares plus his royalties and payments from Capitol Records.

Everyone was asking for him, so demand was now outstripping the number of days in a year for Dean. The fact that he still found time to contact us amazed me.

Meanwhile he was harboring a secret passion to own his own Italian restaurant and had noticed the Alpine Lodge bistro up for sale in Las Vegas. He went into co-ownership with the then-owners and renamed it Dino's Lodge, complete with his name and image above the door. The front entrance soon featured on the popular weekly television series *77 Sunset Strip*, boosting both public and celebrity interest. An instrumental jazz LP, AN EVENING AT DINO'S LODGE, was released some months later.

He returned to MGM to star with Susan Hayward in the gritty drama *Ada*, an examination of the deep machinations of behind-the-scenes politics. The film company had acquired the screenplay rights of the Wirt Williams novel *Ada Dallas*, and Dean had one of his strongest dramatic parts to date in governor Bo Gillis. Location shooting took place in the US Government offices in Sacramento and Dean went there for interior and exterior shoots. This was the very first time that a motion picture company had actually filmed inside the government building.

Even though *Ada* was far from light-hearted, Dean still managed to include a song "May the Lord Bless you Real Good", which did not appear out of context of the story.

He pushed his character very hard in this story and director Daniel Mann said of Dean in this film, 'he is one of the most easiest and prepared professionals I have ever had the pleasure of directing.'

The Clan reunited on film for *Sergeants 3* (you'll notice that all the Rat Pack movies have numbers in the titles and that those numbers don't appear as words... *Ocean's 11, Robin and the 7 Hoods* and so on...) and with our membership now steadily increasing, the months of frustration wondering what the future would hold for the club finally paid off as we began to show signs of success.

Dean's recordings were still providing him with substantial sales, with songs such as "Sparkelin' Eyes", "Giuggiola" and "Somebody Loves You", with the inclusion this year of one of his most successful and lush collection of songs on DINO – ITALIAN LOVE SONGS.

This was exactly what the album title implied: Dean singing Italian love songs. This, his penultimate album for Capitol, came with sleeve notes announcing that this was just what his admirers had wanted all along! He'd spent three days in September recording those dozen beautiful renditions of songs, some of which I can even remember my Italian Grandmother singing to me (or to herself) when I was a child!

I classify this album as my very firm favorite from Capitol – the inexplicable genius and orchestrations of Gus Levene, together with Dean's voice, which was nothing other than perfect when he recorded these songs; all in all, an amazing combination of music and voice which remains unsurpassed. The album was released in February 1962 and entered the American charts the following May, staying there for a period of sixteen weeks. For this production, Dean had re-recorded two of his hit songs, "On An Evening In Roma" and "Return To Me", giving them a bigger, more sophisticated sound with elevated presentation values.

This was *the* definitive Italian collection for Dean, which he never surpassed in his entire recording career, although he would continue to include the occasional Italian style song in his repertoire.

Spread over the course of three days in December (18th, 19th and 20th), Dean entered the Capitol Tower for what would be his final set of songs for that record company.

He had been with them since the autumn of 1948, with a surprising list of just over 300 titles for the period. As is the case with all artists, some songs were very good, some he would rather not remember, and some were big hits, making the compilation a very varied selection of songs of all moods and rhythm for a man who had long since proved he could sing like the rest of them.

'I can sing just about everything quite good, perhaps not the greatest voice, but I do my best and you cannot say much else after that. I've had a good time doing that, which is nice.'

With his contract now ending, he spent these three sessions recording another gorgeous set of popular and beautiful songs, this time set to cha rhythms, arranged by the master Nelson Riddle, whose orchestra played superbly. Dean again did his unique best, his own inimitable phrasing well-suited to the arrangements for this set.

CHA CHA DE AMOR was released in America in March the following year with the UK release the November after.

Dean had already felt a couple of years back that he needed a change of situation with his vocal work, and had been considering offers with some of the record companies since then. Considering several options and financial deals, the place he ended up seemed an inevitable one: Frank had created Reprise Records.

In late 1961, Dean told us he was signing with Frank's label and requested that Frank, Sammy, Peter and Joey be honorary members. He told us too about his family and asked about ours, saying that Jeanne, his daughter Claudia, and his parents had all spent time in hospital, but luckily, they were all back home and feeling a lot better. He had been quite concerned at the health problems they had all been through.

Dean said he was pleased we were working hard for him. Even with our not having been in operation for two years yet, we already had members overseas and things were generally looking favorable. He mentioned a London visit to film his cameo with Frank for *Road to Hong Kong* and hoped to meet, adding that he hated flying but accepted when he had to do it for his work. Ultimately, he apologized that the meeting didn't happen due to his family commitments in Germany.

He did say, however, that he'd been at the Savoy Hotel in London for two days, where one of the guests was Hollywood restaurateur Mike Romanoff. He'd managed to pull off some practical jokes with Romanoff by cutting his expensive cigarettes into pieces and his ties into shreds!

Sinatra's Reprise, 'to play and play again', had signed up a myriad of artists with a unique feature: each and every artist had the advantage of actually owning outright their recorded works and masters. Each artist therefore had the prerogative of releasing their work as and when they wished (or not at all if they so desired) merely loaning out the actual tapes to a company that would do all of the distribution and selling to the public.

This was unheard of in the record industry, for all artists on all labels had no say or any rights in what happened to their recordings - but at Reprise this legal innovation came into being and at precisely 3.30pm on the afternoon of Tuesday 13th January 1962, Dean signed his name to a thirteen-year contract.

But even Dean himself was yet to realize just how illustrious and successful his new era would become with this label; it did not occur to him at that time the phenomenal achievements he would experience in those thirteen years.

Exactly one month to the day after his signature appeared on his contract, he recorded five songs: his very first was entitled "Senza Fine", written by Paoli and Wilder, being the love theme from *Flight of the Phoenix*, with orchestration by the fine musicianship of Neal Hefti (later of *Batman* fame). The remainder of songs, also with Hefti, at this session were "Just Close Your Eyes", "Baby-0", "Dame Su Amor" and "Tik-A-Tee, Tik-A-Tay". This latter song was to become his first regular issue, announcing in the press *Dean Martin's On Reprise!!*

They were released as singles, although "Senza Fine" seemed to lose itself somewhere for a while and was not issued as a regular single for either the American or United Kingdom markets.

For the future, Dean's management would carefully work out the release schedules for both singles and albums: he would record batches of songs at a time and all would be chosen for albums of songs, with singles being used for the usual heavy promotion within the industry.

With his initial five songs, even then he threw in a smattering of the Italian style ballads – but he changed his theme entirely for his second studio visit when he taped a dozen songs all in one day, on February 26th. He'd decided to record an album of French-inspired style songs, gathering them all together and with the impeccable talents again of Neal Hefti, Dean really embraced this theme, even remarking at the end of a song '…there's some good stuff around here, Frank!'

FRENCH STYLE was a good selection of songs for his first Reprise album release and in my own personal opinion, I always thought that this was one of his finest albums for his new company, but, strangely, it did not do very well and was not one of his best-selling releases. There was little if any marketing for it. I have wondered why ever since, and have considered whether or not it was down to the public's reception of the album's cover image – where a not-entirely serious Dean had adopted a beret and a cigarette-holder! There had always been a conflict for the public with Dean the actor/comedian and Dean the serious singer – it was as if people couldn't marry the two.

Very few of the companions and staff at this time realized that he was suffering from arthritis in his spine, a painful and aggravating condition. He told no one about his problems and suffered in silence, taking medication recommended by his close friend Mack Gray. His life was so very busy now and he felt he had no time to complain or bother too much about his health at the age of 45. This was a habit that he was to keep throughout his life: he detested any medical issues or hospitals and would leave things to the last minute before he would do something about it.

It seems many of us have a phobia and in Dean's case, this was his - plus his other worries of travelling in elevators or on an airplane.

After two years of existence, the International Dean Martin Club published its first complete film list, detailing to date all the information of Dean's films. This was issued to all of our members, along with the regular monthly newsletter.

Slowly but surely, we were gaining more members, and we were able to supply a selection of photographs of Dean, which his office had provided for our use.

At Dino's Lodge, however, there was trouble.

Even though it regularly attracted icons such as Judy Garland (but not Dean himself), his partners had been found mismanaging the business and Dean sued, receiving damages, but his demands to remove his name and image from the fascia were rejected. He was able to bring in his brother Bill to manage things, and he did so until the venue eventually closed as business dried up.

His film career now garnered the attention of Hollywood royalty.

Marilyn Monroe asked for him (and no one else) to be her leading man in her next picture with 20th Century Fox, who then made him an offer of $300,000. *Something's Got to Give* was based on the film *My Favorite Wife* which was in turn based on the poem "Enoch Arden" by Alfred, Lord Tennyson. Fox were eager to recoup their losses for *Cleopatra* and they saw the joint billing of Monroe and Martin to be the way towards it.

Dean liked Marilyn immensely and she greatly admired Dean's looks, his singing and his manner. She was the top actress of her time, infamous for her temperament but nevertheless in great demand for her work. She had that wonderful status of being known, like Dean, by her first name only, so it was a match made in heaven.

Dean's advisers did warn him that she was renowned for various temperamental tantrums and complications, but he was personally flattered that she'd asked him, even though the script, he felt, wasn't what he wanted to do.

'I felt like I was going backwards but how could you say no to her?'

As production commenced, so did the problems.

Marilyn continually arrived late or sometimes not at all, causing nightmares for the film executives. The budget was expanding by the hour for every one she lost them, and eventually the studio issued a suit of $500,000 against her for breach of contract, announcing that she had been taken off the film to be replaced by Lee Remick.

While she was still adored by fans worldwide and in their millions, her exquisite charm was wearing thin for the studios. The very next morning, Dean himself announced he would not be making this film. Fox had no choice but to close down production, and attempted to sue Dean for every cent that had been spent so far on the movie (only a few feet had been shot so far) plus an extra $1million thrown in for 'exemplary damages'. With the demand of over $3,339,000 on his head, Dean counter-sued for $6,900,000, citing 'fraud, oppression and malice'. He stated, too, that he had no objection to the talents of Miss Remick, but his contract stated otherwise.

It was, he stated, Marilyn or no one.

Several weeks later, Fox agreed to continue production with both original stars but no sooner had the cameras started to roll again that Marilyn was in hospital suffering a miscarriage. She then descended into a severe and uncontrollable depression and never returned to the set. The production was finally cancelled on 11th June 1962 and on 5th August that same year, Marilyn was found dead at her home.

Something's Got to Give was never completed and Dean and Fox settled out of court. Fox did however overhaul the entire production and remounted it as *Move Over, Darling* with Doris Day and James Garner in 1963. The footage of the original version was released in 1990 as part of the one-hour documentary *Marilyn: Something's Got to Give* then re-edited again in 2001 for *Marilyn: The Final Days*.

TWELVE

Watching The World Go By

Dean now went straight on to his next film *Who's Got the Action?* for Paramount, another comedy, this time about a gambling husband whose wife (played by the beautiful Lana Turner) was sick and tired of his losing money on the horses.

As part of his agreement, Dean again would record the title song for a single, amongst other tracks that took on multiple genres, including Latin and Country. With fine arrangements by such talent as Don Costa, Gus Levene and Neal Hefti, he slowly moved back into the charts.

His popularity in Europe was growing (as our club membership could attest to) and there was a (now long since defunct) radio station called Radio Luxembourg that was using Dean's recording of "One More Time" as a theme to one of its regular features where listeners wrote in about their most hated record – and I'm pleased to say that none of Dean's ever featured!

We also had a feature on the club in the magazine *Cherie* in 1963 and we held our own top ten record poll: members wrote in with their top ten Dean Martin songs and the favorite chosen above all others in this instance was "How Do You Speak To An Angel?".

The tape cassette format was introduced in the United Kingdom this year and UK label Pye Records stated that they would not be issuing stereophonic versions of Dean's albums unless his sales improved.

EMI Records' mail-order company, World Records, asked us to compile a special album for them for release sometime in 1964 and this was to comprise songs taken from previous Capitol releases, and songs chosen by us for their UK customers.

As far as British television was concerned, we did not see much of Dean's work, although the BBC screened *Laughter USA* which included some vintage Martin and Lewis segments.

Among many others shows and appearances, Dean had been the guest with Martha Raye on *The Bob Hope Show* for NBC TV on 14th April 1963, and had taken Jeanne to see Frank in concert at the Flamingo, Las Vegas. He also hosted a Dick Powell Theatre production and was the first competitor for the Frank Sinatra Annual Golf Tournament for November 7th, keeping him very active with his work and the occasional --if not indeed rare-- private function.

The Frank, Dean, and Sammy trio had found their act by now and were pulling in huge audiences in towns like Chicago, and, of course, their adopted home, Las Vegas.

Sammy and I met briefly in London and he talked with such verve about his working relationship and friendship with Dean, saying he was a perfect gentleman and a complete prankster, and said he did very little but laugh when he was in Dean's company. From photos of him and Dean together, and where they are with Frank, you can clearly see this relationship.

Two further films were now scheduled for Dean, *Boeing Boeing* with Frank, and *I Love Louisa*, but shortly after this announcement, Dean was admitted to hospital suffering from exhaustion, not surprising when you looked at his working schedule covering the next four years!

Returning home a few days later to rest and recuperate, confirmation came (which Dean was expecting) that Frank had sold out his complete ownership of Reprise for it to merge with Warner Brothers Records (meanwhile, many miles across the globe, it was noted that Dean's version of Johnny Cash's "I Walk the Line" had reached number three in September...in South Africa).

If you take a careful look at the film *Come Blow Your Horn*, you will see a disheveled tramp wander past as he is presented with a piece of steak by Frank Sinatra. Only on the screen for a few seconds, Dean makes the cameo appearance here that only he can – even in that fleeting moment, as he goes past the camera, you know it's him.

Dean then made a dramatic change in his character roles, choosing to play the part of Julian Berniers alongside Wendy Hiller and Geraldine Page in Lillian Hellman's original story *Toys in the Attic* for United Artists. This disturbing story was presented on the screen in an excellent version of the play, the first written by Hellman in almost a decade. Dean's brutal portrayal shocked quite a number of critics: they simply weren't used to seeing him tackle such an extreme role.

He reverted to type for *Who's Been Sleeping in My Bed?* with the delectable Elizabeth Montgomery. This film now marked the completion of the original Martin and Lewis contract that producer Hal B. Wallis adjusted when the two stars parted company back in 1956, so there was no longer any obligation to revert to Paramount.

He switched to Warner Brothers for his next film effort, again with Frank Sinatra, teaming with Bond girl Ursula Andress and Anita Ekberg for the Robert Aldrich-directed western comedy *4 For Texas*. Produced by the SAM Company [Sinatra, Aldrich, Martin], the film was to originally have cast Dean with Gina Lollobrigida, but, as she was unavailable, the title was changed from *Two for Texas* to its familiar title and the subsequent four actors with equal billing.

Opposed as he was to too much travelling outside of California, Dean had declined to go to Broadway for the grand opening night of *Toys in the Attic* at the Hudson Theatre, but asked me to attend, which I duly did.

With Dean Martin's star rising ever higher, he was cultivating the relaxed, drunk image more than ever but at the same time working much harder and diversifying into many roles in his film work. His recordings too were moving towards more sophisticated attitudes all round, with carefully planned issues and promotion. What little time he did have for relaxation, he would sit at home and watch television or perhaps rest in a steam bath for an hour or so before his next commitment, playing as much golf as he could possibly fit in between.

He was now part owner of the Sands Hotel in Vegas, with

his own production companies and real estate businesses: he had become partners with Laurence Harvey and Frank Sinatra for a restaurant, the Bistro, and he was a major shareholder in RCA and many more investments that gave him an excellent income, not including his payments and royalties from his films and recordings.

The original Reprise offices had gone now and were incorporated within those of Warner Brothers at Warner Boulevard. But the label was still attracting some of the biggest names in the recording world, as well as licensing material from abroad.

Although by mid-1963, Dean had had four albums and a gathering of singles issued, there was not much headway towards chart positions related to sales. He continued to sell in reasonable quantities, though, as each release became available in stores around the world.

He hosted the original show *The Hollywood Palace* on Saturday 7th March 1964, which gave him more coverage on the small screen; he began to consider making more of a presence there but was conscious that over-exposure would be a detriment.

He was invited to the famous Grauman's Chinese Theatre on 21st March to make his handprints on the sidewalk outside and with his mischievous humor he made sure his shoe prints were there as well!

Dean continued to increase his workload all the time, regardless of his health (he continued to have his arthritic problems and occasional intestinal infections.) Nevertheless, he loved to stay up late and sleep late when he could and, of course, watch television, finding inspiration in commercial breaks and soaking up ideas that he could use himself. He played golf and tennis, had always been a good boxer, swimmer and tennis player, and although he was a past master at portraying relaxation, spare time was becoming a rare commodity.

This was just one of the reasons Dean gave out such an air of laziness. He worked hard, maybe even harder than the average artist, but as he worked, he made his act look easy because of the way he did it. He'd come to a film set prepared and ready, sailing through it while cracking a few jokes -- wherever he was, and whoever he was with. The end result was a unique, professional entertainer, with a charming and relaxed persona presented to the public.

Although his personal life with his wife and children was in a reasonable situation now, he was still seen on numerous occasions with a woman on his arm.

This seemed to contradict with his stance that he had no time for complications, yet by encouraging extra-marital dalliances, he incurred exactly that.

From a working viewpoint, all his affairs, no pun intended, were dealt with by his management. He performed what was asked of him, and expected everyone to accept that fact and leave him to do his own thing as and when he wished.

He was quite often found difficult and aloof by many as a result but this was only at the first instance: once you had accepted his mannerisms and general attitude to his own life, he was found to be likeable and effervescent in his approach.

Dean had always been a loner – not lonely, that is something entirely different – and few people who were associated with him, either in his career or his private life, were able to get through to him. Through to the man inside, what he thought, what he felt. Only a small handful of people, primarily those in his own family, found the way into his domain of thoughts and deeds.

'I know I'm arrogant and argumentative. I've pushed people and businesses to get what I wanted. In this business, there's no way you can sit back and wait for that something to happen. You have to push hard for what you want.'

With continued appearances at the Sands Hotel, he also stood in for Nat 'King' Cole when the famous singer became ill at Christmas.

Meanwhile, we had completed the compilation for the World Record Club: the song list was finalized, as were the sleeve design and notes. I chose the title LET'S BE FRIENDLY, a song included on the album, and it was released 15th June 1964, eight days after Dean's 47th birthday and to coincide with his 21st year in show business.

Coverage for this album included an interview by me with Dean. EMI did us proud with some splendid publicity for the release as well as for our organization. This was our very first album release that we had had the chance to work on and, unbeknownst to us at that time, we were to have many more opportunities to do so.

Dean had also recorded quite a number of varied songs with Reprise, working with his pianist and arranger Ken Lane, who had agreed with Dean at the singer's home all but one of twelve tracks required for a new album.

Going through numerous manuscripts, Ken came across one that he and Irving Taylor had written in the 40s entitled "Everybody Loves Somebody". Playing a few bars on the piano, Jeanne immediately remembered the tune as one of her favourites from a few years back. Frank himself had recorded it for Columbia on 4th December 1947 but had not had any particular success with it. Dean remarked that, following Ken's piano rendition, it was 'quite nice' and that if Jeanne liked it, it was good enough for him! He'd actually already sung it, way back in 1948 for an edition of *The Bob Hope Show*.

DREAM WITH DEAN – THE INTIMATE DEAN MARTIN was released in the US on 4th August, with the UK release following a month later. It was one of Dean's most sophisticated albums, and unusual for the fact there was not the normal full orchestral backing, but just four top musicians, namely Irv Cottier on drums, Ken Lane at the piano. Barney Kessel was on guitar, and Red Mitchell on bass. Together, they created Dean's very first Gold album, reaching 15 in the American charts on 29th August and remaining in the charts for 31 weeks.

It came in the wake of *What a Way To Go!* (originally titled *I Love Louisa*), a 20th Century Fox release with a stellar cast that included Shirley MacLaine, Robert Mitchum, Paul Newman, Gene Kelly, Bob Cummings and Dick Van Dyke.

He had also filmed two segments for a travel extravaganza special showing some of the world's top nightspots. Dean was seen relaxing poolside at his home then taking a drive as two of his hit songs "Return To Me" and "On An Evening In Roma" played in the background. Its title depended upon which country you saw the film; as it had three: *Songs of the World*, *World by Night*, and the suggestive *38-24-36*.

More studio time followed and Dean was now – finally--considered a best-selling artist, which led to the idea of teaming up with Bing Crosby to record BING, DINO AND DIXIE. Reprise even scheduled a catalog number (RS6127) and designed the cover for the Dixie-land style album but sadly, the artists were never together for long enough to record at the same time, so the whole project was scrapped.

Just over a month later, with Dean having to specially record his songs for the soundtrack of the film *Robin and the 7 Hoods*, he included amongst them an up-tempo version of "Everybody Loves Somebody" at the suggestion of his record producer Jimmy Bowen. Jimmy liked the melody and was convinced it could be a big hit if they were to and give it a sing-a-long approach, something in the music industry which was beginning to prove popular. His singles sales were moderate at this stage but with this, Dean hit the jackpot. The hit version went to number 1 in America and gave him his first Gold single for Reprise, the press calling him *Beatle-buster Martin!* for knocking the British pop combo off the top spot, a feat that no one else seemed to be able to do. Reprise had a winner on their hands and released a new album EVERYBODY LOVES SOMEBODY – THE HIT VERSION securing another Gold album.

Frank, Dean and Sammy had an intriguing idea to record some songs calling themselves the Bumblers, but nothing came of it.

In 1964, we issued the first edition of Dean's discography, also choosing the front cover photograph for an album to be released later in the year entitled THE DOOR IS STILL OPEN TO MY HEART. Dean had contacted me directly inviting me to his home (he had been in London for a mere three days this year shopping!) but around a week later, work commitments meant he had to cancel.

Rumors of Dean and Frank coming to England for concerts were unfounded and didn't form any part of the workload that had been scheduled for the next five years ahead.

Once again, though, his personal life could not be said to be as mapped out: Jeanne had no social life and complained most bitterly about her lack of time with her famous husband. His children saw even less of him and only heard him on the radio. It was off to school or college when their father had maybe only come home an hour or two earlier, going straight to bed. He very rarely saw them or shared breakfast with any of them, even his wife.

With his monogrammed clothes laying around some of the rooms, they knew when he was home. He was not the tidiest of people, very often leaving clothes around. When he wasn't working (a rare occurrence), he and Jeanne would be in bed by 11.30pm, but he would stay awake to watch late films until the early hours.

He had always had the habit of eating fast (one of the reasons he had developed an ulcer), and suffered indigestion frequently. Numerous times over the years, Jeanne would try anything to slow him down. He would eat the average meal twice as fast as she or anyone else did which always concerned her.

With his massive popularity in the recording scene, Capitol sought various ways of making money by re-issuing numerous songs from their large back catalog of his recordings with them. They were reluctant to choose unusual or little-heard items, instead they tended to issue 'best of' compilations which, admittedly, did sell in large quantities, although they did not in any form reach the giddy heights of Dean's Reprise material.

His tremendous successes in the US meant numerous compilations were appearing on licensed releases on the Tower and Pickwick labels. However, in 1965, EMI had created a brand-new budget label called Music For Pleasure, in collaboration with Paul Hamlyn Limited, and the very first UK album to be issued was MFP1001 THE DEAN SINGS, a solid collection of his singles, some quite unusual. But just to confuse everyone, this collection was exactly the same as the former THE DEAN SINGS AGAIN album via World Records, but for a different cover.

The label itself was to become one of the most successful budget series ever, enabling the availability of mostly re-issued material from hundreds of artists across many labels. It continues its success today, backed by the efficiency and years of experience of EMI Records.

Meanwhile, our society remained popular and busy, and we increased the annual subscription to ten shillings from 1st February 1965. Membership was steadily increasing year-by-year now, and we were becoming more popular as we increased our international advertising.

Frank and Dean led the parade for the late trumpeter Conrad Gozzo this year, with Dean being voted the *23rd Best World Singer* by UK pop newspaper *New Musical Express* and Dave Dennis from the 'pirate' radio station Radio London, chose "(Remember Me) I'm The One Who Loves You" as his *Pick of The Week* for two weeks from 14th June. These little snippets into the public's awareness of him showed he was within their consciousness.

As one mere example of Dean's record sales, his single "The Door is Still Open To My Heart" sold over 400,000 copies, remaining in the American charts for eleven weeks and reaching number six - with even a UK chart entry at a more leisurely 42! With Dean's eventual release of another album, HOUSTON, he was made an honorary citizen of that city in Texas.

We were privileged enough to attend the recording sessions for HOUSTON, a wonderful insight into a typical working day for Dean. He was always so relaxed and effortless, not one for demanding take after take.

During the late sixties and into the seventies, there was a

significant boost of material around from Dean: Both Reprise and Capitol were coming out with numerous releases – all to whet the appetite of the record-buying public. THE LUSH YEARS, DEAN MARTIN DELUXE, DEAN MARTIN HITS AGAIN and YOUNG AND FOOLISH were just a handful of the many releases on the market at this time, although the bulk of these were issued for the American market.

But, as everyone was now well aware, it was not just Dean's records that were blasting his name to the top all around the world. He also had his films, cabaret, and guest spots everywhere.

NBC kept on at him to attempt a friendly persuasion to launch his own television show but he simply wasn't interested. As a way to stave off their advances, he demanded certain conditions, some so unusual and out of line that he genuinely believed no executive in their right mind would accept them.

'I told them that if we were gonna do this, then I'd own the shows. And if I didn't want to sing in any of them, they weren't gonna make me.' Dean had a wry smile on his face as he told me this, the outcome of his demands of course well known. 'I said I'd be at the studio for one day a week and I'd suggest the guests. I never imagined they'd go for it!'

But go for it they did.

Even Dean himself had failed to recognize the magnitude of his status in this business, or see how far he had progressed. Neither did he realize just how much his associates respected his achievements so far.

THIRTEEN

That Lucky Old Sun

With a contracted fee of over $34,000,000, the Dean Martin Television Show first aired at 10pm on Thursday 16th September 1965.

Dean seemed happy, although he appeared to wander around the show on screen as if he had never been on television before, with jokes like: *I got picked up the other night on suspicion of drunk driving. The cop asked me to walk a white line. I said not unless you put a net under it*, and parodies of songs: *In your Easter bonnet, with all the frills upon it, you'd look a bit peculiar in the men's room, my dear*, or: *Return to me...I've a sink full of dishes*, and *Take me in your arms...I'll never make it to the car*. That was the sort of thing that Dean told his audiences he'd do: he'd play with the material he'd been singing for years, would ad-lib, crack endless jokes and occasionally fail to finish a song.

His guest stars were giants in the industry: John Wayne, Orson Welles, Bob Newhart, Frank Sinatra, Sammy Davis Jr, Dom Deluise, Rich Little, Jimmy Stewart, Foster Brooks, Tony Bennett -- to name but a few. They, along with Dean, readily parodied themselves, sometimes in outrageous wigs and even in drag. Dean also showcased newcomers such as the effervescent and beautiful Goldie Hawn and welcomed British stars like Petula Clark, Marty Feldman, Stanley Holloway and Peter Sellers. The roll-call went on and on and was, quite simply, impressive.

With a regular series and weekly TV exposure, his record sales increased and he garnered more recognition than his films could achieve.

When asked a few weeks later what he would do if NBC did not renew his first season, he replied by saying that he'd made up his mind for regular television and would go to ABC or CBS or, if no networks wanted him he'd stick to his recordings, his cabaret and movies.

'After all, that's what I'd done already, made sure that I'd have several strings to my bow, you know, not relying on just one thing in this business. I don't think you can do that if you really want to be successful in this game. Diversification is the name of it and I like to think that I tried all chapters of this and did the best I could.'

The best that Dean Martin *did* do was bring in the television audiences in their millions – and he did so with the public loving his devil-may-care attitude. Every show topped the Nielsen ratings, and there was never any doubt that NBC would renew his show for future series.

Into the second year, he and producer Greg Garrison formed their own company to produce the shows, with a staggering (for the time) weekly budget of $200,000. Dean himself was receiving $50,000 a show, plus massive investments from his shares in RCA, NBC's parent company.

Dean's rota for taping his segments for each show was always the same: the guest stars and crew would rehearse their parts (usually with Greg standing in for Dean) to get everything timed and set. Dean, of course, used to learn his lines by having three tapes made at the studio: one for home; one for golf; a third for wherever else he may be. He possibly spent more time than his guests in learning his lines, rehearsing whenever he had the chance, and then walking onto the set on the Saturday to have his own contributions filmed and finished, ready for the completed shows to be transmitted the following Thursday.

So many people thought he was a miracle man, coming in to the television studios in the morning and knowing all his lines and where to stand, sit or film the next take without having been with them all week.

'I found learning my lines pretty easy to do from having to learn the words of songs, so my TV show was no different.'

Dean kept his actual studio rehearsals to a minimum. While he knew the script verbatim, he insisted on cue cards at all times when he filmed and made sure that the audience knew he was using them. It was all part of the act. He also enjoyed the spontaneity that came with performing with guests for the first time. Rehearsing with them, he felt, would water that down.

Part of his job too meant he had to socialize.

And he hated socializing.

Being at home or in his hotel room with a TV and a glass of milk was how this superstar enjoyed himself. Dean was rarely found at Hollywood functions, although when the necessity arose, and where it may have been beneficial to his career, along he went.

Jeanne became somewhat used to the idea of having to socialize by herself. Her husband was all too often away with his work and if he was with Frank, Sammy, Shirley and the CClan, she knew it may be some time before she would see him at home again. As Dean himself said, 'Where else can you go out and do a day's work, have lots of fun with the girls and the guys and get well paid for it? You tell me where else anyone can do that!'

With this appealing atmosphere, anyone could see what Dean Martin meant, especially when his professional and relaxed approach showed up so well on screen, particularly in films like 1963's *Robin and the 7 Hoods*, sadly the last film the Clan made together and, in fact, the last musical for Bing Crosby.

A somewhat quieter but stronger story came next for Dean when he signed with Billy Wilder for the film version of Anna Bonacci's stage comedy *Dazzling Hour*. Released in February 1965 as *Kiss Me, Stupid*, he starred as cabaret singer Dino opposite Kim Novak as the wonderfully-monikered Polly the Pistol. Peter Sellers was signed as Orville J Spooner but because of the talented British comedian's increasingly bad health with his heart, he had to be replaced by Ray Walston.

This was a shame, as I had personally followed Peter's career from his early days with Spike Milligan and Harry Secombe in the BBC Radio series *The Goons*. Dean had done likewise and they did eventually work together on an episode of Dean's TV show.

The songs for *Kiss Me, Stupid* were supplied by George and Ira Gershwin, one of them entitled "Sophia" which Dean recorded for Reprise but was never generally released to tie in with the film. The music was scored by renowned classical conductor Andre Previn.

This was classified as an 'X' film for its day, because of the suggestive and sexually-charged scenes. Dean's status had really moved to higher spheres: he still owned property and estates that would make a book on their own in their paper capacity; investments he had made (and not including his career) were now making him a very wealthy man. This enabled him to easily part with $20,000 to celebrate his parents' 50th wedding anniversary and lavishly furnish his rambling $600,000 mansion in Beverly Hills – although at this time only four out of his seven children were actually living there (Deana, Gina, Ricci and Dean Jr).

All of his children had always been devoted to him and some years later I was fortunate enough to talk with Deana, who lavished such honest and loving praise about her father that it was hard to be unmoved.

He would willingly offer to write notes to his children's teachers, excusing them for their homework if they wished, although they hardly ever took him up on his offers!

On one occasion when Craig had failed his woodwork examinations, his sisters told him that Dad would be very annoyed – but when Dad saw the reports, he just simply said, 'Well, he ain't gonna be a carpenter!'

It was usually Jeanne who controlled the children's discipline and organized the home routine. She was a lady that preferred to be the wife and mother as opposed to partaking in the glitz and glamour of Dean's world, although she would have liked to have taken part in just some of his socializing. She was a stickler for impeccable manners, teaching all seven children to be polite at all times, and how they should behave inside and outside of the family circle. When asked to pass the bread at the dining table, she would expect just that, but sometimes

Dean himself would be liable to throw a slice or two on to their plates just for the kick of it all.

That was Dean's way, which does not mean he had no interest in family manners. To the contrary, he was strict, but believed that they should all go on their own way and decide what they would like to do, with his guidance and advice, for what it is worth (he added).

He was happy that they were all content with their various careers and lives and, without any singing lessons, their father proved to them and everyone else in the world that you can make it by sheer hard work, a lot of luck and, in Dean's particular case, a natural flair for entertaining (and with over forty million people watching his weekly television show, who could argue with that?).

He always did want to entertain, but he also wanted it to look easy, so he worked extremely hard at looking laid back and relaxed and, of course, he became a global success in everything he cared to do.

If there was a rare day in which he was not working, he would be off to the golf course, as he liked to play a few rounds before the dew went and before too many people arrived; but if his mind took him off that idea, then he would sometimes lay in bed until nearly lunchtime!

Then, of course, there was Dean Martin's mammoth capacity for drinking.

A complete myth.

There was only ever apple juice in that glass tumbler. It was a prop, nothing more. His drunk image was just that, an image manufactured by the man himself in the early days of his career, simply because he noticed audiences loved the stance. He became synonymous with booze and encouraged it. Even some of his peers believed he was drunk, he was that good at it. Yet at the same time, I believe it became something of a burden for him: people expected him to be drunk so he simply had to keep up the act.

'If people see me as a drunk, let them,' he told me. 'I sure couldn't hit the right notes if I was as stoned as they say I am. I could never do a good show like that.'

The Dean you saw on chat shows or being interviewed wasn't the Dean at home. The times we spoke on the telephone, he had none of his stage drawl. His act was his act, his private life away from the cameras and the microphones was one where he could relax.

But relaxing wasn't easy: his success at work was not matched by his personal life. He had reached such a pinnacle of work and engagements that he spent less and less time with Jeanne. She understood the drive in him, but at the same time would have liked to see more of him at home and not have him so distant, in both mileage and emotion.

Tensions built up again, but he had no desire to go to any functions with Jeanne and, as a result, she became very upset so they parted again. But like last time, this was a brief separation: Dean agreed to cut back on some work and things were patched up between them. Although they both agreed that the money was more than nice, it seemed Dean was working himself just a little too much and Jeanne did think that he could afford to cut back on some of his commitments. As a result, the film *Community Property* with Margaret Rutherford, Ann-Margret and Frank Sinatra was never made, neither was the previously mentioned *Boeing, Boeing*.

He continued his recording sessions for Reprise, however, with such wonderful songs and albums like DEAN MARTIN HITS AGAIN (originally to be titled YOU'RE NOBODY 'TIL SOMEBODY LOVES YOU), "Red Roses for A Blue Lady" and the classic "Welcome To My World", a song he used frequently in his TV shows.

But although Dean did reduce his workload, he continued his cabaret and other appearances, including a guest spot in the western series *Rawhide*. He was also approached to see if he would consider a series of films in which he would play a character called Matt Helm, the hero of the successful super-spy novels by Donald Hamilton.

The Sons of Katie Elder for Paramount came next, though, a very strong western in which he again starred with John

Wayne, together with Earl Holliman and Michael Anderson Junior. Filmed in Durango, Mexico, the film was originally going to be called *Durango*. The Durango Country Club golf course entertained Dean in between shoots, and he actually got his first hole in one! Dean even cooked a pasta meal for the director and cast on the set, but forgot to add vegetables to his heavily spiced dish of spaghetti and fetuccini. As a result, local doctor Pedro Peres was called in because they all had excessive stomach pains!

A further collaboration with Frank (and Deborah Kerr) led him to film the comedy *Marriage on the Rocks*, with Cesar Romero, (future Joker to Adam West's unique Batman), and soon-to-be *Star Trek* icon DeForest Kelley). Frank's own daughter (and Dean's god-daughter) Nancy featured in the cast but it seemed to me that most of the actors seemed uneasy in this venture. Perhaps that was just the way I saw it, but something didn't gel, although it did have moderate success at the box office.

FOURTEEN

Don't Be A Do-Badder

Dean's recording manager Jimmy Bowen had arrived in London in early 1965 with his fiancée Keely Smith, and I spent a couple of days with them whilst she recorded some wonderful songs at the Pye studios under the expert direction of Tony Hatch. Jimmy he said he enjoyed working in the UK, finding the approach by British technicians to be far more relaxed but nevertheless as professional and dedicated as any other studio.

'The atmosphere is less charged,' he told me. 'You guys get the job done.' I asked him, too, about working with Dean. 'Oh, he's a laid back guy. You know that. A couple of takes more or less and it's there.'

On any further recordings from Dean, Jimmy said, 'It would be great to get new material down, but he seems reluctant to commit himself to any more recordings.'

Unaware of the fact at the time, it was while I was with Keely that she told me that she was the 'little voice' on the record that Dean had made (called "A Little Voice"). She remarked how easy and lovely he was to work with and that she would have loved to have recorded some songs with him.

I was also told that future Dean Martin albums in the UK would now be in Stereo as well as Mono. This was excellent news as this indicated his British sales were increasing much more!

Dean had been interviewed for the National Guard sessions, a series of fifteen minute shows for American radio to help promote the National Guard; light-hearted chat interspersed with some of his popular recordings.

He also did a three-week season at the Sands Hotel and turned down another film, *Luv*, that had been provisionally scheduled for the autumn.

With Dean's record releases, nothing else could describe his success in this field other than stupendous! DREAM WITH

Dean, Everybody Loves Somebody, The Door Is Still Open
To My Heart, Dean Martin Hits Again, (Remember Me) I'm
The One Who Loves You, Houston and Somewhere There's
A Someone had given Dean seven Gold Albums (for a million
sales each) in succession up to October 1965, a feat no other
artist had achieved, and an event that also happened in the
midst of a semi-explosion in the music business where there
were such changes in style.

Dean took all of this in his stride. He was astounded at the
conveyor-belt of hits he was having, but at the same time he
recognized that it was success and ensured that he recorded
songs that were very typical of the times.

In the period of two years from June 1964 through to mid-
1966 he sold in excess of 3,415,000 singles, plus a staggering
collection of over 2,899,000 albums, making him the hottest
artist on Reprise.

With his deal now completed for a series of six Matt Helm
films, co-produced by his own company Meadway-Claude,
work began on *The Silencers*, based on the novels *The Silencers*
and *Death of A Citizen*. Intended as America's answer to James
Bond, the Matt Helm films were just as removed from the
Hamilton novels as the Bond films were from the Ian Fleming
works. They even 'out-gadgeted' the ridiculous inventions
from Q Branch. This was Dean at his relaxed, caricatured best.
He played the part to perfection and every film in the series
bordered on comedy with a moderate amount of danger, thin
plots, bikini-clad girls and lots of action. Dean even sang
parodies of his songs in the films where he could. He recorded
a special set of songs for Reprise for *The Silencers*, also
including some powerful instrumental tracks on the same
album, released in the US on 8th March 1966.

Such was the success of *The Silencers*, a full range of Louis
Marx and Crescent toys were made available to tie in with the
film. Locations were filmed in the Columbia ranch and street
area which was rebuilt to look like a residential New Mexico
town, complete with a Bel Air Hotel and swimming pools. The
fast automobile chases took place at Santa Fe, New Mexico,

and Phoenix, Arizona. In the course of filming, five stuntmen were hurt: one of them, Tom Henessey, had three front teeth knocked out and had his head heavily bruised by Dean during a fight scene.

Interestingly, the out-and-out comedy spy series of *Austin Powers* decades later seems to owe more to Dean's secret agent than EON's more successful take on James Bond.

In the closing weeks of this year, Reprise in America decided to have what they called a *Dean Martin Month* (it was actually a two-month period) when they issued two new albums, THE DEAN MARTIN TELEVISION SHOW and THE DEAN MARTIN CHRISTMAS ALBUM with a massive publicity campaign commencing 1st November and lasting until New Year's Eve.

His first picture for Universal was the comedy Western *Texas Across the River* with Alain Delon and Joey Bishop.

Next came the second Matt Helm movie, *Murderer's Row*. We attended a special private showing at the 20th Century-Fox Private Theatre, 31, Soho Square London on Wednesday 25th January 1967, prior to the film opening in the UK. We brushed shoulders with the cast and crew (but not, of course, Dino!). Matt Helm's Slaygirls were in attendance, too. It was a great start to 1967. Several locations were used for this film, among them the picturesque Isle of Wight. Dean had invited me to come to the shoot, to watch him film and to spend some time with him afterwards. It had intended to be an all-expenses paid event for me, with hotel accommodation and something like 3 weeks' worth of filming for the star. Dean cancelled not long after the invite, citing increasing workloads, but I took up Columbia's kind offer and watched the UK filming anyway. All the scenes filmed in and around the hovercrafts were with a body double. You don't need to look too hard to see, in the finished film, that it's not Dean! The Isle of Wight hovercraft that was used was re-named 'Matt Helm One' after the filming.

A sort of family affair, Dean's son Dean Jr appeared with Desi Arnaz Junior and Billy Hinsche, all three making the pop trio Dino, Desi and Billy, who were enjoying reasonable success in the music market themselves at this time.

The following month, in February, we supported Pye Records with their *Dean Martin Week* from Monday the 13th, then collaborated with them for a 45rpm one-sided single issue of "I'm Not the Marrying Kind", complete with an introduction from the man himself. The release was limited and is now a very rare item.

Meanwhile, Dean was voted *Music Man of the Year* by the Academy of Country and Western Music in Los Angeles, but the award was collected on his behalf by his daughters Claudia and Deana on 6th March. And talking of daughters, my own was born just two days before! Dean congratulated my wife and me, and in June even sent over the same brand of doll that he had been photographed holding on the front of his HAPPINESS IS… LP. Carole still owns the doll to this day and remains proud that Dean gave it to her as a present.

Pye now began to issue cassette tapes, and Dean's first album re-appeared in this new format as ZCK4-44022.

We issued an interview with Dean via our newsletter for July and this created quite some excitement with the members (he had agreed to answer a series of set questions from me over the telephone).

With Reprise, Dean was now talking of recording an album of songs in the Hawaiian style, but nothing further came of this project. Prior to this in 1966, Dean had proposed a religious type collection that was even assigned a catalog number and title (RB6189 OLD TIME RELIGION). Again, nothing had come of it – but was an intriguing concept.

At a charity concert in Los Angeles, Dean donated $350 to hear Bobby Darin sing and one of Europe's offshore 'pirate' radio stations, Britain Radio, featured us during September, which again boosted our status somewhat. Also, the teen magazine *Diana* gave us a large feature, giving details of our club and our aims for the future.

As part of a deal he had made with Universal Pictures, Dean made another film for them entitled *Rough Night In Jericho*, teaming himself with the beautiful and well-known Jean

Simmons and an up and coming actor called George Peppard who was beginning to make a good name for himself. Peppard would find fame ultimately as the cigar-chomping, wise-cracking Colonel John 'Hannibal' Smith in Stephen J Cannell's 80s action series *The A-Team*.

As Alex Flood, this was the very first time that Dean actually 'died' in character on film, as this was something he had always balked at before. His part was described as 'very heavy' and he gave an excellent performance as the antagonist, treating Simmons' character with such poison.

Nancy Sinatra was finding her own way in the industry, and her hit single, "These Boots Are Made for Walkin'" has since gone down in history. Dean guest-starred in her TV special *Movin' with Nancy* in 1967, fitting in his recorded sequences in between his own shows and Reprise studio bookings. One such song could almost have been the theme to his acted persona, although this was generally by the public and not him: "Little Ole Wine Drinker, Me" was more of a hit in Europe than it was in America when it was released in June of this year.

Incidentally, the song that Dean had had re-mixed for Nancy to sing in his original recording of "Things" reached number one in Sweden that same July, and remained in the chart for five weeks, having never been issued as a single either in America or the UK.

Capitol Records USA released their first-ever boxed set in October, and it was aptly named THE DEAN MARTIN DELUXE SET, containing three albums of songs all previously available.

Meanwhile, his weekly TV show for NBC was still charging up the ratings, his studio band being Les Brown and His Band of Renown.

Pennsylvania-born Les started his career as a band leader in 1936 with 'Les Brown and His Blue Devils', becoming 'Les Brown and His Band of Renown' from 1938. Performing with stars such as Doris Day, Tony Bennett, Ella Fitzgerald, Nat King Cole and Dean Martin, to name but a few, Les worked with his band until 2000. Les himself passed away aged 88 in 2001.

We'd been in contact with Joel Guldin, who chairs the Les Brown Big Band Festival[2] committee (and hosts an annual event at the Williams Valley High School in Pennsylvania, where Les Brown Jr. appears) and he'd mentioned to Hal Espinosa, who was Les' lead trumpet player for many years, of our own association with Dean Martin.

We were very fortunate to chat with Hal about his own career, about working with Les and, of course, knowing Dean.

'Dean Martin had his own show on NBC, only one of eleven different variety shows that were being produced around that time. In those days musicians worked on multiple shows. They were staff bands and most studios had them: NBC, CBS and so on. It was the same with movie studios, too, and MGM had its own: the MGM Studio Orchestra.'

Hal was in Las Vegas for six years prior to moving to LA in 1969. When he arrived in LA, Butch Stone, saxophone player for Les Brown (and who was also the musician contractor for the band), had heard about Hal from somebody and wanted to see if he'd be interested in performing with them.

'They were going out on the road for three weeks,' Hal said, 'and their lead trumpeter was on staff at NBC and so the studio wouldn't release him for the tour. That same musician also used to work on *The Dean Martin Television Show*. I accepted the offer and joined them on the tour.'

Les liked the way Hal played and so, whenever cover was required, he'd sub for NBC.

At the turn of the 1970s, NBC got rid of their staff band, meaning Les was able to hire whoever he wanted. Hal continued: 'Les used the majority of the members of his band for the NBC recordings and that's when I started on a regular basis for *The Dean Martin Television Show*. I'd previously

---

2 *For more information on Les Brown and the festival, please visit lesbrownfest.org.*

worked on the Bob Hope Specials, going around the world entertaining the troops, but with Dean's show it was based solely in Burbank, California. Thursday evenings we rehearsed but Dean was never there. Greg Garrison would pop his head around occasionally.'

Dean would be in his dressing room, watching the show on a monitor (there'd be a stand-in for him on the soundstage). But he knew his lines, knew his cues and when he came out for the show's recording, it'd be liked he'd rehearsed properly.

'Musicians are their own worst critics,' Hal laughed, 'and it's got to be perfect - so anytime somebody didn't come in on cue or cracked a note then they'd ask Les to stop and start again, even though others in the band couldn't always hear it. Les would also pick up where a note was out and after a while Greg would get on the podium with Les and say, 'We're not making records here, Les – just do it one time, and that's all you need to do!' Greg was a real businessman, he was saving money!'

Hal did admit he found that way of working a little frustrating because he wanted his own performance to be perfect but when he went home and watched the show, 'I couldn't hear any of the goofs so I knew it was ok.' (Many years later, Hal would realize that what he thought wasn't great at the time wasn't so bad after all!)

Hal didn't see much of Dean during the recordings but remembers the entertainer as being very laid back and that he never took himself too seriously. While Hal himself never appeared on screen, he said, 'The shows were a lot of fun to do and Dean was a happy guy. He was unique. There really was no one like Dean.'

That relaxed approach filtered down to the crew and Hal fondly recalled one particular day: 'We [the band] often used to dash over the road during a 10-minute break to a Mexican restaurant. It would take 6 minutes to get there and back so we only had 4 to down our drinks. A girlfriend I was dating back then had some sweatshirts made up one time: on the back we'd had printed 'The Dean Martin Speed Drinking Team' (which was what a few of us called ourselves!)' On the front was a martini glass design with their respective names below it. One was made up for Dean (who of course never joined them) and Hal presented it to him.

'Dean got a kick out of it...thought it was great!' Hal laughed.

Ken Lane, Hal remembered, was a nice guy and very quiet. 'One time, we all got up to start filing out for a break. We were soon questioned as to where we were all going...and much to our embarrassment and laughter we'd all misheard someone say 'Hey, Ken!' as 'Take ten'!'

Of Les Brown, Hal said, 'He was good musician, easy going and, like I said, he liked the way I played. He was nice to all the guys in the band but never hung around with us, never showed up at band parties. I think that was because Les belong to the Bel Air Country Club that attracted big stars and musicians, so he preferred to associate with them. But all the same, he was a great band leader and I've never had anything negative say about him.'

We asked Hal what Les would have thought about the band still going (now with Les Jr) all these years later. With sincerity, Hal replied, 'I think Les would have loved to have his son carry on the sounds of the 'Band of Renown'.'

Prior to his Burbank years, Hal worked with many East Coast bands and, after the army, joined Woody Herman's band. But Woody broke the group up after a year so Hal started with Tommy Dorsey, rejoining Woody some time later when that band reformed. At that time Bill Chase was playing lead with Woody at a good $175 per week with Hal on a little less. 'But then Buddy Morrow's band offered me a higher salary. I was going to work in Basin Street East with Peggy Lee in 1963 in New York but I got a call from a friend in Las Vegas to work the Dunes Hotel on a higher pay rate - so I left for Vegas before Peggy's opening night.'

Hal was a jobbing musician so there was no question he wouldn't take it. He worked in Vegas for the next 6 years then moved to LA to join Les.

'I figured I'd play 'til I was about 50 years old then get a real job because I was having too much fun as a trumpet player!'

Hal's enthusiasm for his career was infectious and talking to him made us see that one can live a dream if they try hard enough. *Do You Love Me* was a 20th Century Fox picture starring Maureen O'Hara. Dick Haymes played a successful singer with designs on O'Hara's music school dean. But it was Harry James as the smooth trumpet player who got the girl. On seeing the movie, Hal said to his Dad, 'I want to be a trumpet player! So he bought me a $40 coronet. In High School I was once embarrassed by my music teacher...he said when I played I sounded like a billy-goat! So I started practicing four or five hours every day. I remember too I would stand in front of bandstands and the trumpet section would stand and play. The power of the sound felt like my hair was blowing back!'

And so at 17 years, he knew that's what he wanted to do and when he eventually played for Harry James himself, he related his stories to him - Harry loved the anecdotes. Likewise, he had always played the Les Brown classic "Leap Frog" at school and vowed one day he'd play it with Les Brown himself - and he did!

He stayed with the Band of Renown until 1975 and a couple of decades later Hal moved away from playing entirely: 'I'd done sessions [including a few of Dean's country songs as well as tracks such as "It's a Good Day" and "I'm Sitting On Top of the World" and tracks for The Mamas & The Papas] and film scores [notably *WarGames* for Arthur B Rubenstein and *Forrest Gump* for Alan Silvestri]. Playing at dances were fun even though you knew that the audience wasn't really listening to the music. But the 'phone kept ringing and I kept on working. When I did stop, my friends and colleagues carried on calling me 'the trumpet player'. I still get called that to this day! I became the Musicians' Union president and even after I'd put my horn down I was still working with the guys I used to play with, but this time negotiating contracts for them.'

He helped many musicians over the 10 years he held the position and made sure he never took any playing offers on mainly because he didn't want to take work away from other people. Jazz, Big Band, Sinatra and so on were always his preferred tastes but he met highly-talented artists from backgrounds such as classical, hip hop and reggae. The role, however, was very intense and he felt burnt out after a decade.

We asked Hal, a genuine, good-to-honest gentleman, if he felt he'd done everything he wanted to do in life. His simple and encouraging response was: 'Yes.'

He did wonder though who would be interested in what he'd done but we can safely say that talking with him in 2018 about his career that has spanned decades was rewarding and gave a glimpse of a work ethic that reflected determination, success, hard work, kindness and honesty - and who wouldn't want to be interested in that?[3]

****

A worry for Dean was his mother Angela, who had become seriously ill. Her love of charity work had to be cut back and Dean ensured the finest treatment money could buy would come her way. She and Guy Crocetti had been living in a beautiful home Dean had bought them in Westwood and while Guy had been suffering with pancreas trouble for some time, he was able to enjoy his retirement with Dean's support: the strong Italian upbringing shone through and he could never be accused of forsaking them for anything. He continually asked them what they wanted and they would only have to say and it was done.

Both his mother and father would attend some of his stage performances from time to time, but now, with Angela ill, Guy longer had the heart to do anything. After spending some happy years at Westwood, it was decided that his parents should move nearer to Dean and reside at Doheny Drive.

---

[3] *Backstage photos of* The Dean Martin Show *from Hal's private collection can be seen in the DMA Books publication* Dean Martin – A Discography *by Bernard H Thorpe.*

Whilst working at the Sands over the Christmas period, Gail had assured her father that Grandmother was in reasonable health and that she did not really need any more gifts, even though she knew that her son just loved giving his parents endless items.

Whilst staying at his hotel in Nevada, Dean received the fateful message that his Mother had died in the early hours of Christmas morning. He raced back to his home devastated, but with unique dignity, he laid her to rest at the family plot in the Westwood Memorial Park.

FIFTEEN

Gentle On My Mind

Amongst all the glitz, glamour, and false existence in the world of show business, it was very easy to forget that Dean Martin, the total entertainer, could not have kept up the pace of his work if he had been true to his stage persona: these long-standing stories of excessive drink had never been true. Years of dark and ominous tales are really to be laughed about, mostly found in tabloids looking for a story or a hook to grab the media's attention.

Contrary to those 'drink' jokes that would be spread around (a lot of them by Dean himself) he would drink healthily and ensured that he took daily exercise even without any of the fancy equipment he could have purchased. One always smiles when thinking of Dean drinking milk! That's not to say he was tee-total. He enjoyed a good scotch and soda but rarely drank privately. While he adored being the entertainer he was, at the same time he wanted to keep away from the outside world and not allow anyone to see the true man (although he always said that what you see on the television screen was his real self).

Jeanne said many times that she never really knew her husband, even after all those years they were together, but it was particularly intentional for Dean to do this. Brought up to believe it was weak to show emotion, to shake hands with people was generally not his style – he would sooner place his hands on your shoulder as an expression of affection.

If he was disinterested in a social gathering or similar atmosphere, he was known to sit away from everyone, pretending to be drunk, tired, or both. No matter what he felt inside, good or bad, it was a rare chance for Dean Martin to show emotion to anyone.

Yet for all his exercise, he continued to suffer with arthritis in his spine, and with stomach problems and anxiety.

He had now completed his third Matt Helm *production The Ambushers*, this time with Senta Berger, Janice Rule and Beverley Adams, scoring yet again another smash across the world, although a little short off the mark from the first.

The film went before the cameras on April 24th in Mexico, with Hollywood work all completed in 44 days, two days ahead of schedule. The two previous pictures had given Dean a gross profit of $25million (a fact relayed to him whilst he was filming).

He was looking at a further film with Columbia (*How To Save A Marriage...and Ruin Your Life*) as well as signing on for a production with James Stewart, together with an unprecedented $34 million for a three year deal with NBC for his television shows. That amount of money proved the status of Dean Martin now: he could do no wrong in his career, and it was also because of his tremendous popularity that the association was getting so busy.

Throughout these months, he had raced ahead with his Matt Helm productions as well as *How To Save A Marriage...and Ruin Your Life* (originally titled *Band of Gold*) with Stella Stevens and Eli Wallach. He returned to the Western genre in style with Racquel Welch and James Stewart in *Bandolero!* for 20th Century Fox (accompanied by a wonderful and expressive score by the genius that was Jerry Goldsmith). Another dramatic Western followed alongside the great Robert Mitchum for Paramount's *Five Card Stud*. For this production, Dean agreed to record the main title as a Reprise single release, going in to the studios 23rd July 1968 to lay down just this one song.

He was working practically non-stop, which was, admittedly, due to demand, but he was unhappy with his health and was still, naturally, devastated by his mother's death.

He sought an outlet for his problems by finding solace outside the marriage and rumors once more spread around town that he was to divorce Jeanne. The tabloids ran stories that he had thought nothing of his parents, and these vicious and wholly unfounded stories caused him much upset. He was in a nervous state and it was a great tribute to his inner-self that he could actually show his talent to the public and yet be so strung-up inside, not sure of perhaps which way to turn. He worried about his father even more after losing his mother, and, after a marriage lasting more than 53 years, Guy passed away 8 months later. He died of heartbreak: he could not cope with life without his beloved Angela and, although Dean tried to do everything for him, it seemed absolutely nothing worked. He was finished, and died a sad and broken man, his only consolation perhaps being that Dean had really made it in the world, a famous and household name.

Guy was buried with his devoted wife on 1st September in the Westwood Memorial Park in the family mausoleum, having spent the last few weeks of his life in a nursing home. Dean, of course, working at this fast pace, seemed to take just about everything in his stride: but inside, he was complex and felt so screwed up, so unsettled. His career was practically perfect but he couldn't cope with the loss of both parents and then, on 20th October the same year, his brother Bill died from brain cancer. Bill had worked for Dean as manager of his brother's York Productions for a while (as well as being in charge of Dean's Lodge, of course).

Although each personal tragedy affected Dean greatly, he portrayed the swinger and drinker persona with ultimate ease, publicly dating numerous women but strangely, keeping most of everything else in his private life away from the world.

Again, he attended more recording sessions, having completed all songs for GENTLE ON MY MIND prior to taping "Five Card Stud", whilst Reprise issued the first volume of his greatest hits in May this year, followed by volume two the following August. It was also decided to re-issue some of his hits on 'Back-To-Back' singles and they appeared around the same time as the release of "Gentle On My Mind" on 17th December 1968 (although the UK had to wait until the following February).

Dean's original deal with Columbia was for six Matt Helm

super-spy films. He'd completed *The Wrecking Crew* (working title *The House Of Seven Joys*) with Elke Sommer, Sharon Tate, and that esteemed British actor Nigel Green, but broke his contract when he refused to do any more (via Meadway-Claude Productions).

Having started production on 3rd June 1968, *The Wrecking Crew* was eventually completed the following November, amidst complications and delays. Producer Irving Allen then began preparations for the next Matt Helm entry. But *The Ravagers* never saw the light of day. Matt Helm's movie future was decided. I thought this was a pity as these films showed the relaxed and casual Dean Martin, with a total laugh at spy films in general, with the added bonus of Bondesque action and girls by the dozen!

Columbia still retained the rights, however, and went on to produce a one-season TV series, *Matt Helm*, that debuted on ABC in September 1975. Dean of course didn't reprise his role: it instead went to Anthony Franciosa, who had previously co-starred with Dean in *Career*. There were rumors in the mid-noughties that either Amblin or Dreamworks had secured the rights to the Hamilton books but nothing ever came of it. Bradley Cooper more recently became linked with the role. To date, Mr Helm remains a spy who is definitely out in the cold (although the novels have since been republished by Titan Books). There was a brief re-awareness of *The Wrecking Crew* in 2019 when it was featured in *Once Upon A Time In Hollywood*, Quentin Tarantino's homage to Hollywood's fading Golden Age.

The BBC had negotiated with Dean's management for a series of his renowned television shows to be screened in the UK. Although the four they showed (9th and 30th October, 27th November, and 26th December) were superb, the BBC advised us in early 1969 that they wouldn't be showing any more under the deal as they had had very little audience engagement at all.

I found this very disappointing: he was liked in the UK, but, I felt, always underrated, and it seemed this type of variety show did not appeal to our market like it did in the US.

But his popularity was still considerable and the club gained many more members and acclaim as a result of the shows being aired over here.

When Dean sent me copies of his new album GENTLE ON MY MIND in November, I naturally played this collection of songs and was quite taken aback at his astounding version of John Hartford's song used for the title. In my opinion, it was a far superior version by Dean than I had ever heard by any artist previously, and I was absolutely convinced it would make a single here and sell very well.

Naturally, the unique way that record companies behave, I was told that I was biased in my opinions and attitude towards Dean in general. But I had this very strong feeling in my heart that if this song could be released as a single here, it would get into the UK charts.

But Pye weren't budging (to be honest, why would they?) yet I still felt strongly about it. I was told numerous times that Dean Martin was mainly an album seller, a comment I did find strange when I thought of the many singles that had become big sellers, even though they did, admittedly, all make chart entries.

It took many weeks of negotiation and persuasion with Pye records in London who, in turn, had to consult with Dean's office before I won my battle on this suggestion. I was not concerned with the flip-side of the single. It was the fact that I was 100% sure that "Gentle On My Mind" could and would make it as a single.

Finally, they announced that the single would be issued 24th January 1969 and, without writing several pages just on this subject, with the work and excitement that this caused, the record actually reached number 2 in the UK charts March 1st and stayed there for two weeks! Moving down after a fortnight, it stayed in the charts for a total of 23 weeks, including a meagre re-entry in August at number 49. I tried my hardest to get Dean to appear here as a promotional tool, but he could find no time in his very busy schedule. Whether he would have actually come over had he got the time is something we'll never know.

The BBC's weekly music show *Top Of The Pops* usually had the artists perform live in the studio (albeit miming on some occasions to whatever chart single they were pushing) but with Dean they showed various photographs on screen whilst the record was playing and sales (plus our membership) gained a tremendous boost for this year, with our being almost unable to cope with the sacks of mail we were getting.

Conversely, I had also forecast that "Gentle On My Mind" *wouldn't* fare well as a single in America and, unsurprisingly, it did not gain any chart entries, achieving only reasonable sales. Pye themselves suggested a follow-up single after the success of this issue, but I believed there would be no point in anything like this, as it would not produce any results. My premonitions seemed to be proven right yet again, because although they did release a single ("By the Time I Get to Phoenix" coupled with "Things") on 23rd May, it didn't do well at all.

Dean called me when news reached him of his success in the UK with "Gentle On My Mind", saying too how very grateful he was for our continued work and support of his career. In all the years I worked on behalf of Dean, it never felt once like a job. It was a pleasure from day one.

With the UK success of this single, it seemed to make certain people sit and take notice of my remarks that Dean did make hit singles and could do it here as well as America. On Monday 2nd September, the inimitable presenter Desmond Carrington included a 15-minute segment on Dean on his BBC Radio 2 program *Roundabout*, giving Dean more UK exposure.

The music publication *Melody Maker* announced that "Gentle On My Mind" was the most played song; the club had its first society meeting Sunday 19th October 19th and the US-trade paper *Billboard* gave a special tribute to Dean. Meanwhile in the US, Capitol issued THE BEST OF DEAN MARTIN plus DEAN MARTIN'S GREATEST! (different compilations of THE BEST OF DEAN MARTIN, VOLUMES 1 AND 2 appeared in the UK).

After almost a year's gap in recording now, Dean taped ten songs for his new release album and the title song (Merle Haggard's "I Take A Lot of Pride In What I Am") appeared as his new single in 22nd July, reaching only number 75 in the American charts, although it did wander around the chart positions for four weeks! He had recorded all the songs for this album over two days (11th and 12th June) and a second single lifted from this set of songs did not chart at all.

Back in Nevada, Dean took a 10% stake in the Riviera Hotel and agreed to appear there on an exclusive basis. This was a new chapter for him, allowing him to go on stage when he wanted to, and by now, his fortunes were unalloyed: as well as the Riviera shares, he also had numerous other assets. These included investments in the LA Rams, and real estate assets (he owned several homes and apartments as well as being the largest individual landowner in Ventura County). He also owned a handful of production companies, and property businesses, and a large batch of RCA holdings, with numerous other investments and deals always circulating. He also held total controlling interests in his television shows, and several films, as well as complete ownership of every song recorded for the Reprise and Warner Bros. labels.

None of this money or fame could save Dean's marriage to Jeanne. His affairs with younger women (all averaging around 20 years old, he was 52) were making the news, especially when he was seen regularly with Gail Renshaw. Rumors of a break-up with his wife abounded, and when asked what she thought was going on, Jeanne commented, 'I do not know what he is up to. He cannot seem to make up his mind what age group he is interested in.'

But several weeks later, the day before he made his appearance at the Riviera Hotel's 14th anniversary on 11 December 1969, he finally filed for divorce.

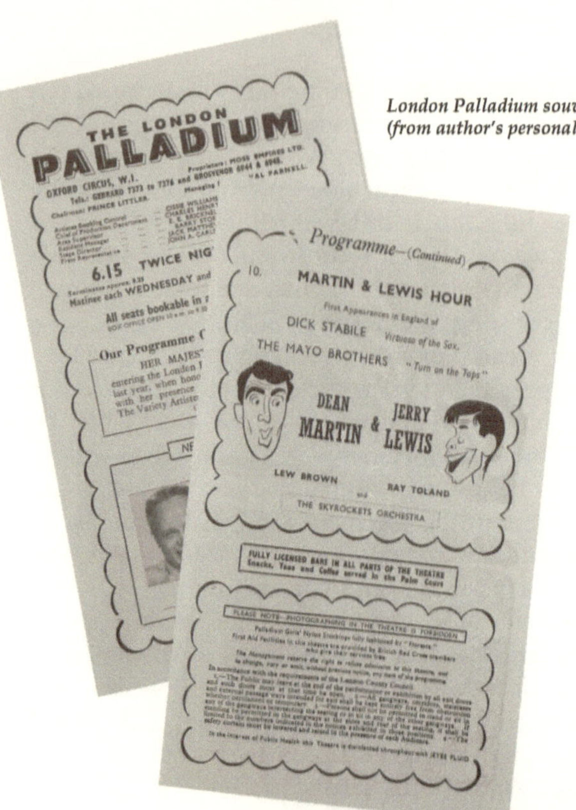

London Palladium souvenir brochure, 1953
(from author's personal collection)

Dean being fitted with traditional Scottish dress, Glasgow Empire, 1953 (from author's personal collection)

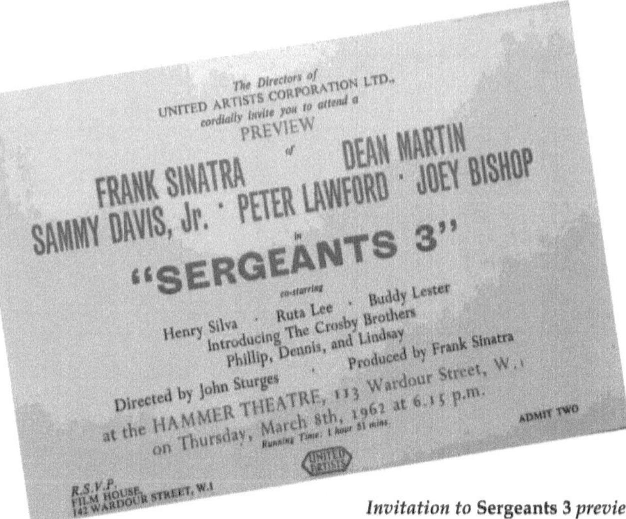

*Invitation to **Sergeants 3** preview screening, 1962 (from author's personal collection)*

Dino's Lodge, 77 Sunset Strip, Las Vegas (from author's personal collection)

With Joey Bishop, 1967 (from author's personal collection)

With Frank Sinatra, 1964 (courtesy Warner-Pathé)

THIS IS YOUR FAVOURITE—DEAN MARTIN—WITH HIS
WIFE JEANNE AND THE SEVEN CHILDREN.
Photograph by kind permission of Dean Martin and Bernard Thorpe.

(from author's personal collection)

*c1970
(from author's
personal collection)*

Dino

August 18, 1964

Bernard H. Thorpe, President
The International Dean Martin Club

Thornton Heath
Surrey, England

Dear Bernard:

We have just received the album, Let's Be
Friendly, and the family and myself thank you. We
enjoyed it and also the sleeve note comments.

We are sending you our three most recent
releases. If you already have them perhaps the
Club may find use for them.

Thanks again for the thoughtful congratulatory
cables.

Best wishes,

DEAN MARTIN

DM:erh

4 For Texas, 1963
(courtesy Warner-Pathé)

Various DMA publications, 1960 - 2010

Working version of the first edition's cover, art by Steve Caldwell, 2017
(courtesy Chinbeard Books)

Robin and the 7 Hoods, 1964 *(courtesy Warner-Pathé)*

*With Frank Sinatra, 1964
(courtesy Warner-Pathé)*

The author, 1983 (courtesy Croydon Advertiser)

Trade announcements, 20 ORIGINAL HITS, *October 1976, Warner-Reprise*

With Jimmy Stewart, c1972 (from author's personal collection)

Bally's, Las Vegas, July 1991 (from author's personal collection)

Apollo, London, June 1983
(from the author's personal collection)

c1989 (from author's personal collection)

London Palladium, July 1987 (from author's personal collection)

One of the very last photos of Dean, 1995 (from author's personal collection)

A selection of the DMA's compilations, 1964 – 2003
(EMI / Warner-Reprise / Charly)

"Thanks Bernard - Dino"
(from author's personal collection)

SIXTEEN

A Million And One

Gail's the girl for me, Dean reportedly said. *Jeanne might get the ranch, you know, I could never find it anyway!*

His quips belied his real feelings.

He was starry-eyed over the beauty queen, the Virginia-born Miss World USA titleholder and runner up in 1969's Miss World competition. They'd first met backstage at the Riviera in late November 1969 when she asked him to pose with her for a photo. They dined at the Riviera's exclusive gourmet restaurant Delmonico between shows and had a nightcap in Dino's Den, an intimate cocktail lounge off the casino area, following his midnight performances. After a photo was released whilst they were having a meal together, the media in general just could not wait to hear the sound of wedding bells, hungry for something new about Dean and his love life.

But after all the coverage and publicity, the engagement lasted just over four months and it was officially announced that there would be no marriage.

Dean's appearances at the Riviera continued unabated. 'It's New Year's Eve every night when he's in town,' said Marty Klein, the Versailles Room *maitre d'*.

A typical day for the him when he played the Riviera included a 10am breakfast with golfing partners Tony Frabbiele and Don Cherry, tee off at 11am sharp (he was an eight-cap handicap golfer who gave his best high note for a sub-par round), breaking for 1pm lunch at the clubhouse and a return to the hotel at 4pm for a rubdown and a nap. He'd prepare three hours later for the dinner show and go on stage for 10pm at the Delmonico, followed by a midnight show in the Versailles Room. 2am the next morning often meant a gathering in Dino's Den where a couple of impromptu songs with pianist Alice Darr would occasionally take place as well as a story-swapping session with celebrity pals who dropped in from other hotels for a late drink. Then finally, at 3am, it was bedtime in the luxurious Dean Martin Suite.

No wonder his ulcers never got a break.

Looks like I can forget eating Italian sausage for another year, he was heard to groan.

One evening, American football quarterback Joe Namath dropped by the Den, having seen Dean's midnight show. He'd been struggling with his new career as an actor and asked Dean for some tips.

Dean suggested Joe just relax and try to act natural.

'Relax?' came Namath's reply. 'I'm so relaxed I can't stand up. I drink five quick Scotches before I go before the damn camera, but I still feel like the whole of Kansas City line is comin' straight at me.'

Dean's response? 'It must be your brand of Scotch.'

In June 1970, Dean was seen at the Delmonico in the company of another woman, 24-year old Catherine Mae Hawn. He seemed more at ease with his new partner and took her on to numerous local functions and eating houses, remarking on one occasion to a reporter that he would have to leave earlier than usual to 'burp [his] girl'.

In the midst of all the coverage he was getting about his love life, his work continued at a fast pace. He'd signed with Universal Pictures to star alongside the great Burt Lancaster in *Airport,* the film version of Arthur Hailey's best-selling novel of the same name, and looked forward to having a strong part again, with the added bonus of being able to work with a fine actor like Burt.

He was right. His role as the Boeing 707 pilot Vernon Demerest was a very dramatic one. Producer Ross Hunter had seen the potential in casting Dean.

'When I first saw and read those proofs,' said Hunter, 'I immediately saw one man in my mind's eye: Dean Martin. I knew he would just have to play the jetliner pilot who has to cope with a maniacal bomb-carrying passenger who wants to blow the plane up in mid-air. I distinctly remembered Dean's dramatic role in *Some Came Running* and, once I had signed him, I cast the rest of the film from there.'

Dean agreed to do this part before he had even read the script, and it became one of his favorite roles.

'Dean was a great actor,' continued Ross. 'People just didn't give him credit for being as good as he really was. They saw him in that Matt Helm picture and others like it, but he was a very serious and professional man. He knew everyone's lines and everyone else's part as well as his own. He was anxious to rehearse in his own way and get everything right. I telephoned him at home one night: I'd just seen the dailies when he gets the case with the bomb in it from Van Heflin [who played Guerrero, the suicidal maniac] and he did it with so much authority and dignity, I just felt compelled to thank him and congratulate him for his expertise.'

An astonishing tribute to Dean, considering the weight of the rest of the cast in this gripping thriller, which included Lancaster, George Kennedy, Barry Nelson, Jean Seberg, Helen Hayes, Jacqueline Bisset, and many more. Locations at St. Paul Minneapolis airport were proving problematic, with temperatures at 45 degrees below zero at times.

Box office receipts proved the film a resounding success. It had cost over $12 million and had good returns all around the world, spawning a series of airplane disaster movies (culminating in possibly the best tribute of all, *Airplane!*).

My wife and I attended the Royal Charity Premiere at the Odeon Leicester Square in London on Wednesday 22nd April at 8.15pm in the presence of their Royal Highnesses, the Duke and Duchess of Kent.

Dean, of course, didn't go.

Those of us who have followed the life and career of Dean Martin, know that if he had never been a singer he could have made it as a straight actor. But then singing is a form of acting anyway: the way that each song is expressed is a total and unique action of phrasing for each individual. Listen to the voices and styling of, for example, Sinatra, Sammy, Madonna, Nat 'King' Cole, Dusty Springfield, Michael Jackson, Rod

Stewart, Barbra Streisand, P!nk, Billie Eilish…just a handful of examples over the decades, but each artist has their own unique way of song interpretation.

Dean himself always had that certain style and manner all of his own right from the beginning. His acting, too, was different. He was practically an expert on making it look so easy. Even in comedy he made it look so casual.

I'd go so far as to say that he was underrated as a comedy performer, adding that he was possibly one of the world's greatest and funniest comedians, although people who perhaps have not witnessed all of Dean's talents might say 'but he's only a singer and an actor, surely not a comedian'.

Even after he split with Jerry, he continued to put his finely-tuned comedy to good use in various forms as he progressed through his career.

There's a great scene in the 2008 picture *Transporter 3*, where Jason Statham's character Frank Martin (and it only just occurred to me writing this, of the marrying of Sinatra's first name with Dean's surname!) is fishing with his friend, Inspector Tarconi (François Berléand). Tarconi talks about the highly developed French sense of humor, to which Frank Martin responds:

'With respect, the French think Jerry Lewis was a genius.'

'Well, he *was* a genius,' says Tarconi.

'No, *Dean* was the genius.'

'No, Dean just stood there with a drink and a cigarette.'

'My point exactly,' Statham's character continues. 'Anybody can fall down and get a laugh but how many can do it standing still with a drink and a cigarette?'

Writers Luc Besson and Robert Mark Kamen clearly knew what they were talking about!

To attend a Dean Martin recording session was a chance to see not only a singer doing great things with a song, but to witness his comedy antics with the musicians and staff as he recorded six or eight songs in one session, perhaps to return the next day to complete another handful for a new album. But there was always the smile and the ability to make the whole room fall about in fits of laughter. The few sessions I was fortunate enough to attend, I remember the joy the technicians and I experienced as we all sat listening and watching the man himself.

It was while completing *Airport* that Dean realized he was now among the elite handful of entertainers in the world who could demand big money for anything they cared to do. He had reached the top of his profession.

When making films, Dean always disliked the delays involved with the production. He hated waiting to be called for his next scene, so he tried to avoid this by pushing for his scenes to be in the can as swiftly as possible. On one occasion, he completed a film well before the completion schedule, which naturally pleased the studio execs.

By this time in his life, Dean Martin had done most things he had wanted to achieve in show business and he was beginning to gradually slow down the pace of his career, reducing his television appearances as well as his visits to the recording studios. With the completion of *Airport*, he was only to make another five films for the cinema.

This was through choice rather than a dwindling popularity. Dean felt pleased with his accomplishments in the past thirty years; he did the best work he could and found satisfaction in his career at all levels.

Asked once why he never tried Broadway or the dramatic stage in general, he replied in a way that sums him up entirely, but is somewhat ironic:

'I just did not want to repetitiously speak the same old lines night after night. Besides, anyone that gets to Broadway usually looks to making it to Hollywood. Well, I did it from Hollywood first and had the luck to be successful from there, so that was satisfying for me. No, I don't knock the stage, it is just that I have never particularly liked the theatre anyway.'

The irony I mention is in reference to his stage act. Listen to his segments on the live Rat Pack shows at the Sands in the early 1960s: he usually starts with the same gags and the same songs. Jump to his last concert appearances in the 1980s and he hasn't changed his act, save for a few contemporary lines here and there and a different song or two.

Career-wise, Dean could not have been in a better position, but his personal life was in utter turmoil. Legal complications were starting to appear as his lawyer went through his estate and investments with his accountants and management in preparation for the split after 24 years with Jeanne. Now his hands were tied in his personal situation, but everything had to be legally transacted and it was a matter of time before things were finalized.

His sound recordings continued to appear both on Capitol and Reprise, with such items as "Tracks Of My Tears", "Come On Down", "Cheatin' On Me" and LET'S BE FRIENDLY now seen in the record stores, along with a spectacular boxed album set of records and cassettes containing five dozen songs from the Capitol era.

Work continued in earnest for the DMA as I completed this set for EMI's mail order division World Records. The sixty songs I chose for this project gave a wonderful insight into Dean's Capitol career, and I had full say in which songs were chosen, as well as the design and sleeve notes. The release was planned for January 1970.

We also assisted the BBC in a 45 minute tribute to Dean for Radio 2, transmitted 2nd June, linking with the club's tenth anniversary.

As a surprise, Dean invited me to visit him at his home in Beverly Hills. It was only a couple of days, but my wife and I were treated like honored guests. Having Dean cook us meatballs and pasta was an experience not to be missed. My own Italian mother was a stupendous and proud cook when it came to traditional cuisine and I never dared tell her Dean was a chef of the first order! When Dean mentioned that he had 'ordered' Frank to come see me, I didn't quite believe this was all happening! But sadly, Frank's commitments elsewhere meant he was unable to be there. Dean spoke of purchasing a new Spanish style ranch, suggesting we come back one day and ride with him. He also said he was beginning to think of retirement as he wanted to spend some time with his horses and generally ease up on most things. *After all, I'm 30 now*, he was prone to say when anyone asked him if he was serious about giving it all up. When I asked him about his Reprise contract, he confirmed he'd renewed it up until 1975.

That wonderful Marty Robbins composition "My Woman, My Woman, My Wife" became the title (and single release) of Dean's brand new album for August, with a batch of country songs recorded in Hollywood on 27th and 28th May, again under the expert supervision and production of Jimmy Bowen. Dean continued to demonstrate his prowess and knack for songs by recording them in just a couple of days – an achievement not many artists managed, but the end result was perfection, although this album only managed to struggle to number 97 on 12th September, remaining in the same chart for twelve weeks.

He had backed away from recording with a full quota of musicians: these days he would mostly put his voice on tape with just a small group and Ken Lane, with the orchestral backing mixed in later. And that was the way Dean wanted it. His television shows were still peaking and had entered syndication too, meaning Dean was on virtually every week of the year. He did not like repeating his part in a show – at the most he would act his role twice, as he wanted spontaneity with each song, each joke, each sketch: he worked best that way. Large white cue cards were in front of Dean all the time he was working but he never needed them. It was part of his act, joking he couldn't see or read the writing or the spelling. He'd wander or stagger in front of the cameras and audience holding a glass half-filled with apple juice, and sing a song, some of the time not actually completing the words or, if he did, replacing them with his own amusing parody.

'I just have never understood when people say that acting or singing is hard work. Learn your lines and sing the words and that's it, it's easy. Try standing on your damn feet all day dealing black-jack and see what the difference is. Now that comes hard! If you cannot be bothered to go to see a film, then the artists' work is lost to you, but on television, there is no effort, you can sit back and just watch that screen and the program is there with you.'

Now, of course, there are any number of Dean's movies on satellite or streaming channels, as online uploads or on DVD, so the medium of television has meant his statement is of its time. Being the advocate of TV viewing as he was, I wonder what he would have made of the saturation we now all have of the small screen?

Unfortunately, as the new decade continued, his health was against him. His ulcer was causing a lot of discomfort, but although he was strongly advised to enter hospital, he twice refused, saying he didn't have the time. Unable to overcome the pain while in San Francisco, he finally relented and had surgery for the chronic condition.

During the course of 1970, the UK arm of Warner Brothers created a new label called Valiant. This was to be a budget label representing various artists whose material would be re-issued at a lower price than the original (not unlike EMI's Music For Pleasure).

A handful of albums appeared from other artists (these are now very rare indeed), and such a release was planned from Dean's back catalog. Dean took umbrage with this, objecting to material he owned being re-released at a cheaper price. Although a catalog number was allocated for Dean's issue (VS145), it was never released, and strangely, the other albums that had been released by fellow artists were quickly withdrawn.

One of the places Dean had never visited was the fine continent of Australia. He had never had any particular desire to visit, but was asked if he would appear in a series of live concerts. As expected, he refused, citing his workload was too much for such a tour. The point in fact was that his aversion to travelling stopped him saying yes, even if he had the time. So, sadly, Australia was denied that talent but his TV and film work was readily repeated across the continent. We had numerous members in Australia at this time and our membership was growing steadily. We opened our own small office in Beverly Hills, giving us local facilities to Dean's office, and had another DMA meeting on 15th November in London, while the man himself was gathering finance for charities. A Joe E. Lewis tribute raised $75,000, his appearance for the Roger Baldwin Foundation for American Civil Liberties Union accrued $200,000, and in an on-stage appearance at the Riviera hotel, Frank Sinatra joined Dean in a surprise walk-on.

As 1971 came into being, the entertainer 'par excellence' (as one magazine referred to Dean) recorded more songs for release, forming his new album FOR THE GOOD TIMES, an apt title considering his present success. Having taped these ten songs 29th and 30th September 1970, with the release for February this year, he only recorded a further 18 for Reprise for the whole of the year, sure signs that he had slowed down his song output.

SEVENTEEN

My Own, My Only, My All

Over the next few years with Reprise, Dean was to record even less, his popularity in the charts now waning. He had spent his time working much harder than most of his peers, and was still half-threatening to retire.

I'll do that around 1975 I guess, Dean had said, *then I can sit around all day and do nothing but watch television! But no! I gotta get up in the morning and do something!*

More and more album compilations appeared from the Capitol stable to compete with Dean's output on Reprise. I suggested to EMI an album of songs Dean had recorded with other artists in his Capitol days (such as Nat 'King' Cole, Margaret Whiting and Peggy Lee), and while they never even acknowledged my ideas, shortly afterwards, an album did appear with similar content. Entitled NAT, DEAN AND FRIENDS, I put it down to a remarkable coincidence.

The club was given a big feature in *Woman* magazine but our newsletter distribution was somewhat suspended early this year due to a 47-day postal strike in the UK. When the strike ended, we combined two issues for our members.

After a long break between films, there were almost two years before *Something Big* was to appear, in which Dean struck a deal with 20th Century Fox for yet another western saga, this time bringing him to work with Brian Keith and another former Bond girl Honor Blackman.

Filmed entirely on location in Durango, Mexico, this was 108 minutes of very 'vigorous' action (according to the publicity manual!) and Dean was quoted as saying *this is a great fun film.*

Advertising slogans stated that *everybody wants to do something big once in his life*, but unfortunately this was not one of Dean's big box-office smashes, although it gained larger audiences across America than in any other country. Nevertheless, it gave Dean another chance to play the villain, a part remote from his previous role as the dashing airline pilot. Although there was a song composed by Burt Bacharach and Hal David for the title theme, it was performed not by Dean but by Mark Lindsay, lead singer of Paul Revere and the Raiders. After filming had wrapped, he visited Hawaii and was quite taken by the islands and their people, even taking time out to watch Jack Lord film an episode of the hit police drama *Hawaii Five-O*.

'I was pretty impressed,' he told me later on. 'Jack was a good guy. Really professional. We hit it off and he suggested I should do a guest spot.'

Dean of course never did appear in the series but he did ask me to make Jack Lord an honorary club member. We duly did so but never ever heard from Mr Lord!

From Dean's recording sessions at the end of September, it was not until 12th April that he recorded again, this time only three songs, with another gap until mid-November for a batch of ten more, for an album with the most unimaginative title ever for Dean: DINO. The album included Dean's second version of Baker Knight's "The Right Kind of Woman". His original version was recorded with the other two songs in April, none of which have ever been issued in any format, at the time of writing this.

With meandering record sales, the album struggled to chart in the US in 1972 - and was in point of fact the last of his albums to ever chart, only ever reaching an abysmal 117. A stand-out track was the Kris Kristofferson-penned "Kiss the World Goodbye" but, for me, it was the Belvins' "Guess Who" that cried out to be released as a single. The aforementioned lack of album sales meant Reprise wouldn't entertain the idea, a reluctance I understood but I did unsuccessfully argue the notion that a single may have boosted album popularity.

Meanwhile in Europe, Warner Bros issued a series of double albums entitled THE MOST BEAUTIFUL SONGS OF DEAN MARTIN, with 23 songs. It used low-grade packaging (a bright orange cover with a smaller version of the photograph used on Dean's Christmas album). But it was altogether a grand compilation, even including Dean's duet with Nancy Sinatra on "Things".

Still romancing Cathy Hawn, Dean made a surprise visit to London on 11th May (just for shopping, he told us) and returned home on the 16th, having stayed at the Park Lane Hotel and managing to escape the prying ears and eyes of the media.

Trundling along with our newsletters, we changed our format slightly and reduced our page size from the original A4.

Health-wise, Dean was suffering from ulcers again, and the arthritis in his back made him dependent on pain killers. His recent vasectomy had given him enough hospital time to be getting on with, he complained.

After a year-long argument relating to non-payments from *Airport*, this was finally settled and his dues were cleared: he claimed and received his 10% of the profits after film costs were all paid. Dean always considered this one of the 'most interesting' films he'd made so it was a shame that the remuneration difficulties somewhat marred his experience.

'Working with Lancaster and all those guys, it was great fun. There were sequels? Well, I sure didn't see them and I wasn't asked back. I don't know if I would have said yes, anyway,' he told me some time later.

During 1972, he was unhappy with the arrangements at the Riviera, whose management insisted he perform two shows per night for each night he was to appear. As they were set on him doing this, tempers flared, disagreements arose and Dean walked out. He simply didn't want to do two shows a night. Whilst things were settled amicably, he did not appear there very often during the remainder of his contract.

Additionally, his accountants and lawyers were gradually clearing his problems relating to his impending divorce from Jeanne.

Within the DMA, we were always looking for ways to promote Dean as much as we could and, after many negotiations, the BBC actually showed an episode from Dean's

NBC series on 21st April starring Tony Bennett and Zero Mostel. Our meetings this year were successful and these were held 30th January, 26th March and 13th August. I guess you could compare these to the modern day fan conventions, albeit on a much smaller scale. We had guest speakers, showings of very rare footage (remember, this was pre-internet!), panels, and memorabilia stalls. A typical meeting lasted from around lunchtime to 10.30pm and we welcomed fans from around the world. On one occasion, we were delighted when Dean recorded an audio greeting for us to play to our guests, saying (as per his usual sign-off on his TV shows), '...keep those letters and cards comin' in'.

After much persuasion, BBC Radio 2 had a *Dean Martin Week* from Monday 31st July and this proved a tremendous boost to our society and, of course, to Dean's record sales. Meanwhile, a format change was made to his regular television shows and producer Greg Garrison suggested some alterations, mainly toning down the scantily-clad girls and sexualized remarks in general. Times were changing and the US did not want this suggestive type of comedy any more.

With numerous ongoing negotiations concerning Dean's affairs, it was agreed between Jeanne and Dean themselves that to offload some Inland Revenue problems, they would sell their ranch to the state to avoid paying too much tax. They appeared amicable and eventually, a divorce was granted to them on 12th December 12th: they had been married for 23 years. Dean spent this Christmas at the ranch before it was sold off.

Now he was out on his own.

After so many years married to Jeanne, he had chosen to leave her – for good this time – no going back after a few days or weeks like he had done many times before. Although he was now involved with Cathy, his mind went back a while and he thought of those times when he had been alone once before, when the million-dollar partnership with Jerry had finished.

They had both felt then that things had to come to an end;

he'd left his partner over 20 years ago now and struck out on his own for a different and (he hoped) more successful future. And now he was alone again, even if for different reasons, yet the feelings were the same. All those years of familiarity with his beautiful Jeanne, his children growing up - and he had broken away from all that of his own choice. Whether he regretted it, only he knew, but there was a fondness and love for Jeanne that I don't think ever truly went away, even though he seemed infatuated with Cathy.

His solitude, his privacy, his desire to not let anyone in, meant very few people understood him or realized how this jarred with his stage act or working persona: he was such a pleasure to work with and be with, but there was no way the average person could penetrate that outer shell. He remained for all of his life a man that kept himself at a distance, only letting you in if he wanted to...yet he would give his all to you on stage in front of untold numbers of people.

He had made his mind up to marry Cathy and now in the coming year he knew there were many things in his personal life to be re-assessed and thought out. Problems he hated, but now he had put himself in this position, giving thought to the many complications divorce and marriage bring to all of us. Jeanne was given both their Californian homes (Beverly Hills and Palm Springs) with contents from both, and with the biggest alimony settlement at that time of $6.5 million. She also received a couple of sleek cars, portions of his stocks and shares, and proceeds from various other assets. Dean was very amicable in his settlement with Jeanne: he wanted to ensure that she would never be in need of anything for the rest of her life.

From my personal impressions about Cathy and Dean, there was a strong feeling that this would not be successful. Something told me that this would not be right and that it would not be a case of 'third time lucky'. However, I made no comment to him regarding their forthcoming marriage. It was not my place to do so and he would have been extremely offended had I even dared to.

Jeanne and his family could not understand what he was doing: he had everything he had always wanted, a tremendous career and home life with seven lovely children and a loving, beautiful, attentive wife. But no more.

With all of the legal tangles and complications taking their time to be ironed out, Dean was content to sit back and wait for all this to be concluded...after all, that was what he was paying heavy fees for professional people to do!

But Cathy was impatient and unwilling to wait. She walked out, telling Dean she was fed up waiting for him to decide on a wedding date. But the date was finally arranged and, amid the typical Hollywood glamour, the wedding took place on 25th April 1973 at the Beverly Hills Hotel in a room specially converted to a Catholic chapel. Sasha (Cathy's six-year old daughter) was chief bridesmaid and Frank was Dean's best man. The bride wore a peach French Chiffon gown made of satin with lilies placed in her hair. We weren't allowed to take photos but it was certainly a lavish affair. Dean acknowledged my wife and me being there and we definitely never expected any further exchanges, but were overjoyed when he brought over Frank Sinatra to say hello! Mr Sinatra, much to my surprise, knew who we were, what we did, and didn't seem at all fazed that we were even there! I felt somewhat humbled that Dean would have even reminded him of us.

Cathy and Dean bought a house in Bel-Air and she was soon to have it completely re-styled just to her liking. Dean had taken a break from cabaret for a while but returned to his stage with vigor, yet had no desire for continuous film-making now, and no roles came along for him that he had any inclination to follow. He was losing interest and those roles didn't grab him like they had done a few years back when he admitted to enjoying making the most of them. Dean was not a person to bother watching many of his rushes (the filmed sequences were approved before the final edit) and was mostly inclined to leave that to his people to check over for him. If it was not possible for him to return home when he had finished his day's filming, he would have his own trailer to reside in with all his facilities and comforts awaiting that next call.

His daughter Deana suggested to him this year that he should write his autobiography, but he stubbornly refused, having no wish for a publication of this nature. Knowing full well that over the years there had been so many untruths and exaggerated stories and fantasies written about him, he felt that it would make not a jot of difference if he *did* write his life story. I couldn't see that he would have had the patience to sit down and write one anyway, but it nevertheless would have been quite something to have read about his life from his own unique and rarely heard point of view.

Meanwhile, he had asked me to change the name of the club, and so, at Dean's behest, we formally became The Dean Martin Association on Monday 2nd April 1973. We remained the only official world organization on his behalf, gaining new members all the time and continuing to promote and publicize Dean to the best of our ability. We received positive promotion when we were given a three-page feature (written by me) for the November edition of the magazine *Listen Easy*.

After all these years, we have become very well-known and quite the advocate of Dean, offering information and assistance to any member of the public or organization that contacted us, as well as the occasional record album or single that was issued at our suggestion. This was more work than perhaps could have been imagined but it was all very much worth it!

Some of the more spectacular pleasantries of the job were attending those illustrious film premieres, meeting numerous stars, and getting to know the many people who starred and worked with Dean.

And once more, that word *retirement* reared up again, not only from his own lips but in the press. His record sales were diminishing and his box-office returns at the cinema weren't great.

Be Honest With Me

In between all the work that Dean was still relatively happy to do, he was still suffering from his ulcers and relented at last, admitting to Cedars Of Lebanon Hospital in early July for treatment. He had to overcome his dreaded fear of all things medical and it seemed he would sooner rely on his addiction to Percodan than seek medical attention. His face was becoming quite bloated and he was not looking like the handsome Dean the world knew.

I could always understand his numerous remarks in the early 70s about retiring (even amidst all the joking) but he had committed himself to a lot more work at this time, so, luckily for his admirers, there was no chance he would be leaving the business for a long time yet. He continued his shows but they did not have the same appeal as before, and ratings were sliding. Variety shows in general were losing favor: public taste was changing and, like so many things, this genre unfortunately seemed to be losing face, with or without Dean Martin. Its days were numbered.

At the very end of December 1972, Dean had taped a dozen songs in the studio, ten of which made up the album SITTIN' ON TOP OF THE WORLD for release 29th May. Photographs for this album were taken by his son Ricci. Again, this album didn't chart, even though there were familiar compositions such as "I Wonder Who's Kissing Her Now", "Ramblin' Rose" and Charlie Chaplin's "Smile". Dean recorded another five songs on 25th July, coming back on the 26th for three more. On 10th August, he taped "I'll Hold out My Hand" but this was not included on the 14th December album "You're The Best Thing That Ever Happened to Me". To date, the missing song has never been issued anywhere. EMI Records in the UK managed to release THE VERY BEST OF DEAN MARTIN for the Yuletide season on Capitol, which remained a steady seller for a good few years.

Dean managed only one film in 1973 and he went to Universal Pictures for producer/director George Seaton, the screenwriter and director of Airport, so Dean was in familiar territory for this one. The Western *Showdown* co-starred Hollywood legend Rock Hudson, and Dean gave a strong and dramatic performance in his favorite genre. It sold to packed houses upon release in the US even though it did not get many favorable comments by the critics (comments that Dean never listened to anyway). Henry Kissinger had visited the film set and was very taken with Dean's professionalism and unconventional laid-back approach.

Although Dean was pleased with the story, circumstances seemed compelled to doom the outcome: he had insisted on only working on this particular film for twelve weeks at $25,000 a week because of other commitments, but production was held up for weeks when Hudson suffered a near-fatal accident during filming. With no disrespect to his co-star's injuries, Dean was fuming: he was desperate to get this production in the can as fast as possible - but it wasn't to be. Then, to make matters worse for Dean himself, his beloved horse Tops (with whom he had starred in every one of his solo Westerns) died under him. Dean, in a rage and very upset, walked off the set (later giving his 15-year-old horse a funeral). Universal informed him that unless he returned, they would slap a $6million suit on him. But again, like he had done several times before with any legal threats or demands, all was settled amicably between his management and the studio.

Thus *Showdown* was finally finished after such problematic circumstances, leaving a very disenchanted Dean Martin, whose waning interest in films was worse than ever.

I suppose no one could blame him. After almost thirty years, Dean could financially afford to sit back on his television and cinema history and reap the rewards of an even longer illustrious recording career.

I asked him about this particular period in his life, mentioning to him that he seemed to have dropped the *retiring soon* comments.

'I always have a reason for getting out of bed each morning, otherwise you just die, y'know? You have to have something.'

At the end of 1973, Cary Grant attended the Gala opening of MGM's brand new brilliant Grand Hotel, which featured Dean Martin as the first billed entertainer to appear. As someone remarked later, when Frank Sinatra is in town the hotels are full, but when Dean Martin plays Las Vegas, he fills the town.

This was certainly true when Dean performed in the Celebrity Room, a part of the $100 million fantasy complex that only Metro-Goldwyn-Mayer could ever dream of. The 2,100 rooms and 376 suites were just part of Nevada's latest and most spectacular building, towering into the Las Vegas skyline.

Dean, now one of the world's richest and most popular all-round entertainers, was part of all this when he signed a deal with MGM for a package consisting of five films plus exclusive cabaret appearances.

Health problems loomed again and he continued to suffer the usual stomach and back pains, once again relying on his addiction to counter the agony. Furthermore, Cathy was becoming extravagant, spending so much of Dean's finances that he was becoming concerned. Several times, he picked her up on her lavish spending, always ending with bad arguments. True, he was not exactly short of money, but he did not like to see anyone wasting it, particularly if it was his. He had always kept himself in a huge range of clothes when he was younger, but he found in his later years he did not need so much and therefore had only a minimum wardrobe, so he did not understand why Cathy wanted to purchase so many clothes. She would purchase a dress in perhaps twenty different colors. This seemed to be the thing to do as far as she was concerned, when she had gone from earning a handful of bucks a week to becoming the wife of one of Hollywood's richest men.

Perhaps it was the age gap, too, that meant they never saw eye to eye on this. And, in a repeat of both his previous marriages, she was unhappy at home. Why? Because if Dean wasn't out performing, he was at home watching TV. He would frequently sit at home watching the small screen for hours whilst his young wife would be wearing a dress costing around $2,000 or more, with nowhere to go.

Dean wasn't happy. He was unsettled, but was not telling a soul about it. He'd suffered from depression before and it was something that was rearing up again. Coupled with his addiction to painkillers as well as the conditions he hoped they'd resolve, it was clear that something had to give.

So what did he do? Increase his Vegas appearances, of course, allowing Dino to hide behind Dean.

His television shows were not the same as before, and no matter how devoted an admirer you were, everyone admitted that they needed something...so again Greg Garrison worked out a new formula. From *The Dean Martin Television Show* it went to the (essentially clip-driven) *Dean Martin Comedy Hour*, to be later regenerated as *The Dean Martin Celebrity Roasts* after initially appearing as a segment in the variety show itself. In essence, no matter what the format, it kept Dean on TV.

He had made so many shows for television, even before his 1965 series began, and had always been a regular guest on other shows, so there had been plenty of coverage for plenty of years. I have talked of the unprecedented success of it all and even Dean himself was surprised his shows had lasted so long: top of the US ratings every time, thousands of letters all requesting replies from Dean that neither he nor his office could honor. They did send most our way but we didn't have the capacity to respond to every one, and we had to tell his office it was a support arm we couldn't easily continue. On one particular show, he jokingly asked the viewers to send in their piano lids...and dozens turned up days later at NBC. He found this extremely funny but was politely advised by the studio that perhaps it would not be a good idea to repeat such requests!

Running until 1984, *The Dean Martin Celebrity Roasts* would generally be an hour of friendly insults and remarks made by a gathering of star guests to the man or woman of the hour, hosted by Dean, who would add his remarks about his guest before handing over to that same celebrity to finish the show. This was filmed within the MGM Grand Hotel and again became popular for Dean (he could film his show and appear in cabaret on $170,000 a stint for a minimum of six weeks per year – and he had his own private apartment there, too).

Two particular comedians semi-regularly took the dais, one being Foster Brooks, the comedian with his 'lovable drunk' act. Rich Little was the other, the comedian-impressionist who effortlessly took on the personas of his peers.

Rich was born in Ottawa in 1938 and found he had a natural flair for impressions while working as an usher in his local cinema, the Elgin Movie Theatre. He moved into acting then became a DJ, incorporating his talent for mimicry into his shows. LPs followed, some satirical, but one was an interpretation of Charles Dickens' classic *A Christmas Carol*, playing all the roles himself in the guises of various Hollywood stars.

As a result of various club work and his recordings, he was asked by Mel Torme to audition for a new variety series and, successful, he debuted on American television in 1964 for CBS' *The Judy Garland Show*. He quickly became a staple of TV, appearing on numerous entertainment and talk shows as well as taking on dramatic roles.

He was working at the Tropicana in Las Vegas in 2018 when he spoke to us, performing in a one-man retrospective show.

'I play lots of clips with some humor to go along with it. I do a whole thing on Dean.'

We asked him if such a retrospective format was a conscious decision or one driven by audience desires.

'I perform for older people, those who were around when the shows were done. Young people, they don't know about Dean, or Frank Sinatra or John Wayne, unless they're interested in the past.'

Certainly, the younger generation may be aware of the names of these classic stars, but not necessarily who they were or what they accomplished. That said, Rich pointed out that he was aware of teenagers who had actually seen *all* the *Roasts*.

'Comics today are very crude. They use the 'f' word all the time. It's more observational now than jokes.'

The Dean Martin Celebrity Roasts, while encouraging insults about the main guest star, were never crude or blue and that made the humor more palatable, more accessible and all the more funnier.

'I did 24 in all, more than anybody. There was a lot of pressure performing in front of the greatest comedians and actors of all time. Apart from the millions watching, just having [the stars] on the dais was enough to really unnerve you. To stand up in front of Lucille Ball, Orson Welles, Jack Benny, John Wayne...that was pretty terrifying in itself. You had to concentrate on what you were doing and not let the presence of these people bother you.

'Some people who did the *Roasts* when they looked down the dais, they actually panicked and so there were a few who were cut to a minute or taken out of the show completely.'

Rich performed in front of his idols. He grew up watching them, admiring them and impersonating them - and here he was, in Las Vegas, doing all of that in front of them. He didn't consider himself and idol, an attitude that really showed how Rich Little is genuinely and sincerely humble regarding the success he has had. He never showed off, never threw an ego around and his gentle manner and honesty was clear.

'Dean didn't have to rehearse for the *Roasts*. That was very important to him. He didn't like to rehearse. I'd done his variety show then moved over to the *Roasts*. He was in studio for and hour and a half or so when he did the variety shows and just wasn't the type to sit down and talk. He may have just put his head around the door of the Green Room and say 'How are you, pally?'

'Dean was at his best when things went wrong. He had the ability to ab lib. He wanted things to go wrong then get out of it. He was a man who only did what he wanted to do and he didn't care anything about Royalty or anyone with authority or presidents or anybody. He didn't want to rehearse, just wanted to get it over with. He never took anything seriously. After his son died he want totally down-hill - he was just a shell, he'd gone.'

Rich has also appeared in various American drama shows such as *Police Woman*, *Love American Style*, *Hawaii Five-O* (as a James Cagney-style murderer) and *The Flying Nun* (as an accident-prone priest).

'I enjoy acting. My background is theater and I always wanted to be an actor before becoming an impersonator. I love doing something dramatic.' Rich added that he would love to do more if he could.

His book *Little by Little: People I've Known and Been*[4] is a tremendous read and recalls many of the people he admired and worked with throughout his career. He recalls the funny things that have happened to him. But he'd never write a straight biography.

'My [personal] life is not that interesting,' he said. 'I've been married four times, and I've got the greatest girl now, so you just gotta get lucky. I made a few people like me or laugh and forget their problems and I was able to entertain. During one or two hours on stage, people forget their problems and remember the great actors of the past. As Cary Grant once said, 'It's great.''

So much of the camaraderie and remarks made in *The Dean Martin Celebrity Roasts* and on stage were very much in-jokes, old pals acting out a comedy. A lot of the gags were lost on the viewers; one perhaps had to be part of the clique to appreciate the comedy. Dean kept some sort of order in all of this mayhem, and again his shows were going up in the ratings. This was something that he was now used to hearing but not necessarily expecting, especially in these trying times with so many younger entertainers coming up fast behind.

However, Dean complained that there were just too many

---

[4] 2016, Dog Ear Publishing

'drunk' jokes about himself in the scripts, so these were eased off gradually. The audiences filled the area in front of the celebrities (usually to packed capacity), all adding atmosphere to the shows. Certain scenes were filmed back in the studio with the same props, re-arranged for better continuity, and finally edited to present the show ready for transmission.

Dean's first wife Betty had received $2,400 a month from her ex-husband since 1949 which had now ceased, the amount hardly noticeable to him the way his present wife was spending money!

In the headlines was the other Dean, his son, who had been arrested for being in possession of firearms. He'd collected some as a hobby and the authorities released him soon after when he produced a genuine arms certificate, stating he was a collector.

Meanwhile, his father now started work on the first film under his deal with MGM entitled *Mr Ricco*, in which he played a lawyer defending an accused killer involved in a spate of police murders. This was a strong character role - but Dean's heart was not in it. He could not concentrate on his lines, his depression swamping his waking thoughts. Yet he completed what was actually a good film, together with a good storyline, but he announced that he would do no more films for MGM, once again breaking a deal. It was a pattern that had followed him for his entire career.

MGM didn't promote the film with much publicity and it fell by the wayside to become an interesting yet largely forgotten entry to the early 70s police/action movie genre. It was never going to be a *Dirty Harry*, or a *French Connection* or a *Death Wish* but it is of that ilk - and sorely underrated.

Rumors appeared here and there that a possible concert tour with Sammy and Frank was in the offing but nothing came of this; the three artists were involved in commitments that would not enable them to get together at the same time.

With Dean's latest album issued quite some time back, there was now a distinct lack of recorded material for those admirers of the mellow Martin sound, who naturally felt starved of their favorite singer's renditions , even though his sales had diminished of late. In between breaks from his television and cabaret work, he managed to go into the recording studio at the end of November to lay down ten tracks including "It's Magic" and "Love Thy Neighbor". With these, he had finally come to record his last-ever songs for release on the Reprise label.

Although his contract was not officially expired until 1975, Dean had recorded enough songs to fulfil his commitments under that contract and of course rumors started that he would soon re-sign with another record company. A strong contender at the time was thought to be RCA, as he held quite a considerable stake in that company. But these ten songs he recorded were shelved and not released within the normal time-span – no issue date was arranged by either side.

If it had been possible for him to retire in 1975, as he had jokingly threatened many times, he would have had no financial worries or concerns. But retirement was out of the question for him, at least for a year or two. He had contracted himself for further cabaret and television work if nothing else.

NINETEEN

I Still Get A Thrill Thinking Of You

It had now been two years since a new album had been released, and Dean's collectors and admirers were becoming impatient at the lack of products. There was no way that Dean Martin was going to have the commitment he had previously had with any chapter of his career - he just did not want or need such fierce output now and to all sensible admirers of his work, they had to be reasonable and realize that he was an entertainer whose ratings pull or sales figures were becoming less headlining.

The DMA entered its fifteenth year of representing Dean's career, and I began work in assisting EMI Records for a Capitol album for the summer season with the theme of memories. In conjunction with Kodak, we made a selection of songs by Dean to reflect this, with the public invited to send in their memories, with records and photographic equipment as prizes. The album tracks were now finalized between Capitol and me, with the front cover a collage of small pictures surrounding a larger central photograph of Dean, with the inevitable title, MEMORIES ARE MADE OF THIS. An unusual twenty-track compilation (most were half that length), the album was issued on 9th July 1975 and became the BBC Radio 2 *Album of the Week* for 22nd July.

We had an international poll amongst our members this year in which we asked them which was their favorite character part that Dean had played in a film so far. When we eventually sorted the answers, we were somewhat surprised when it turned out to be the part of Dude in *Rio Bravo*. In my personal opinion, with the popularity of his spy films, I would have thought the top choice would have been Matt Helm - but it reflected the choice of the public and just goes to show that we all see Dean in different ways!

With such a variety of characters throughout his films, Dean time and time again showed the public that he was not just a fine singer but he also made a damn good actor and comedian. Joey Bishop said, 'What a pity Dean is such a fine singer…he is also the greatest comedian ever!'

Perhaps Dean's talent with comedy is not at the forefront of his repertoire because he portrayed the best of his funny lines and sketches in his own television shows over the years, and they never had the worldwide distribution that they warranted. I always thought that this was a terrible pity, because it was Dean himself who did not allow his shows to have blanket coverage around the world. It was only in America that we had these weekly showings; the rest of the world had to have erratic, broken scheduling. When we played these shows at our meetings, I was surprised that some people didn't appreciate his song parodies. When I mentioned this to him, he quite rightly said, 'Bernard, if they wanna listen to me sing properly, tell them to go buy my records!'

With so many years working for Dean, I suppose I had the envious position of perhaps being part of Dean's extended 'team'. I typically kept a low profile in the representation of Dean and his life and career, but at the same time always ensured that we served the man and his members with as much professionalism and sincerity as possible.

Over the period of those last eighteen months we had issued various items of merchandise such as t-shirts, sweatshirts, pens and the like, plus authorized posters which all sold very well. We had withdrawn our membership cards to cut down on costs, and ran another poll asking them for their favorite Reprise song to date. The result? "Gentle On My Mind". Meanwhile, Dean carried on with his appearances on television and in his Vegas shows, and also attended the Linda and Paul McCartney party aboard the Queen Mary liner at Long Beach, heading the 'conga' with Cher followed by Tony Curtis, Bob Dylan and many others!

Late this year I was asked by Reprise to co-produce the very first compilation album of Dean's songs specifically for the UK market, so I began work on song selection and sleeve design for this innovative release scheduled for release later in 1976.

Initial instructions had come from Dean's office for me to manage this project, as he had insisted in his contract that his product would never be re-issued on the Reprise label as a budget item, so therefore this album, even though it was a compilation of all songs previously available, had to be normal price. The album was to comprise twenty songs, leaving scope for a second similar album possibly for release in late 1977. I commenced work on this project in the new year which gave me ample time among my numerous other commitments for Dean to finalize the album overall.

In their personal lives, Cathy and Dean continued their relationship as husband and wife, but the problems were building up and they seemed to be at odds all the time. There did not seem to be any improvement between them and they were both now feeling very unsettled and unsure. Dean had yet another operation for an ulcer and, after recuperation, he resumed work at the MGM Grand, carrying on with his favorite occupation in his business, his cabaret shows.

It was sort of 'homely' to relax and watch him, and I relished the chance to witness him perform whenever I was able. He could stand on that stage, presenting his jokes and songs in the inimitable atmosphere of the Celebrity Room, being fully at ease with his audience, letting them all become a part of his world, even if it was for less than an hour most of the time.

But with his personal life again in turmoil, things were a little bleak to say the least: continuous differences of opinion and his wife's extravagances meant the marriage was no longer salvageable and Cathy moved out of their home in late June, leaving her husband once again in a confused and depressed state. He had thought that perhaps with a little more perseverance on both sides they could have made it, but it obviously was not to be. Once again (but this time after only three years) he was to go through the trauma of divorce. There were people around him who could have warned him where things were headed but, in any case, they both knew that this situation just could not go on.

Even living on the other side of the world from Dean, I had

sensed from the very beginning that something was not quite right for him when he decided to marry Catherine Hawn. It is difficult to explain, but I did not feel as if this union would last. Perhaps because I had come to know Dean a little more than the average person, his calls to me were rarely about his public and professional life, often chatting about family and home. By sheer chance, it seemed my feelings were right and they eventually divorced in February 1977. Settlements between them were quickly dealt with and completed. But the media had a different take: whilst staying at Mort Viner's home, Dean was inspecting some guns and one accidentally went off, injuring him in the hand and needing twenty stitches at the hospital. With his current wave of depression, a couple of newspapers exploited the false notion that he had attempted suicide.

Dean had always been the target for negative press, fueled by his 'drunk' stage persona. When he was pulled over by the police for dangerous driving, he was of course considered to be drunk. But the truth of the matter was that he had taken an excess of pain-killers which caused him to drive erratically. Dean said, 'If I drank as much as I say I do and as many people think I do, then I would not have even been alive after forty years of age, would I?'

No matter what his personal or public affairs were at any time, the public adored him and even though there was a shortage of live concerts and films now, together with the lack of new recordings, they still loved this man.

Since those times with Jerry Lewis, Dean had made sure that the work was continuous. Sometimes things were hard, but he had that passionate determination, maybe because of his Italian heritage, to work hard and play hard and be rewarded with acclaim and success. He had always dreamed of success, particularly as a singer, but he wanted to be able to tackle most areas of show business and be as good as he could be overall. Even he had to admit now that he was a phenomenal success in the true sense of the word.

Even though they had only seen each other on less than a

handful of occasions, Dean and Jerry never really got together. Their careers never crossed paths again, and Dean was never the sort of man to chase after anyone; he liked his own company and did not feel the need to be with anyone, male or female, at any time. He was content being around himself and doing nothing, unless his work called. Then he would wholeheartedly throw himself into that project and without doubt.

But although Dean and Jerry had not worked together since their break-up, both entertainers were doing an incredible amount of solo work. If they had seen each other, it was merely a passing glance, and Dean did not acknowledge any notes or messages that Jerry left (something Jerry did even before they properly knew each other). Over 20 years had gone since by they were the world's biggest team, and perhaps the hugely talented Jerry had not quite made it to the same dizzy heights as his former partner - but he was not doing too badly!

Jerry loved the technical aspect of film-making and was a wonderful comic. I had the good fortune to meet him just once in the 70s and he spoke lovingly of Dean, and I found him to be a warm, character, if somewhat mischievous and sometimes a little curt. He continued to make films and appeared in cabaret numerous times (and had a terrific resurgence of popularity with his show Damn Yankees in 1995). However, he became an advocate of the telethon and he had a yearly Muscular Dystrophy charity show, raising millions of dollars for this crippling disease. But it was his show for 1976 that was to give him the shock of his life!

On 5th September, he had commenced his latest television marathon-seen by so many millions of people right across America. This was a live televised event, this time taking place at the Sahara Hotel, Las Vegas, and Jerry was hoping to exceed over $20 million, beating previous years by far. He had managed to procure the services of no less than one Francis Albert Sinatra and, after an elaborate introduction, Frank walked on and performed a couple of songs, livening up the proceedings somewhat.

When he finished these songs, he mentioned to Jerry that he had a friend who he'd brought along who may help to attain more money for his cause. He pointed off to his right and the camera panned in to see Dean saunter on, totally unannounced and unfazed by the uproarious applause of the audience, to hug Jerry for the first time in two decades.

I thought it was about time, didn't you? Frank was heard o say, as the two continued to embrace, both of them lost for words, if only for a few seconds. But it was not too long before Jerry asked Dean if he was working.

Sure, at the Megam, now and again.

Megam! Jerry repeated, knowing full well that Dean meant the MGM Grand. Remembering this was live television, you could see Jerry well up but Dean, ever the closed off person, held back his emotions. Dean told me years later that he did struggle to keep it straight.

'Seeing the kid again? Yeah, it was a blast and I had to pretend to stay stoned so as to not let it out.'

He was a past master at this, never showing emotion if he could help it. Nevertheless, he soon showed everyone that he was the great entertainer, as he took over the show. Frank had given them each a microphone, where the former partners chatted briefly before Dean joined Frank in what he called a *meldy* of songs. This certainly made the money pour in: the impact of such three unique entertainers on stage together was big enough, but the historical event of Martin and Lewis appearing together like that was absolutely enthralling for viewers, production staff and anyone else involved. Frank had actually managed to keep it totally quiet that Dean was even in the building and it surprised more than the public when Dean walked on. As was usual, Dean screwed up his lyrics, made jokes and pretended he couldn't see the cue cards and kept getting closer to the cameras.

The entire event was something that could never happen – but it did and only the great Frank Sinatra that could have organized it.

After this Martin and Lewis reunion, there was much rumor within the industry that perhaps they may work together again, even in a film, and director David Puttnam tried to contact both artists for such a proposal, but nothing ever materialized from either men.

A little while after this event, Jerry sent a message to Dean's management asking if they could get together, even if only for a meeting for old time's sake. He eventually received a somewhat vague comment saying perhaps it would be nice to see each other again, but after a few attempts at a further reunion, Jerry had no response from Dean nor his management at all; no one on Dean's side ever got around to even suggesting a meeting of any sort and so it never came to fruition.

This was a part of Dean Martin that few people could understand: he rarely thought of organizing something himself and regularly left such things to his staff. This left many people frustrated and annoyed, as they would often receive no response at all. This wasn't really blatant rudeness, it was something that he just didn't deal with. It took me a while to get used to this, to not take any silence personally but to accept that was simply his way.

That frustration spilled out into the correspondence the DMA received. We received so many letters daily, some requesting more than the normal from Dean, sometimes requesting money – lots of it – and some asking for things that were just not possible, such as personal home visits by Dean. We responded to these alarming and bewildering requests professionally and courteously and had little or no comeback. We did have a few fans who came to our UK offices genuinely expecting Dean to be there. When my team told them that Mr Martin was a) in Hollywood and b) didn't accept personal visits anyway, they seemed rather annoyed and almost didn't believe what we were saying!

But we dealt with all aspects of fandom as best we could, hoping to enlighten the enquirer about the amazing talent that was Dean. I sincerely hope that we assisted Dean in his own personal life and his career since we were established in 1960 and that we certainly continue to do so as long as possible. The DMA will always exist, perhaps not as it used to, to honor and promote the name and artistry of Dean.

TWENTY

I'm Sittin' On Top Of The World

With the numerous projects that we had undertaken up to 1976, we knew we were furthering Dean's career when our latest efforts with his first compilation album for Reprise became very successful[5]. As well as song selection, I also had the privilege of designing the complete front and rear sleeves. I chose a blue background, mainly because it was Dean's favorite color, with the title in yellow and orange. It was my intention to make this album stand out in the record store racks, because after all, that is what sleeve design is all about…something that catches the eye amongst all of the other issues.

There was some disagreement between me and Reprise in London, as they wanted to call the album LITTLE OLD WINE DRINKER, DEAN, but I found this offensive, pushing further the continued negative and wrong opinion that Dean was nothing but a drunk. The title I decided on, I left with them for discussion, leaving it in their hands to see if they could suggest something more suitable (which they did not!). Meanwhile, I submitted my complete project, the full choice of twenty songs and the sleeve design and title included, over to Dean for his approval.

He called me after a short while, confirming his acceptance of it all and telling me he was very pleased with my tremendous efforts involved with this special release. His office followed this up in writing to both me and Reprise in London. Later, however, the London office disagreed with three or four of the songs I had chosen and decided to replace them with some of their own suggestions. Being very concerned with this, I could see that if this happened it would soon become their project, not mine. I informed the London

---

[5] See also Chapter 28, pg. 231

office of my concerns, advising them that I did not agree and would consider informing Mr Martin, mentioning his own approval of the project as was.

Further time elapsed and eventually I was informed by Reprise that they had been instructed by Dean's office that my original song choices must stand. Having settled that problem, the album was prepared and set for release on 27th August 1976, but then later amended to 28th October (which I was very pleased with, as it was nearer the Christmas selling season).

Now pushing my luck, I suggested a national television advertising campaign, but Reprise UK did not consider this viable. But after many weeks of determination, I did persuade them to test-advertise in the local Tyne Tees television area. They were unconvinced by my passionate claims that this album would go Gold, and they were wary of my complete faith in Dean Martin's sales appeal, even if it was for the Christmas selling period. I was strongly informed that if this album did not sell in reasonable quantities to cover their considerable TV advertising costs they would pull out of all mass advertising and treat the album as an ordinary release. Regardless, I was convinced the executives at Reprise here thought I should have been locked away at my almost demented (their word!) faith in this album. I was that sure that Dean's name on the cover would sell the records by the box-load! They still didn't believe me and I still wonder what was said in their board meetings at the time about the lunatic in South London who seemed convinced this American singer could still sell records!

They did ask (perhaps just to humor me?) for my prediction about which position the album would reach in the charts. I stuck my neck right out and stated it would reach number 2 in the UK by the end of the year. Amidst stifled chuckling, they were mystified about why I did not say number 1. Considering the time of the year, I reasoned, there was nearly always a seasonal album that found itself at the top of the charts, which meant there was never a true number 1 in late

December most years, a fact that I thought such executives should be well aware of if they were worth their salt! Once again I was considered eccentric with this outrageous forecast and I did begin to wonder if I'd finally overstepped the mark!

Naturally, the DMA worked very hard at promoting this release with the special Christmas edition of the newsletter enclosing a copy of the actual record sleeve (LP not included!) to every one of our members across the globe, as well as a full color quad-size poster of Dean.

TWENTY ORIGINAL HITS became Dean's very first Gold album in the UK and – wait for it – reached number 2 in the charts! The album remained in the British charts for five weeks and was a proud moment for me and the DMA – a fine reward for all those months and months of work and sleepless nights on this project for Dean. Maybe the only slight disappointment was that Reprise in California tried to arrange with Dean's office for me to go to Nevada to give the Gold disc to Dean myself, but after some attempts at this, nothing came of it. The idea was for me to walk on stage in the middle of his act in Vegas and present it to him! Instead, it was posted to his office by Reprise in January 1977 and hung in the hallway of his home. I often wonder what became of it after his death.

I visited many parts of the United Kingdom as part of the promotion, which included radio interviews on various BBC stations, and I met many members on the way. I hope that my personal efforts helped to make it go Gold!

TWENTY-ONE

Wrap Your Troubles In Dreams

With his third marriage on the rocks, Dean was in no mood for anything. He'd scrapped any possible films that may have been in the pipeline, and his depression fueled his lethargy. His dependency on painkillers also spiraled his mood into a terrible slump.

Was this the price of fame?

Many before him and many after have gained top stardom and then fallen, but Dean, through some sense of strength, kept his position as a well-respected and highly regarded individual, even if that didn't include Cathy. Those three short years of marriage were a repeat of his past and one wonders if he had been aware of the patterns and perhaps attributed them to himself.

Yet with depression (let alone his ulcers and arthritis) almost crippling his health, no member of the public would ever see past the stage persona.

By mere coincidence, in the midst of Dean's problems, I too suffered a great loss when my dear father, Henry, died on 26th October 1976, five days before my son's fifth birthday. Amidst all the excitement of TWENTY ORIGINAL HITS, this tragic event for my family dulled the happiness at the project into which I had put so much of my time. There is a great chunk of your life that goes when you lose your parents, but life and all that entails has to go on and I was thankful that he had had a great and wonderful life. He is forever in my thoughts.

The Celebrity Roasts continued on NBC (Dean was the recipient of his own roasting earlier in the year), along with a special clip show of them, hosted by Don Rickles. Meanwhile, Dean, throughout the year, managed to pull himself on to the stage for his cabaret appearances. He also recorded the first of his seasonal Christmas in California specials.

19th November saw the divorce from Cathy complete and, although they divided the property in half, she did not come away with anything like the settlement Jeanne had been given previously. She only received $2,000 a month for just three years, with Cathy's daughter Sasha (from her previous marriage) receiving only $250 a month until she was eighteen or got married, whichever was the earlier. Dean also agreed to pay her school fees but cancelled the adoption order.

The future for Dean Martin, the 'total entertainer' as he was so rightly called many times, looked strange: he was not shy in letting people know he was not too bothered with films or recordings now, although he continued with his cabaret and a reasonable number of specials and guest spots for television. Although his net worth was now in its millions (at one time it was thought he had accrued around 34 of them, if anyone could be bothered to count --and Dean was the last to worry about such matters) his status did not concern him too much. He hated unnecessary wastage with money, but at the same time he used it to soften his life and enable a carefree existence. That was what he paid his management for, he considered, and they surpassed themselves in keeping him away from the drudge of routine operations and decisions, allowing him to concentrate on facing his public.

Yet that reliance on those around him meant he had little idea what was going on behind the scenes. Trust, it seemed, was something he bestowed easily to those in control of his finances.

Everyone in show business, in fact in any walk of life, has their share of good times and bad, and Dean experienced more than his fair share of both. But a very fortunate situation takes place when you get to a certain degree of prestige within the business: If you are at the top and you are able to stay there, then talent, hard work and luck must go hand in hand.

Dean was highly respected by everyone (in and out of his business) but even after all these years and even his own death, I must say that today, I believe Dean Martin is extremely under-rated in parts of the world – and the UK is unfortunately one of them.

Certainly, he played to packed houses in his London concerts in the 80s, to great acclaim, and always attracted long queues at cinemas. He sold large quantities of records, too, but there are so many people who still insist that he was just a drunk who took little care or pride in what he did.

To them, all I say is this: just look at his achievements over the years. That usually makes them lose their words, especially when I quote facts and figures, as most people do not even realize just how much work he had done! Nevertheless, I know some people walked away from me thinking I had just exaggerated his achievements and went on too much about him. But Dean had that charm and consistency and has managed to secure an immortal niche in the world of entertainment forever. I can imagine many readers thinking that I perhaps praise Dean too much…but why not? Has he not given so many millions of us so much pleasure?

I don't deny he had many faults, like most of us have, and perhaps I am blinkered because of my association with him, but (and I alluded to this in my introduction) I don't want to linger on his bad points. This recollection is a celebration and appreciation of Dean, of all that he achieved, and the legacy he left us with.

Dad is always so gentle and understanding, his daughter Deana was quoted as saying. *He makes us all feel so important. He always has time for us and I think that that is the nicest thing that can happen to me particularly, but for the rest of us as well. Some of us have often wondered if we will ever find a man to measure up to him. We know why he has been so successful in his career. It's because of his manner and attitude to people. It does help, you know.*

And heaven forbid I ever even begin to consider I was anywhere near as close to him as his children were. Of course I wasn't. It would be ridiculous for me to even think I was! Yet I understood what Deana said and, in my own small way, I like to think that in my professional life, he was the nicest thing to happen to me as well and the respect I have for his family is immense.

It had been two years since Dean had been in a recording

studio, and continuing disagreements with Warner/Reprise meant that several songs he'd recorded remained unissued. After months of discussion, nothing seemed to be resolved and Dean opted to take them to court for around $1.5million. They remarked that his recent record sales were too low to warrant any new further issues on the Reprise label and so they had no interest in releasing anything further. Dean on the other hand stated that they had not given him a reasonable opportunity to release his recordings!

Meanwhile, Reprise UK had asked me to prepare a second album compilation in follow-up to their surprise success of TWENTY ORIGINAL HITS. But now with the arguments raging between Reprise in the US and Dean, the project was scrapped entirely and the album that I had produced became the first and last compilation for Dean on that particular label. That said, I didn't think a second volume would have sold as much as the first, but nevertheless, it was a shame we didn't get the chance to find out.

After many months of arguing, the problems were settled out of court between Dean and Warner/Reprise, stating that just one more album would be issued on that label to clear all legal contracts between them. So, with the split from Cathy and the split from Reprise, it seemed there was more uncertainty regarding the public's expectations. Yes, he continued with his beloved cabaret but it seemed unlikely there would be any new material forthcoming in the way of recordings. Dean's career, it seemed, had peaked, and couldn't climb any further.

He had moved over to Laguna Beach since the divorce and was leading a bachelor life again, being seen in several of the classy clubs and restaurants - with a new woman on his arm every time, it seemed. The media reported later that 'he was madly in love' with Peggy Crosby and that a wedding would take place soon but neither Peggy nor Dean made any comments about such remarks. Admittedly, he had been seen with Peggy on a number of occasions since his divorce, but nothing was ever forthcoming and they eventually parted as good friends. Ever on the hunt for more gossip, the tabloids also ran with the rumor that he was to re-marry Jeanne, but neither side commented on such news: they had always been good friends, even since that divorce, and it did not seem likely that they would get together again in that way. Yet Dean continually stated that he loved Jeanne and when true love is there, does anything really ever dampen it? Even a divorce? Perhaps I'm just an old romantic!

For a man now reported to be worth around $90 million (amusing how the media bump up the worth of entertainers each time!), Dean was now working with more live concerts outside of Nevada, appearing in New Jersey in late May 1977 for five days, Washington for a day and then arriving in Chicago on his birthday for four days on stage there – all with his friend Frank Sinatra.

Frank had on a few occasions tried to persuade Dean to go to London for a series of shows, but even he was unable to get him there! And if Frank couldn't do it, no one could!

Dean attended a sad event in August this year when he went with Tom Jones to the funeral on the 17th of Elvis Presley, the King's death triggering one of the biggest and spectacular affairs ever in show-business. Millions of people all over the world went into meltdown, mourning for days as soon as the news broke of the demise of this superb man who had been given countless accolades in his amazing career – ones that would continue long after. It was a sad loss to the entertainment industry and, in my opinion, a totally unnecessary death at such a young age. He had everything to live for but the richness of his life took a toll on him mentally and physically.

The DMA held a special meeting for June, and we had a reasonable attendance, giving prominence (naturally!) to TWENTY ORIGINAL HITS and Dean's 60th birthday. It proved to be our biggest gathering to date, with something like 1,000 people in attendance. We used to hold our meetings in a hotel (long since demolished) in South London, and this was one of the more enjoyable aspects of the DMA.

Meanwhile, Dean had renewed his contract with NBC for a further two years and, along with his various live appearances, returned to another season with the MGM Grand in Las Vegas.

In the UK, there's an annual tradition called the Royal Variety Performance. It's a show that attracts and showcases the top talent of the time. Held at the illustrious London Palladium, stars around the world are invited by Royal Command and 1977's was to be something extra special - because Her Majesty Queen Elizabeth was celebrating her Silver Jubilee Year. But more importantly for us (!), I had been informed to a great surprise by Dean's office that he, along with Bing Crosby, had been provisionally penciled in for top billing.

Dean arranged his hotel booking for ten days in London, allowing for rehearsals and time for a look around this city (something he had never had the time or opportunity for, but something he had always longed to do). He called me to ask for my availability as he intended to visit our offices while he was here. I'd just appointed a personal secretary, Jayne Kempsey, and I think she nearly fainted when I told her!

Bing had been on holiday in Spain, however, when a great tragedy occurred. He had collapsed on a golf course (Crosby's favorite pastime), dying almost immediately from a heart attack.

With the Royal Variety Performance already scheduled for transmission on 4th December and, as usual, given great publicity in the UK press, the organizers were obviously shocked by this news. To make matters even worse, Dean's management announced that because of a heavy workload and the sudden death of Bing, he would not be appearing. This annoyed the producers and the Royal House: this was just too much to turn down a Royal invitation, but Dean had made his decision and it wasn't going to be changed.

Even in the wake of Bing's sad death, Dean continued his workload, and *Christmas In California* was broadcast on NBC with Crystal Gale co-starring.

Continuing his bachelor life, Phyllis Davis (then the star of *Vega$* with Robert Urich) was his latest flame and, unlike his other dalliances, he became very protective of her. One time when she was asked to pose topless, Dean insisted that she kept herself covered up, a request she honored for him during their relationship.

Meanwhile, back in our world at the DMA, we considered arranging a trip to see Dean on stage at the MGM, but costs proved prohibitive for bulk bookings so Jayne had to sadly abandon the plan. However, our membership still continued to rise steadily, even though many had not taken kindly to Dean's cancellation at the Royal Variety Performance.

Even though he was not making films or recordings, support for his career via the DMA progressed without question through 1978 and we were now well established. It was pleasing after all these years to be able to see Dean's association was successful and, with the marvelous support of the man himself plus those many members we had all over the world, we were even more determined to work harder to keep the name of Dean Martin at the very forefront of great international entertainment.

With the agreement settled between Dean and Reprise, songs were finally being selected for a new album to be released this year and, contrary to the continuing media speculation, Jeanne and Dean were not planning to re-marry - but they were seen a lot together and when Dean held a special 21st birthday party for his daughter Gina, Jeanne was present too, the family spending the entire weekend at the Palm Springs home of Frank Sinatra.

Dean's television appearances had a resurgence: he guest-starred in 'Angels In Vegas', a two-part episode of the phenomenally successful series *Charlie's Angels*, in which he seemed well at ease playing a character called Frank Howell in and amongst the atmosphere and crap tables of Las Vegas. He was very happy and sociable whilst filming with Kate Jackson, Jaclyn Smith and Cheryl Ladd and, by all accounts, had most of the cast in fits with his jokes and antics on and off set.

He recorded a second *Christmas In California*, too, and agreed on a final selection for Once In A While, a new Reprise album. These were 1974 vocal recordings by Dean in Hollywood but backed with 1978 orchestra and singers taped in Nashville. This release finally closed the deal he'd made with Reprise, which now cleared him of any further work on that label. As part of the agreement, sadly, our Twenty Original Hits was now deleted here, along with most of the other albums in the catalog. From then on, all the original master tapes were (and still are) held in bond at Warner Brothers, but with Dean (and now his estate) still holding the outright ownership of the recordings.

Other record companies did not seem to be interested in signing him, and in any case Dean himself was not interested in recording any more songs. He occasionally remarked that he would ease up on his work (and yes, even retire!) but his work schedule this year seemed to tell the exact opposite story. MGM had supplied him with a four-bedroom house within easy reach of the Grand, and he now increased his cabaret dates throughout this year and into 1979.

TWENTY-TWO

What Could Be More Beautiful?

A very surprising out-of-the-blue and welcome invitation came from EMI Records in very early 1979, when they asked me to choose sixteen of my very favorite songs that Dean had recorded for Capitol over the years.

A somewhat daunting task, I may say, because so many of them were my real favorite songs, absolute classics in my opinion, and to try to select just sixteen seemed impossible. But given the chance for another compilation album, I began work on this with great pleasure. Presumably there was confidence in me that I could put together another good solid selection!

There was a paper shortage in the UK at this time which meant restrictions on magazines and newspapers (it seemed the record industry was not directly affected too much, with the number of issues appearing from all the companies) but we still managed to distribute our monthly newsletters, as we had reasonable paper stocks ourselves, owing to forward thinking by Jayne!

Contacting BBC Radio, we asked them if they would be prepared to feature Dean this year somewhere around his birthday and link this with the new album I had just completed. We eventually persuaded them and had a *Dean Martin Day* on Radio 2 on 1st March - but why they chose that day and not one nearer Dean's birthday in June remained a mystery. They were able to feature one or two songs from the new album, but being as it was not actually released then, it acted as something of a preview, which helped with eventual sales, of course.

But the BBC nevertheless put together a great presentation, with many programs during the course of the day playing Dean's songs. Numerous enquiries at the BBC further boosted the DMA's membership, too. I did try and convince Dean to record a greeting for the BBC but, while he was appreciative of the dedicated day, his response was a resounding no.

The new EMI album finally appeared in the stores Monday 8th June, the nearest we could get to celebrating Dean's birthday, and I sent him copies for his own collection. I had remarked several times to Capitol that so many of the songs they had recorded with Dean were really his 'classic' recordings and so I thought that an ideal title for such a collection had to be THE CLASSIC DINO which everyone at EMI agreed to. The disc became a best seller (for a compilation) and remained in the EMI catalog for over eleven years, a record in itself for such a release.

The DMA was featured in a two-column spread in the local newspaper *The Croydon Advertiser*, letting their readers know that we had one of the most famous and successful clubs of this nature in the world at the time, and for an equally famous and successful man. Executives at the newspaper offices were surprised that such an organization was still going strong after almost twenty years, and that it was somewhat unusual for such a big American entertainer to have his headquarters in South London.

We had such marvelous and loving support from Dean and his office and so many times he helped us with the things we needed for promotion. It was always so very exciting when a delivery arrived from his address in California. And those late evenings when our house 'phone rang and he was there on the end of it? ...truly amazing.

I felt very privileged and humble.

As a singer, Dean racked up over 13 million sales with his Reprise releases between 1964 and 1976, an achievement then-unequalled by any artists of his caliber. He could now look back on this unique period in his recording career with pride, with a fabulous library of songs across multiple singles and albums. We must remember that in those days, an artist had to actually sell a million copies before a Gold award was given - and Dean had received plenty.

The 51st Oscars ceremony this year was presented in part by Dean with Racquel Welch, and he looked well as he walked on stage, pretending to stammer with nerves and awe as he stood next to his beautiful co-host.

Nowadays, his famed weekly television shows were in syndication and a further guest role appeared, this time in the episode 'Dean Martin and the Moonshiners' for the short-lived Claude Akins police comedy series *The Misadventures of Sheriff Lobo*. He also did a special at the San Diego Animal Park and a guest spot in *Vega$*, then filmed his third Christmas special.

NBC put together *The Best of Dean* as a two-hour special collected from his TV shows – but it oddly leaned more towards the comedy angle. I would have thought at least a handful of songs in this production would have been more the 'best' of Dean as we knew him. Nevertheless, it was great to see his antics once more.

So ended another busy year for Dean. His health was not what it once was, and his eternal battles against his back and his ulcers never let up. It hardly seemed he would consider retirement, even though in the midst of all this activity he still muttered that he would stop altogether soon! As well as seeing Jeanne quite regularly, he was still dating various women around town and seemed quite content in leading this type of life for the time being. He said little to anyone about how he really felt, but continued with his usual devil-may-care approach to his work and appearances. His commitments still warranted so many events for some time ahead; concerts and television were his mainstay now and he had no desire for film-making any more, no matter what he was offered. The media continued their aggressive assault on his love life, informing each and every one that he was 'due to marry Jeanne soon', but again, neither of them made any comments on this continual barrage of nonsense.

Our boxed album set from World Records was now reduced to four albums instead of the original six, but also with each album now in its own picture sleeve.

Dean requested another five copies of THE CLASSIC DINO album from me, and these were sent direct to his home.

As 1980 appeared, Dean had made appearances in the

Shirley MacLaine TV special *Every Little Movement* and although he was his usual pleasant and amusing self on screen, he was showing signs of strain. Nevertheless, it was another chance to see him on television, transmitted in May of that year.

I contacted Mack Gray, concerned that Dean was looking unwell again. Mack was a wonderful gentleman who had been with Dean for most of his solo career, and who had done great things for him. He had guided him through his singing career and became a close confidante, helping Dean with so many decisions that he had to make. Mack assured me that Dean was listening to his doctors and told me not to worry or let our members be concerned. We used to have regular communications from Mack, giving us so much intimate and confidential information and we always used this with great discretion, Mack knowing full well he could trust us with such insights into Dean's life and career.

On 21st November 1980, a great disaster struck Las Vegas. Fire raged through the MGM Grand, a 26-story luxury resort with more than 2,000 hotel rooms. It started in the Deli restaurant and claimed the lives of 84 people, leaving an additional 650 injured and massive parts of the building devastated. At the time of the fire, approximately 5,000 people were in the hotel and casino. The rebuilding and redecorating was to take several months before it could re-open to the public again. There was a considerable loss of revenue to the company and Dean was shocked by the tragic event and was later invited to inspect some of the damage caused by this terrible tragedy.

Otherwise, he had ended the year with a visit to NBC for another Christmas special. This time it was studio-bound with Beverley Sills, Andy Gibb, Erik Estrada and Mel Tillis as his guests. While he was his usual upbeat self on camera, he once more looked tired and weary.

Continuing with his various television spots and other concerts, Dean had flatly refused any film roles but it was to be ex-stuntman Hal Needham who actually persuaded him to come back in 1981 for a reasonable part in an ensemble cast for the story of a cross-country car race - and Dean came through this comedy with flying colors, together with his friends and co-stars Dom Deluise and Sammy Davis Jr. Burt Reynolds headlined, followed by Farrah Fawcett, Jack Elam and the wonderful Roger Moore in a brilliant pastiche of his Bond persona (even getting to drive the model of Aston Martin made famous by Sean Connery in 1964's *Goldfinger*). Produced by Albert S. Ruddy for Golden Communications, *The Cannonball Run* was directed by Needham and distributed by 20th Century Fox.

The DMA was working steadily now: not much of Dean Martin was heard or seen (particularly in the UK) but with *The Cannonball Run*, I foresaw and hoped for a renewed interest. The film was attracting a generous box-office across America, eventually grossing over $150million.

Dean had contacted me earlier this year for a copy of Joan Collins' autobiography and ten more copies of THE CLASSIC DINO. I avoided asking him what he was doing with them all, but he expressed the immense pleasure he'd felt when he first listened to the album. He did not mention why he wanted a copy of the Joan Collins book.

As Dean was no longer under any commitment to record any songs, it came as quite a surprise when he suddenly asked me to send him a list of around 25 that I could suggest for him to record. I chose a collection of 30 that I thought would be nice for consideration: mostly those he had never recorded before plus a handful that I thought would be an idea for re-recording in a different style. Some weeks later he did acknowledge my suggestions, remarking that some of the songs I had listed he thought were perfect. But strangely enough, after all of this, nothing ever happened. It would have been very nice for a brand new album to have those songs (or at least some of them) recorded. I asked him if he was considering signing, and who with, but he wouldn't be drawn on the subject.

Because of continuing health problems, he did not accept

Bob Hope's invitation to attend his golf tournament this year and his cabaret appearances were now becoming less frequent, but he did take part in a ball game at 3am at the Absecons Memorial Field with Frank Sinatra. This took place after an August show at the Resorts International Hotel, and I was invited to watch (but not, I'm glad to say, to take part!). The game raised lots of money for charity, with the teams called 'Ole Red Eyes' and 'Ole Blue Eyes', and it does not take much to work out who captained what team!

But both pairs of eyes were very bright in this match, in which both great entertainers were very active and enjoyable to watch. It was a late night and they were still playing well into the dawn. I don't think I stirred from my bed at the Resorts until it was time to check out! It was an excellent change of pace for Dean and he felt exhilarated and happy that he had taken part in such a game.

A couple of days later, I flew home and Dean was back in Nevada for a five night bash at his favorite venue, the lavish and spectacular MGM Grand, playing to packed audiences in his inimitable style. He said to me he felt renewed and I hoped this meant a return to form for him...and possibly the recording studio?

Although celebrating our 20th anniversary this year, we had bad attendances at some meetings, so Jayne and I were considering dropping the events. Hiring expenses were rising all the time for such meetings, but even though membership was steady and new members joined us regularly, meetings were sadly no longer viable.

Sales of THE CLASSIC DINO were increasing and although signs of Dean himself seemed to be reducing, the DMA continued its efforts to promote him and were very grateful that we had so many members all over the world who consistently supported Dean and his society.

But Dean's health was not as good as it had been a year ago and he was really showing signs of strain. His painkillers bloated him again, and in a rare television interview, his voice was weak and certainly did not sound anything like the famous mellow and pleasant vocal chords that the world had come to know and love. He looked very exhausted and paused quite often when he spoke, something that was sad to see. Looking at Dean Martin as he was in his numerous clips and then returning to the man being interviewed, you could see such a stark contrast. He was at low par and, to make matters far worse, his depression sunk even lower, being totally devastated about the death of the wonderful Mack Gray, aged 75, on 17th January 1981.

Together with his health subsidence and his state of mind over Mack's death, he turned down Frank's offer to appear at Ronald Reagan's Inaugural Concert, but instead remained a member of the audience.

Frank was one of the very few who partly understood his plight and whilst he was disappointed, he accepted that his friend did not want to support him on stage at this glittering event. Dean had never taken any interest in politics but would always work for a cause if he generally agreed with the candidate, although this time he did not have the heart and energy to carry out this request. He went down with influenza and bronchitis shortly afterwards and had to rest at home.

Quite regularly, repeats of his television shows were seen in syndication – which thankfully maintained his household name, but with his health in such a state, many were asking us what was to become of him. What would he do next?

'Yeah, you must take life a little easier...after all I'm forty now,' he laughed, 'and I ain't gonna be forty again!'

Talks were going on for a possible *Cannonball* sequel and Dean had said it may be worth considering. On the small screen, he guest-starred *on The Paul Anka Cerebral Palsy Telethon* with one of his own specials, and made additional appearances with Bob Newhart and Dom Deluise. NBC also presented more clip-oriented material with *Dean Martin Comedy Classics* and various compilation albums appeared across America --the usual Capitol material, nothing exclusive or of particular note.

Reprise UK took another chance with the re-issue on 10th

July of "Gentle On My Mind", but unfortunately this did not repeat its previous success, when I had suggested the original release from the album of the same name. Because of the closing agreement Dean had with Warner/Reprise, this was to be the last Reprise release ever to appear in the United Kingdom.

1st July had seen the glorious re-opening of the MGM Grand, hosted by Cary Grant, with the actor stating graciously that it had been Dean Martin who had been the biggest attraction at this hotel, indeed in Nevada, for many years, and that he hoped he would continue to be for a long time to come.

But luck was not with Dean.

When he resumed his stage appearances, his health was guiding his actions: some hecklers shouted at him and critics remarked that it was a disgrace to expect people to actually pay to see him in person doing practically nothing. A lot of celebrities were in the audience and were somewhat surprised to see that Dean was using up more time talking and telling jokes than he was actually singing. It was sorely noticeable that he was not in the best of health, and he did continue his season there, but would occasionally cut short his show. This meant he would sometimes only be on stage for around 35 minutes, unlike the times he had been known to continue for well over an hour.

With the man himself easing back on his career, the DMA was receiving letters asking why we bothered continuing. I personally responded, confirming I would always keep the organization going, for Dean and his admirers world-wide. What reason would we have to close, just because Dean's career was slowing down? I think I made my point successfully, because we did not receive any more such correspondence.

To make matters worse, Dean had been caught with a gun in his trouser belt. Explaining that it was merely his son's water pistol, the authorities strongly advised against carrying such an article, especially considering the recent murder of John Lennon. Dean, however, foolishly ignored their advice and was later fined $200 for being in the unlawful possession of firearms, as he had continued to carry the gun in his car. He said he needed protection when he went out, but he did admit he was guilty and paid his fine without any further comment. The only amusing end to this saga was the fact that the judge had said that it was nice meeting him!

Two personalities died this year: George Jessel (83) and Norman Taurog (82), the latter having produced several Martin and Lewis films. So many people who had known Dean, or been in some way associated with him were coming to the end of their lives - a thought that made him slump into a worse depression. He was exhausted, in pain, and in a bleak frame of mind that concerned his family greatly. He was rushed to hospital and they operated on his ulcer, the media being informed that it had been nothing but a severe gastric upset. Upon release, he announced that he had cancelled all future commitments, accepting his doctors' advice that he must take stock of himself and cease consuming non-prescription drugs. He went into seclusion and screened himself from all enquirers. Jeanne had visited him at Cedars Sinai Hospital whilst he was there for his operation. With what seemed like a bad decline in Dean Martin's health, out came the media with exaggerated reports that he was very ill, or possibly dying, with only weeks to live, something his doctor had warned him would happen if he did not take better care of himself immediately. Dean realized just how bad things were, but to put the record straight, he did make an official announcement to clear up the numerous reports.

We received many heart-warming get-well messages, which we passed on to his office. However, he took a long break and recovered enough to make a Christmas special again, this time with Buck Owens. On this show, one could see he did look better, although still strained. The operation had taken its toll.

Even though he had rested, Dean's health still caused many a problem. Showing extreme signs of stress and strain, he was admitted to hospital for eight days' rest, under strict instruction to rest properly. The mixture of drugs and drink he was regularly consuming was becoming toxic, not just for his health, but for his reputation: Dean had been drinking more now than at any time in his life. With all the stories of his drunken days being mere fiction, it seemed that now he was letting those rumors become facts by downing alcohol and, even worse, taking it with prescription drugs - something he had never done before. Being so stubborn, it took a lot for Dean to heed his doctor's advice but this time he did, and rested again before he resumed any kind of work.

A return to his cabaret shows in Vegas was difficult. On one particular occasion he walked off stage, clearly struggling, but returning a few minutes later while his band played on. But he was not the same focused and driven entertainer he once was. He was hesitant in his songs and seemed to be somewhere else, leaning a lot on the piano and speaking sometimes so low that he was inaudible.

On his way home from a show, Dean was arrested for irresponsible driving in Beverly Hills. Now that was glorious news for the media: they jumped on this hot information! To think that Dean Martin of all people had been arrested for drinking and driving was all they had ever hoped for! For countless years they had all thought of him as a heavy drinker and now this incident gave them their chance to gloat and spread the word everywhere they possibly could. This sealed it for them: Dean Martin was a drunk!

Only he wasn't.

When he was tested, it was found that he had very dangerous levels of Percodan in his blood. Dean had gone back on the medical advice he was given. Again, he was admitted to hospital and given just six months to live if he didn't change his lifestyle.

For such a stubborn man living with an addiction, this was a difficult situation to be in, but he knew that if he did not do as advised, it would be over. But if he did survive, the thought of never being able to perform again terrified him.

I usually contacted his office if there was any urgent news I needed to clarify, but this time I contacted his family directly.

Within a few days, Jeanne came back and said Dean was very poorly but listening (at last, she added) to the things he was being told. I felt saddened that he had come to this. It was not the way to end such a magnificent career where he was loved by millions. It seemed that he had given up.

Nothing inspired him anymore, and there was nothing else to experience. He had done it all and he was a changed man.

But perhaps knowing this man a little more than some, I felt sure he would not end up like that. I did not imagine he would really give up and had faith that he would eventually be back.

I could only hope my thoughts would be right.

TWENTY-THREE

Only Trust Your Heart

Less than a month later, a letter from Dean allayed my fears. He thanked me for my concerns and for contacting Jeanne; I was so thrilled to hear from him. His general attitude seemed to be much brighter than reported, and it was so nice that he had taken the time to get in touch with me when he had so much more to concern him. This led me to hope that he was indeed gaining strength and taking heed of medical advice.

Dean said he was watching more television than ever now and was reading, too. He'd never been an avid reader, but said he had to admit it was a welcome change. He was making sure he took his medication, getting plenty of rest, and taking things easy. It sounded like he had spent his time reaping the benefits of the advice he was given.

His break from work had done the trick and when Bob Hope invited him to appear on his November 1982 tribute to Peter Sellers (Peter had died July 1980), Dean jumped at the chance of making a live appearance on television again – his first for many months.

He looked so well when he walked on. Bob had already mentioned that Dean had been ill for a while and when he appeared with that familiar walk towards his host, you could see that Dean Martin was back in business. The audience gave a standing ovation in the studio and he sang "Bumming Around" with ease. His appearance was nothing short of overwhelming; you could see the prescribed rest had done him the power of good.

This was his resurgence, and there would be a few surprises now that he was back! He felt renewed and said that he would now carry on with his work, having finally signed for *Cannonball Run II*. He was back, invigorated, and preparing himself for new roads ahead.

His former recording manager with Reprise, Jimmy Bowen, had been vice-president of Elektra/Asylum Records over in

Nashville since 1978 and it was he who persuaded Dean to return to the recording studios for the first time since 1974. With this surprise move, Jimmy arranged for Dean to sign to the Warner Brothers label for just ten songs, and even talked him into travelling to Nashville for the first time ever in early 1983 to record the tracks.

But another piece of news reached me as Dean travelled to Nashville in mid-January 1983. And it was a shock.

For the first time in thirty years, Dean had decided to visit London for a series of live concerts at the Apollo Victoria - and I just could not believe this. I really thought his office was having me on and I'm surprised I didn't ruin my working relationship with his team by asking them to repeat what they were telling me. But they insisted it was correct, confirming that he would arrive here in June, and said they would keep me updated!

After completing THE NASHVILLE SESSIONS between 17th and 21st January, Jimmy Bowen was pleased with the outcome of the production, saying that Dean's voice was back on excellent form, although one has to admit that it did have a slight, and understandable, weakness to it. Dean had enjoyed the sessions, with Merle Haggard and Conway Twitty joining him on a couple of tracks.

Dean was determined to get back into things, even appearing live in New York, a place he had never been too fond of, as well as various other spots during the course of this year. He was featured on *Entertainment Tonight* and made a guest appearance on a Dom Deluise special and, of course, he was back in Las Vegas. He also fitted in a charity benefit for the Desert Hospital, Palm Springs with Sammy and Frank.

The Apollo management had allocated us 200 tickets for the upcoming concerts in June and we quickly sent out the good news to our DMA members, giving them the opportunity to buy them through us. Suffice to say, demand was high and we had to sell them on a first come first serve basis, suggesting that when we'd sold our allocation, our members should book with the theatre if they could. The weeks seemed to rush by and my own excitement grew.

Dean's management called me to say he'd arrived at the Inn On The Park in London, and it seemed like he had brought the Californian sunshine with him, as it was a beautiful few days, weather-wise! I had to clear my own schedules for this period, I had been invited to some of the events where he would be appearing.

An unusual but logical decision was for Dean's new album to be released in the UK on 3rd June before the US release (15th) to tie in with his concerts. This meant sales were higher than normal (and certainly continued after his dates had ended). His first and final album on the Warner label was his very first digitally-mastered recording and, as with his previous recordings, he owned those masters outright.

His first function (one my wife and I had to dust off our respective evening dress and tuxedo for) was a 66th birthday luncheon (including a cake!) in Dean's honor on 7th June, hosted by the Princess Royal. Dean sat and listened to the many tributes given to him in the banquet hall of the Mayfair Hilton. Celebrities such as Tommy Cooper, Dickie Henderson, Ron Moody, Peter Goodwright and many others all heaped praise upon this American star who had finally made it to our shores after such a long absence. After all, he had last worked here with Jerry Lewis in 1953, when he'd vowed he would never return!

He did seem somewhat uneasy at this function, something he did not quite anticipate, and he made one slight error in Royal etiquette when he sat down before Princess Anne. Obviously Dean had not intended to break protocol, but even he himself was in awe of all of these people who were gathered there to pay him respect and adulation.

Dean had always said he was no one special, he just happened to be lucky enough to have reached the top of his chosen profession as he had hoped, and compliments made him uncomfortable. Indeed, this reminded me of Dean's embarrassment when I thanked him over the 'phone for being such a good friend and for all of the opportunities he had given to me. He curtly replied by saying that he never wanted any thanks, no matter what he would ever do for me or send to me, then softened by adding it was merely a pleasure for all that I had done for him for many years.

Dean gave just one press meeting at his hotel, but refused all offers for radio or television interviews, even though we and many others tried as hard as we could to change his mind.

Due to demand, his original show dates for seven nights, commencing with his Gala night on 9th June, were extended to a total of ten days, showing any doubters (were there any by now?) that he was still in demand from so many people, with an exceptional following in the United Kingdom.

I arrived nightly for all ten performances and had arranged to meet with Dean on the first Wednesday before the show. I went, as usual, through the stage door, guided by one of his staff direct to his dressing room.

I noted it was sparse, just a table and three chairs, and as I walked in, Dean stood, came towards me and embraced me, his arms as strong as they ever were. He seemed genuinely pleased to see me again.

He asked how my family were. I told them my wife Irene, daughter Carole, and son Elliot were in the audience and Elliot, then only 12 years old, knowing his live act so well, was very excited to see him performing front of him! To my surprise, he asked his staff to call them backstage and greeted them warmly, albeit only for a few minutes, before he and I returned to his dressing room.

As we sat chatting, Dean wearing just his dress shirt and trousers, no jacket nor tie, he thanked me for all my hard work over the last 23 years. He spoke of his prior illness and said that he was going to start working with Burt, Dom and Sammy again. He asked how the club was faring and I told him that we'd had such renewed interest with him being in the UK. I mentioned that many members had asked me to meet him but he shook his head.

'You do it, you meet them,' he said. 'Do it on my behalf, Bernard.'

I said to him that it wouldn't quite be the same and that they'd be disappointed.

'It's impossible,' he insisted. 'I don't do that. I can't do that. Tell them how thankful I am.'

Interestingly, and I wondered if this was due to his anxiety and how poorly he'd been, he was actually concerned that he wouldn't be well-received out on that stage.

'Do you really think they'll like me?' he asked me.

I assured him he didn't have a thing to worry about, pointing out that, as we talked, we could hear the audience chanting 'we want Dean' over and over. He seemed not to have noticed and his heavy-lidded eyes widened as he realized what the background noise actually was. Wall Street Crash, his warm-up act, had a tough crowd to please.

We continued to talk about the DMA and what he had planned in the coming months, and I asked him if he'd considered allowing the re-release of his back catalog (being that he owned the masters). I added that EMI and Warner/Reprise had not seemed too keen on the idea (I'd approached them in 1982). He pondered and nodded as though it hadn't occurred to him (perhaps it hadn't).

'When I get back, I'll see what I can do.'

The 3,000-seat theatre was packed every night and he sang his usual repertoire and told jokes on top form. He was enjoying himself and looked great up there. He told his audience he was so taken aback by the tremendous welcome he'd received. Every night, he was showered with gifts from the audience, plus those given to me to pass on to him at the hotel, which I duly did.

Naturally, the DMA had been planning a massive publicity campaign since the new year, and we sent hundreds and hundreds of letters and publicity notes to every radio and television station in the country, as well as numerous newspapers and magazines, making sure they knew all about us and Dean's acclaimed visit here. His first visit here for thirty years just could not be ignored. We visited record stores throughout the UK, asking them to present window displays to tie in with his concerts.

I knew that a concert was being recorded and filmed, so I suggested a live album plus VHS cassette to be released but this fell on deaf ears. In my opinion, these would have sold very well. The concert footage was eventually broadcast on American cable.

With astounding success at all of these appearances, Dean said he'd be back – but that remained to be seen, as this was a comment he tended to say at the end of all his appearances anywhere on stage. Although he had overcome his terrible fear of flying some time back, he still didn't like travelling so it was doubtful whether we would see him here again. He returned home amidst rumors of a visit in 1984, tying in with a European tour (possibly with Frank and Sammy), but it was all gossip and media speculation.

TWENTY-FOUR

I Take A Lot Of Pride In What I Am

For the many years I had known and represented him through the DMA, Dean was the gentle gentleman. It was incredible to think that he had actually come over to London and visited us, and been a great success every single night. I must admit I was somewhat disappointed that he had not agreed with my requests that he met with some of our members whilst he was here, but it was not to be, no matter how much I pleaded with him.

Yet after thinking about it, I guess I could see his point: he was a shy person around people when he was Dino, but as Dean Martin on stage behind that mic and the apple juice, he was the total opposite. He had never been a person to meet his fans in a pre-arranged face to face situation and he would hardly change his habits at 66!

After a short break at home, he went to Nevada for his Celebrity Room appearances, to be followed by his part in *Cannonball Run II*, filmed in Tucson, Arizona. As Frank Sinatra was to appear in a cameo role, this would be the first time since 1960 that he, along with Dean, Sammy, and Shirley MacLaine, would be together in a movie.

Dean teamed up with Sammy again, their characters this time dressed as police officers (as opposed to priests in the first picture). *So this time I might get laid,* laughed Dean.

In early 1984, he recommenced *The Dean Martin Celebrity Roasts* for NBC but this time they were specials as opposed to the previous weekly shows. He also started reducing the number of cabaret appearances he would make at the MGM Grand.

He made another surprise decision by flying direct to Paris, France for just one 40-minute show at the famed Moulin Rouge on 3rd July. Here, he met with Line Renaud and they chatted about the old times when they'd recorded "Relax-Ay-Voo" and "Two Sleepy People" back in 1955 with Dick Stabile and his orchestra.

Back in the US, Dean and Frank had signed to appear together in a number of shows at the Golden Nugget Casino, Atlantic City, for September but it appeared that there were underhand dealings and fixed card sharking at the tables. Dean and Frank immediately cancelled the complete run, wanting no connection with (or even inferred links to) whatever was going on. Frank firmly stated that he would never appear in Atlantic City again, and never did.

Later that same month, I was invited to the Friar's Club for an honorary show on 13th September where Dean was crowned 'Man of the Year'. Hosted by Frank, tickets were available at $250 each with a meal for $1,000 if required. Asked later why he was chosen as ' Man Of The Year', Dean laughed and said he had no idea...*but I am not going to ask either, they may change their mind! I'm amused because I cannot think of anything particular I have done recently!*

Cannonball Run II had by now completed its rounds in cinemas both in the US and the UK but did not achieve impressive results at the box office, gaining returns for Warner Brothers far below the first film. In 1989, Orion Pictures made and released *Speed Zone*, also known as *Cannonball Fever* (or in Japan, *The Cannonball Run III: Speed Zone*). It featured an ensemble case much like the first two movies but none of the original main cast or crew, bar one: this was Jamie Farr, reprising his role in a brief cameo as Sheik Abdul ben Falafel, the only actor to link the three films together.

Once again, there were rumors of a European tour by Dean and Frank, or at least more visits to London for Dean, but nothing came of the reported concerts from either artist.

I contacted Dean to follow up on our conversation in London about re-releasing his Reprise back catalog but his office replied saying simply that they had 'no plans at present'.

Having put his signature to paper for just the one album for Warner Brothers, it was another surprise when he recorded just the one song for MCA Records entitled "L.A Is My Home". With great production, his voice was soft and smooth, even if a little strained in places. It was used as the end theme for a new TV series which would have Dean making a regular guest appearance in each episode. *Half Nelson* starred Joe Pesci as a private eye and bodyguard to the stars, one of his clients being Dean's character, Mr Martin. With Pesci's short stature, the promotional tag ran as *Half Nelson - a man women can look down to! You'll Love It!* But not many people did. After the 2-hour pilot, only six more episodes were made and the 1985 series was shelved and, to date, has never been repeated or sold outside of the US.

In the UK, independent television network LWT was running a popular comedy series called *Me & My Girl*. Starring Richard O'Sullivan and Joanne Ridley, one episode had the storyline of Dean being asked to appear in cabaret at a business conference. Although he was mentioned, no footage or reference photographs were used.

This really shows the status and staying-power that Dean had and, in many ways, still has. He is often name-checked or referenced in the most unlikely of places: *Grease*, made in 1978, features *Hollywood or Bust* as a drive-in movie; the 1996 action flick *The Long Kiss Goodnight* plays "Let It Snow! Let It Snow! Let Snow!" during a car crash sequence; the 90s comedy series *3rd Rock From the Sun* has the main cast singing a rendition of "That's Amore"; Quentin Tarantino's cult success *Pulp Fiction* has a character ordering a milkshake called 'Martin & Lewis' in the fictional Jack Rabbit Slim's bar, where a photo of Dean is also seen. And it doesn't stop there: the 2008 BBC time-travel cop series *Ashes to Ashes* features a drinking establishment that shows Dean in a painted mural on a back wall; CBS/Paramount's *Star Trek: Deep Space Nine* includes a 'holodeck' character played by James Darren that was modelled on Dean (and Frank) and Darren actually wore to the casting a pair of shoes he owned that used to be Dean's; in 2016, "Volare" opened an episode of Sam Raimi's horror-comedy *Ash vs Evil Dead*; in 2017, the sequel to the 90s smash hit picture *Trainspotting* features a sequence where one character is dancing with a full-size cardboard cut-out of Dean; 2017's *Going In Style* starring Michael Caine prominently uses Dean's hit "Memories Are Made of This"; and in 2022, the trailer for Guy Ritchie's action-flick *Operation Fortune* startlingly remixes "Sway".

The places you can find Dean Martin in modern media seem endless.

As his Las Vegas shows continued (although some of his shows were again cut back on time), Dean also made further guest appearances in a Motown Revue, a Dutch Reagan celebration, a Shirley MacLaine special and another Dom Deluise show. He seemed to be in reasonable health but he was most certainly taking life a little easier, although it must be noted here that he was not getting too many offers for work (a lot of which he was turning down anyway). There was an element of history repeating: as he had come out of his partnership with Jerry, he was second billing in most of his immediate films. In the mid- to late-80s, he was back in a similar position: guest starring, second or even third or fourth billing in shows and movies.

Two more of his working associates had died recently, too: the renowned and highly respected Orson Welles, who had appeared so many times on Dean's weekly shows, and Nelson Riddle, trumpeter and arranger for the Charlie Spivak orchestra back in December 1940 and who evolved his great and superb arrangement artistry for so many fine artists. It would take numerous pages to list his credits, but just listen to his album HEY, LET YOURSELF GO! and Dean's own THIS TIME I'M SWINGIN'! and you will hear just a glimpse of arrangement finesse there. Once again, when Dean heard two more contemporaries had passed away, he realized that the era he had come from and the era he was living in where almost unrecognizable from each other.

Another landmark in Dean Martin's career came when he appeared before the one-millionth person at the MGM Grand – the lucky customer, Michelle Dolan, was taken out of the queue and presented with a special plaque by Dean on stage. She also received a free 3-night/4-day stay at the hotel complex with tickets for other shows thrown in, too. After Dean's show, Michelle and her companion even met him backstage for a brief chat.

Dean had always been the biggest success at the hotel and proved beyond doubt his international popularity. Las Vegas audiences are a cross-section of the population; they come from all over the world to visit this 'electric' town in the desert, where hundreds of entertainers have performed.

In April 1986, the Bally Manufacturing Company bought the MGM Grand, renaming it the Ballys Grand, and later, they would also buy up the Golden Nugget Casino.

As Dean got older, more ailments knocked him down. In January 1987 he was hospitalized with more stomach problems and was forced to cancel pre-booked (and confirmed) engagements in Las Vegas. Further, he acquired a small abscess in his mouth, which was dealt with quickly, after which he returned home to relax.

However, some weeks later, an event took place which was to be the most devastating in his life, affecting his future in every possible way.

His son, Dean Paul Jr, was a pilot for the National Guard and had been reported missing whilst in flight. Evidently, the weather was treacherous and when Dean was told the news, he immediately contacted Jeanne and went and stayed with her and the rest of his family. They just sat and waited for news for an agonizing five days. But when the news did come, delivered personally to the family home by a USAF colonel, it was what they feared the most: what was left of his son's body had been found.

Dean Jr's jet had hit the 11,500 feet high San Gorgonio Mountains, the air-traffic controller having tried desperately to guide the experienced pilot through a massive blizzard. But heavy air traffic hampered communications and it was found after the official investigation that Dean Jr had not heard the Ontario International airport controller's instructions to change course. His last words before the F4C Phantom jet ploughed straight into the side of the mountains was a request for a course change and he sadly did not receive any return communication. Dean Jr was just 35 when he was killed on 21st March 1987.

Nothing whatsoever in any written word can even come close to describing how Dean felt at this time. Nothing like this had ever happened in the family. It was bad enough for him when his dear parents had died, but when he thought of how young his son was, and the tragic situation in which he had died, it all became too much for him. Dean had very small comfort in realizing that perhaps his son did not have enough time to know what was about to happen, but the loss of his son was more than he could stand. He cancelled all work and personal appearances.

With such sadness in the Martin family, once again it seemed that his own problems coincided with mine, because in April of this year my wife Irene lost her mother Connie after a massive stroke. That was a heavy loss for us, especially for Irene, who had been looking after her practically every day as part of her normal routine before Connie had to be admitted to a care home. My own mother was also experiencing bad health at that time but was not taking the medication she had been prescribed, and I was very concerned with her situation.

But Dean himself had gone into a severe and worrying state. He just could not go on: everything had completely collapsed around him and his state of mind told him he just could not work. He could not face anything, he was so shaken beyond imagination.

Jeanne and the children all encouraged him to get back to normal, at least, as normal as was possible. He had to be strong and try to overcome what had happened. He was, after all, a hugely famous and popular person, and he had to resume his career.

Dean, however, was almost ready to disappear.

TWENTY-FIVE

I Feel A Song Comin' On

The very first handful of songs that Dean Martin recorded back in the 1940s were originally issued on the 10" 78rpm format, most of them turning up on a compilations in 1953 and 1954. The American pressings came via Waldorf and Audition, with the UK seeing them on the Britone label, an FW Woolworth exclusive. However, the very first LP record of Dino was issued as a 12" by Capitol in April 1955 (previously a 2-part 10" EP set).

DEAN MARTIN SINGS contained "Who's Your Little Who-Zis", "I'm Yours", "I Feel A Song Comin' On", "With My Eyes Wide Open I'm Dreaming", "Just One More Chance", "I Feel Like A Feather In The Breeze", "A Girl Named Mary and A Boy Named Bill", with the additional tracks not featured on the EPs "Come Back To Sorrento", "Oh Marie", "When You're Smiling" and "That's Amore". By the time the album had hit the shelves, "That's Amore" had already gone Gold so it was natural that it would form part of this initial collection.

Across the pond in the UK, a 10" LP was released October 1956 (in fact it was the UK's first and only 10" of Dino). CAPITOL PRESENTS DEAN MARTIN featured "Who's Your Little Who-Zis", "I Feel A Song Comin' On", "With My Eyes Wide Open I'm Dreaming", "I Feel Like A Feather In The Breeze", "When You're Smiling" and "Muskrat Ramble", "Rain", "Be Honest With Me".

With SWINGIN' DOWN YONDER (T576) released 1 August 1955, we were treated to the first bona-fide studio album from Dino. With Dixie-land arrangements from Dick Stabile, it gave us foresight that Dino could take on a number of different styles. It found its way to the UK some seven years later as DEAN GOES DIXIE from EMI/Encore, then reverting back to its original title for a February 1972 re-release. The US market also had a re-issue (June 1965), renamed SOUTHERN STYLE but with the track "Dinah" missing!

Finally, in July 1991 (August in the UK), the entire album, with never-before-released songs from the same recording sessions or of similar ilk, was remastered for a glorious CD release. Hearing these again in crisp digital quality was incredible, and Dino had never sounded so good.

It was another eighteen months after the debut of Swingin' Down Yonder before we got Dino's next release.

A grand mixture of song styles with the superb arrangements of Gus Levene that truly complemented Dino's lush voice, Pretty Baby hit the shelves February 1957. Amazingly, the album sales were poor. It was evident that he was not appreciated for his talents at that time, even though there were flashes of hit material appearing via his singles. Perhaps Dino wasn't an album seller? EMI's UK mail-order only World Record Club issued it June 1965, but it wouldn't be widely available in stores until April 1969, where it would undergo a name-change to Only Forever.

Capitol followed the tepid release with This Is Dean Martin!, a compilation of singles such as "Volare" and "Return To Me", in October 1958. With Dino's popularity beginning to show, the album sold well. Not a hit by any standards, but it gave Capitol the confidence that he was at least a steady seller.

In a clever marketing move, Sinatra's name shared the cover on Dino's next studio album: Dean Martin With Orchestra Conducted By Frank Sinatra (aka Sleep Warm). With the songs recorded over 3 days in October 1958, it wouldn't be until March 1959 that we'd get to hear them (November for UK collectors). April 1965: the US saw it reappear as Dean Martin Sings Sinatra Conducts, but with "Dream" omitted. It was re-issued complete for the UK market August 1985. Dino had created one of his most pleasant 'mood' projects: a beautiful, soft collection of dreamy songs perfectly suited to Dino's mellow voice. In my opinion, this smooth style was where Dino excelled and he later repeated the exercise for Reprise with Dream With Dean.

During a sweltering Hollywood summer, Dino recorded a collection of snowy, wintry ballads for the November 1959 release A WINTER ROMANCE.

It continued his trend of a well-crafted, relaxed, cosy style. An immaculate, gorgeous batch of songs, it corned the Christmas market and, as a seasonal release, it has been a fairly sturdy seller ever since. It came out in November 1965 as HOLIDAY CHEER (omitting "A Winter Romance") but was returned to its original glory on CD in November 1989 with an extra song from a 1953 session, "The Christmas Blues".

Christmas at the DMA is never complete without Dino's appropriate ballads playing in the background – and seeing as tracks such as "Let It Snow! Let It Snow! Let It Snow!" and "Baby, It's Cold Outside" have become Christmas standards and reappear on any number of holiday compilations year after year, we assume the rest of the world thinks the same!

How sad it is then that Christmas Day itself has been a period of reflection for us Dino fans since 1995…

July 1960 (October in the UK) saw a full soundtrack album from Capitol of Dino's musical with the much-missed Judy Holliday, *Bells Are Ringing*. While Dino only recorded two solo songs for the release ("I Met A Girl" and "Do It Yourself") his duets with Judy on "Just In Time" and "Better Than A Dream" more than made up for it (he had already recorded a solo version of "Just In Time" with a Nelson Riddle arrangement). A happy musical – and one well worth tracking down on DVD – Dino was in fine form and sold very well, arguably because of Judy's presence. BELLS ARE RINGING resurfaced in the US on the STET label in 1982 and sold abominably, but Capitol re-released it on CD in January 1990.

Three months after BELLS ARE RINGING's successful release came a very superb album of twelve songs. This time, Dino was swingin', his immaculate phrasing backed by the great and inimitable Nelson Riddle and orchestra.

THIS TIME' I'M SWINGIN' hit the shelves October 1960, having been recorded the previous May. The UK received it that December, and was reissued by Starline on 27 October 1973, with an alternative cover. Filled with tracks that would become familiar standards for Dino's recorded output ("You're Nobody 'Til Somebody Loves You", "Please Don't Talk About Me When I'm Gone" etc.), the album has stood the test of time and can be considered the archetypal Dean Martin release. These songs have continued to appear on numerous compilations over the years, proving their worth and longevity. 27 October 1973 saw it re-released and it had a new lease of life in 1996 when EMI coupled it with PRETTY BABY on CD.

EMI created a mail-order members-only service based in the UK, the World Record Club [WRC], and heralded their launch with THE DEAN SINGS in February 1961 with songs such as "Aw C'mon" and "Try Again".

A November follow-up, THE DEAN SINGS AGAIN, contained twelve more solid songs, including "Baby! Obey Me!", "In the Cool, Cool, Cool Of The Evening" and "That Lucky Old Sun" among others. It gave us all the opportunity to replace those much-loved, much-played worn out old 78s.

Being Italian, it was inevitable that Dino would record an album of authentic ballads in the Italian style.

The fact that it too him a few years to get there indicates he was waiting for his voice to further mature and for the record-buying public to be receptive to the album.

Gus Levene arranged the rich and lush sound for DINO – ITALIAN LOVE SONGS, recorded at the unique-looking Capitol Tower during September 1961. Released on 5 February 1962, it proved to be a hit album for Dino. The UK had to wait until September that same year.

"Arrivederci, Roma", "On An Evening In Roma", "I Have But One Heart"…it's packed with glorious track after glorious track. This then was Dino's definitive Italian album and my own personal favorite from his Capitol era. I had suggested to

Capitol to release this, remastered and with suitable bonus tracks, on CD – they agreed (at least to the CD part of my suggestion) when they coupled it with CHA CHA DE AMOR in 1997.

December 1961 proved to be the last time Dino would record an album for Capitol, with Nelson Riddle back on arrangement duties. The dozen standard songs were lyrically beautiful, enhanced by Riddle's cha-cha rhythm, faultlessly matching Dino's dulcet tones. CHA CHA DE AMOR is indeed a fine album, carrying on the consistent high quality of Dino's work – how can this man make such fantastic and wonderful albums? It is also one of the best examples of Stereophonic sound. It was re-released on 5 November 1971 and on CD in 2005.

With Reprise on the horizon, the gates were now wide open for Capitol to flood the market with countless album compilations – a good idea in some ways but in others it watered down the quality of the original album constructs. Capitol had understandably prepared themselves and no one could blame them. Business is business! It also meant that I had the opportunity to put together a brand-new collection of songs for them.

I didn't want the standard ballads. I wanted something unusual, different, containing songs not heard since their original 78s releases. I was restricted however with song choices but I believe LET'S BE FRIENDLY was an album that gave a nice cross-section of Dino's Capitol career. It was issued on 1 June 1964 (the closest I could get to Dino's birthday that year) by EMI through the WRC and ourselves. Capitol released their own compilation HEY BROTHER POUR THE WINE in America on 4 December 1964.

With the advent of 1966, we now entered a phase of nothing but re-issues of all Dino's recorded material from Capitol, a natural situation considering he'd been signed with Reprise now for a while.

His career away from the recording studio was sky-rocketing and so it made sense that Capitol would tap into the treasure trove of back catalogs.

8 March 1966: they released, on their Tower label, RELAXIN', a solid collection including "Sparkelin' Eyes" and "Who Was That Lady?", followed on 20 September with HAPPY IN LOVE, a selection of love songs including "Rue Do Mon Amour", composed by Dino himself. This pair of Tower albums are exceptionally rare these days.

THE BEST OF DEAN MARTIN (4 October 1966) was intended as a chart album but didn't make much of a dent. "Memories Are Made Of This", "Volare", "Hey Brother, Pour The Wine"…they were all there plus more, songs that many of us already owned elsewhere. That may explain why it only got to 95 in the US album charts, but remained in the charts overall for an impressive 13 weeks. It was released on CD in May 1988.

Pickwick was a Capitol budget label and it wasn't long before Dino was added to their US catalog with YOU CAN'T LOVE 'EM ALL (January 1967). Once again, a grand collection of songs encompassing a nice range of styles, from "You Can't Love 'Em All", through to "That Lucky Old Sun" and the thumping "Ain't That A Kick In The Head". The Pickwick and US Capitol releases had the advantage: they were available across cassette and cartridge as well as the standard LP, thereby widening the sales possibilities.

LOVE IS A CAREER came from EMI on their stateside label on 5 May 1968. A bargain 14-track collection – unusual for the 60s – it contained a different selection of songs, boasting "You Were Made For Love", "The Story of Life", "Off Again On Again" amongst others. It showed that there was indeed an appetite for variation.

Tower returned on 22 August 1967 with DINO – LIKE NEVER BEFORE. Adopting the approach by EMI, this too contained songs we'd not found before on prior compilations, ten beautiful ballads, crooning classics all. "Beside You", "I Ran All The Way Home", "Second Chance", "Never Before"…

The public were lapping up the albums and Capitol rushed out the very first box set, containing two previously released albums (DINO – ITALIAN LOVE SONGS and HEY BROTHER POUR THE WINE) and the third a new compilation. THE DEAN MARTIN DELUXE BOX SET is an extremely rare and expensive collector's item today, selling very well on its US release 16 October 1967.

Regal was a short-lived EMI label and in late 1967, they issued an album called simply DEAN MARTIN, containing tracks not unusual for a compilation ("Muskrat Ramble", "That Lucky Old Sun" and so on) but because not many pressings were made, it's now an incredibly rare and important release.

Pickwick began 1969 in earnest with I CAN'T GIVE YOU ANYTHING BUT LOVE on 11 January then, a week later DEAN MARTIN SWINGIN' which was a 2-LP set containing the 7-day old I CAN'T GIVE YOU ANYTHING BUT LOVE and 1967's YOU CAN'T LOVE 'EM ALL. YOUNG AND FOOLISH followed the week after!

Capitol fell over themselves by rush-releasing DEAN MARTIN FAVORITES, which was in essence DEAN MARTIN SINGS with "A Girl Named Mary and A Boy Named Bill" removed.

THE BEST OF DEAN MARTIN VOLUME TWO appeared in America on 25 January 1969, containing a mixture of tracks, some lifted from CHA CHA DE AMOR and others.

It peaked at a dismal 145 in the US charts on 22 February, floundering for 7 weeks. Meanwhile, in the UK, THE BEST OF DEAN MARTIN VOLUME ONE was 16-track delight. "Volare",

"Sway", "Pretty Baby", "Sleepy Time Gal", "You're Nobody 'Til Somebody Loves You" as well as the hit that did *very* well for our Dino, "Return To Me"…

This really was a Capitol best of, and arguably no other subsequent compilation could ever come close for many years.

Another scattering of Dino's hits appeared on the 17 July US release DEAN MARTIN'S GREATEST!, while in the UK, THE BEST OF DEAN MARTIN VOLUME TWO closed the year with another superb 16-song LP.

1970 started big! - and the second compilation under my direction. Called simply DEAN MARTIN, this was a mammoth undertaking of 6 LPs containing 60 songs (chosen by me!) with a lovely gatefold souvenir brochure (written by me!). It was an exclusive WRC/DMA release for January 1970. It is now extremely rare. The condensed 4 LP version released a few years later however can usually be found at record fairs and on second hand stalls or thrift stores.

Meanwhile, Pickwick took the baton on 3 March with YOU WERE MADE FOR LOVE, and Capitol on 14 March with RETURN TO ME: YOU'RE NOBODY 'TIL SOMEBODY LOVES YOU, a 2-LP set of most (but not all) of the tracks from for DINO – ITALIAN LOVE SONGS and THIS TIME I'M SWINGIN' (omitting "Pardon", "My Heart Reminds Me", "Until The Real Thing Comes Along" and "Heaven Can Wait"). The set then inexplicably had the first LP removed and re-released as YOU'RE NOBODY 'TIL SOMEBODY LOVES YOU in May, while Music For Pleasure [MFP] (EMI's UK budget label) came along on 17 July with HEY BROTHER POUR THE WINE (not the 1964 US issue).

ONE MORE TIME quietly joined the swelling number of UK compilations on 1 October 1970 but was an intriguing gathering of songs: "Happy Feet", "Bye Bye Blackbird", "A Winter Romance", "Luna Mezzo Mare" and the like.

It disappeared fairly rapidly.

In the US, the Longines Symphonette Society licensed a stack of songs from Capitol for their 5 LP set MEMORIES ARE MADE OF THIS. Like WRC, it was a mail-order only release and, if ordered within a certain time frame, a sixth LP (THAT'S AMORE: DEAN MARTIN'S 10 ALL-TIME GOLDEN HITS) was yours for free! And again like the WRC issues, it is now a very rare collectible. It was released 11 December.

I had approached EMI at the end of 1970 with the idea of putting together a duets album, DINO AND FRIENDS, bringing together tracks he had recorded for Capitol with other artists such as Nat "King" Cole, Line Renaud, Jerry Lewis and Peggy Lee. I suggested 12 tracks. The idea was summarily rejected.

But on 26 March 1971, out came NAT, DEAN AND FRIENDS, with 8 of the 12 songs I'd listed. I would have to assume that this was simply just an amazing coincidence…

MFP brought out WHITE CHRISTMAS WITH NAT "KING" COLE AND DEAN MARTIN for the 1971 seasonal market, clearly riding high on the success of NAT, DEAN AND FRIENDS .There were no duets between the two men, instead a simple sharing of LP space of Christmas tunes.

With the Starline reissues of CHA CHA DE AMOR and THIS TIME I'M SWINGIN', competition was now fierce between the UK and US arms of Capitol.

The US fought back with DEAN MARTIN DELUXE!, a truncated version of THIS TIME I'M SWINGIN' on 15 February 1972 and again on 15 May with I HAVE BUT ONE HEART. The latter compilation was so-named to attract admirers of Francis Ford Coppola's *The Godfather*, in which Al Martino sang "I Have But One Heart" on screen at Michael Corleone's wedding. In fact, the marketing ploy by Capitol was so fixated on the success of *The Godfather* that the cover featured a generic bride on her wedding day with poor Dino relegated to the back cover of his own album!

Another compilation called DEAN MARTIN DELUXE! was released at the same time, a 2-LP set. The US record stores suddenly had a trinity of releases, two of which had the same title!

In the UK, EMI brought out THE VERY BEST OF DEAN MARTIN for the '72 Christmas trade. It heralded the not-unexpected decline in British sales of Dino's material. The same songs across multiple releases? It was inevitable. 1974 saw only SLEEP WARM re-released as DEAN MARTIN SINGS: SINATRA CONDUCTS.

In the UK in July 1975, KODAK launched a national competition in which members of the public were invited to send in their photographs. Winners would receive camera equipment amongst other relative items. The mainstay of the whole competition was the tied-in release of a Capitol album that I had been asked to compile, with sleeve notes by Fred Dellar. The competition name? Why, 'Memories Are Made Of This', of course! Amazingly, one of our own DMA members even won first prize!

The album itself, MEMORIES ARE MADE OF THIS, would be the very last issue of Dino's material on 8-track cartridge tape. A 20-track album made a welcome change and, although I was restricted once again with song choices, I had the opportunity to include one of my top favorites, "Innamorata", as well as some others that rarely got to see the light of day (Such as "Makin' Love Ukelele Style" and "Let Me Go, Lover"). The album appeared at the height of summer, 9 July 1975.

19 September saw another MFP release, WHEN YOU'RE SMILING, an Italian-flavored compilation but one that seemed to miss the mark, even with songs such as "That's Amore", "Buona Sera" and "I Have But One Heart". Why not simply re-release the complete DINO – ITALIAN LOVE SONGS? The MFP effort had minimal sales.

More run-of-the-mill collections in America, but it was not until 1979 when Capitol decided to renew their efforts in making Dino a UK album seller again. It was their delayed response to a certain million-copies-seller of a happy little Reprise compilation called 20 ORIGINAL HITS...

When EMI approached me and said, 'Bernard, we'd like you to choose 16 of your favorite Capitol recordings of Dean Martin,' my first thought was: how on earth do I pick just 16?! Daunting nevertheless, THE CLASSIC DINO was an absolute pleasure to put together. "Me 'n' You 'n' The Moon", "Watching The World Go By", "Guiggiola", "How Do You Speak To An Angel"...it was a tremendously difficult job to sift through so many wonderful recordings. I also did the sleeve notes.

It was released on 8 June 1979 and the LP stayed in EMI's catalog for 11 years – almost creating a record in itself for longevity (especially for a compilation album). It was finally deleted in 1990 and now much sought-after. It would make a great CD release.

With the increase of compilations since the early 70s, it became no surprise that, as the 80s arrived, there would be more re-issues of older compilations – after all, it was cheaper to reissue an existing collection but with a different cover than commission a whole new set of songs. So, the KODAK-related MEMORIES ARE MADE OF THIS fell under this umbrella, as did THE VERY BEST OF DEAN MARTIN (twice). SLEEP WARM had another round but January 1989 saw a US-only CD from Capitol called DEAN MARTIN.

This was a fascinating collection of remastered, Stereo-mixed recordings going right back to the Martin and Lewis years as well as Dino's early solo work. "That Certain Party", "Powder Your Face With Sunshine", "That's Amore", "Volare" and "Ain't That A Kick In the Head" formed part of this 20-track album, as well as much-welcomed studio out-takes. It was quickly re-packaged and re-issued (US: November 1989; UK:

12 March 1990) as part of the 'Capitol Collector's Series', with a beautiful purple CD label that emulated the classic Capitol 78s.

It was also only the second (and last) time that Dino would have any direct involvement in a compilation of his material. Indeed, it's the only compilation where he offered a brief quote for inclusion in the sleeve notes:

The A WINTER ROMANCE re-issue (also in November 1989) had studio out-takes, too. Considered inappropriate by record companies for many years, including out-takes on a commercial release is a fabulous way to get an insight into the flavor of the recording sessions, and subsequent Dean Martin releases would follow the same approach.

In 1989, EMI launched a similar series to their US counterparts' 'Capitol Collector's Series'. Called THE BEST OF THE CAPITOL YEARS, I was delighted to put together a new compilation for Dino's volume as well as write the sleeve notes.

I didn't want it to be the same as THE CLASSIC DINO and I knew too that Capitol wanted to showcase the songs that had made Dino famous. There was then, a fine line between something old and something new. However, the final choice of 16 songs wasn't 100% mine. At the end of the day, it was a marvelous CD and was even the 'album of the week' in Virgin stores toward the end of 1989 (the album was released 9 January). It was wonderful to walk into the Virgin Megastore on Piccadilly Circus and hear "That's Amore" in the air. It was re-packaged (removing my sleeve notes) and re-issued in 2003 as THE ESSENTIAL DEAN MARTIN and is still readily available at the time of writing.

In 1994, I assisted in the release of THE SINGLES for MFP, an unusual collection in that it contained none of Dino's major hits but brought to the fore "Night Train To Memphis", "Standing On the Corner" and others. Meanwhile, HMV (or hmv as it is now) had its own range of store-exclusive albums, under the HMV EASY brand. DEAN MARTIN COLLECTION in 2003 was another half-popular/half-unusual selection of songs, putting tracks such as "That's Amore" and "Who's Sorry Now?" on the same playlist.

Capitol's compilations had slowed however throughout the early part of the 1990s but a major event[6] in the publishing and ownership rights of all of Dino's recordings in 1996 would take things in a completely unexpected but very welcome direction.

---

[6] See Chapter 30, pg. 248

TWENTY-SIX

Twilight On The Trail

Incredibly, after going through the trauma of his son's funeral, Dean Martin gathered himself together and listened to what his family was saying: he returned to Bally's, receiving standing ovations every night. With tears in his eyes (remember, this was a man that thus far, had showed no real emotion to the public), he made a brief reference to the family tragedy and said he would be carrying on for his son's sake, thanking everyone for their kindness and patience. He looked very strained and tired but had forced himself out of his sadness. Having completed ten nights, he returned home for a short rest, keeping in close contact with Jeanne and the rest of the family.

He once again surprised everyone in the midst of all this unhappiness by announcing more concerts in London. Again, this was amazing news again for us and for all his millions of admirers. He played at the London Palladium to packed houses between 6th and 11th July, re-tracing his steps on the same stage he had worked on with Jerry Lewis. Again, he refused all interviews and appearances on radio and television, with his official program this time reduced from the larger-sized edition in 1983.

I met him again, but there was a marked difference.

In the four years that had gone by, he had aged tremendously and I was very concerned. Even though I said nothing to him about it, I think he knew I had noticed. His dress shirt hung around his shoulders and he was stooped, only slightly, but enough to show he was not the same man I'd known for the last 27 years. Time, emotions and life had ravaged those exceptional good looks. I gave him the deepest condolences for the loss of his son from me and my family to him and his, and he asked how my children were. He seemed to brighten when I told them they were now on their own two feet, with school days virtually behind them. We exchanged general pleasantries and he once again thanked me for everything I was doing.

We discussed the future of his association: the format, attitude style and distribution of our literature, plus our approach in general for the coming years. I told him the DMA needed to keep up its prestige, status and establishment of many years and move with the times, as we could never afford to be complacent. He agreed but felt I knew what I was doing and had no concerns. I didn't feel I could ask him about what he had planned or upcoming because he alluded to taking things day by day. But I did ask if he'd given any more thought to re-releasing his material. He said he had not. As he received his five minute stage call, he hugged me goodbye and wished me well for the future.

It seemed somewhat final.

He gave an outstanding performance on all nights, and mentioning his son's recent death to the audience gained sympathy and adulation at this point in his show. He filled his act with the usual jokes and his songs, but it was clear he was never to get over the tragedy, although he knew his son would have wanted him to carry on with his work and be Dean Martin again. In that respect, he was happy, because it did give him some motivation to pursue his career as he did before.

With Dean's tragedy combined with our own family bereavement, the London visit was somewhat tainted. A lot of gloom pervaded in our lives at the present time, as my own mother's health was deteriorating quickly. Because she was never a lady to complain about anything or tell anyone her thoughts, feelings or pain, even I myself did not realize the gravity of her situation. On the rare occasion she had said anything about herself, it was a remark that she just had backaches, her Italian stubbornness making her refuse to see her doctor. Like both Dean and me, we all have that great dislike of anything medical. She had been in poor health for most of this year and I finally insisted on medical intervention:

she had been suffering quietly with lung cancer and died that August in Mayday Hospital, Croydon. Word had filtered up to Dean from the DMA to his office and I received a short handwritten note from him wishing me and my family every sympathy. Again, it was testament to his attitude: here was a man at the center of his vast world with his own pain and suffering and problems, yet he still took a few moments to write a message of condolence.

Frank and his wife Barbara had invited Dean and Sammy to their Palm Springs home for a weekend because of the telethon she had arranged in the complex at the Eisenhower Medical Centre in September. Sammy suggested that they all do something together on stage again, but something different: they had done enough films and recordings and live acts, so a change of approach, he felt, was required.

Frank came up with an idea of an all-state tour, going to places via train that they had never been to before. But after research, it was found to be too impractical. Perhaps the best way to get across all states would be by air. There was a chance that this could make things easier for all three stars, particularly for getting from state to state, so thought Frank. He envisaged they could play to perhaps 20,000 at a time at indoor stadiums and the like, depending on the facilities in each venue. They would need two 'planes because of their different routines of working. Sammy and Dean liked to be in a town the night before they appeared, whereas Frank would turn up as required.

Discussing these points, Dean himself was very quiet: he had not really wanted to involve himself in another country-wide tour, particularly as he did not feel as eager and enthusiastic as he had when he was younger. He seemed uncertain anyway that all three of them could even keep up the pace --after all, Sammy was not so agile as he had been and even Frank had cut back on the amount of appearances now, so Dean did not think it would be sensible or responsible for any of them. Frank and Sammy knew that Dean was a broken man after his son's death. Further, Dean saw that being at a different venue each night would be very contrary to just playing in one place for several nights as he was used to and, understandably, could cope with.

Dean Martin's lifestyle could not be compared to Sammy's and Frank's: obviously, Dean was very wealthy but now dressed simply, taking with him the minimum of clothes and belongings when he was out working live. His two friends were the opposite.

But Dean was in a predicament. He agreed that it would be nice to work together like they used to, and he was never a person to let them down if they asked him for support. However, when the details were finally worked out and they all got together for press conferences at the end of 1987, he was still not really convinced and did not have his heart in it. He agreed nevertheless and 'Frank, Dean, Sammy - The Together Again Tour' was a go: a tour across all US states, no less, plus talk of taking the same tour to Europe. This famous trio together would be like going back 30 years. There had been nothing like them before and there certainly would be nothing like them ever, ever again.

We approached the end of 1987, 1st October to be exact, with a new-style newsletter. Now called *Just Dino* each edition was fully illustrated with articles and features galore. My son had begun a writing career and contributed to them, adding a new 'voice' to the association. Dean commented on the new format and said he looked forward to watching Elliot's career flourish! There was always so much work that could be done for Dean and we were in an exclusive position to be able to carry out this pleasurable role with such ideas and schemes that hopefully would continue to please him and our members alike.

Dean appeared in a segment for the celebration of the Las Vegas 75th Anniversary, screened in November, completing the end of a very mixed year for him. Arrangements were now fully scheduled for the 'Together Again' series of concerts (sponsored by American Express) to commence 13th March 1988. The trio's first appearances were at the Oakland

Coliseum in California, with the shows planned to go on until mid-April, covering various venues, with a break mid-year scheduled to allow them to fulfil other commitment. It would be a grueling tour, with the stamina required of men half their age.

When the tour began, Dean didn't seem right. His voice and his manner were not as they usually were and seemed as if he was elsewhere, mentally. He missed some of his cues and Sammy stepped in with a few missing lines, making a joke of it. But after just four shows, Dean couldn't cope with the punishing schedule and pulled out of the shows in Chicago after appearing there just once on 18th March.

Flying back home, he checked in at his hospital for observation, covering himself for the concert cancellations, then went home for a few days' rest. His two friends were rather frustrated at this turn of events; they understood some of his reservations, but did not quite understand why he had totally pulled out of the schedule. Frank took it personally, feeling Dean had let him down. But it seemed that Dean just did not want to carry on and there was absolutely nothing they or anyone else could do to change the mind of this stubborn man. He was replaced by Liza Minnelli.

Approaching the 1990s, Dean Martin had reached a different state of mind. He had no need to keep on going and proving himself. He had done everything he had wanted to do in his life and was happy with that. He felt within himself that he had no further need to record, make films or tour the country. He was contented to return to Vegas.

But his troubled health was rearing its ugly head again and he was certainly not at his best when appearing at Bally's. During several performances, he was seen to clutch and rub his stomach several times, as well as rubbing his forehead. He maintained his show routine and still sometimes times cut down his show lengths whenever he felt like it, often stopping mid-way through a song. His jokes were short, sometimes he slurred his speech and, on one occasion, he collapsed when he walked off stage towards his dressing room.

Once again the press had a field day; they reported in various publications that he was drunk and falling about the stage. But like Dean had showed us before, it was the drugs for his medication mixed with some alcohol, in addition to not having taken care of himself as he should have done for a person of his age and status. His medication for his ulcers, kidneys and his nerves (the latter brought on by Dean Jr's demise), when he returned home, was administered by Jeanne. His health did improve towards the middle of the year, enough to take Jeanne and two of their children to London for five days for sight-seeing and shopping, ensuring that his hotel and staff firmly understood that he was not in residence should anyone enquire. He felt that he needed this break, and London was a nice enough place to experience a complete change of atmosphere. Even again this year, with Dean often in Jeanne's company, the media frequently informed the world that they were to re-marry. But there was no mad romance here, they were just both very happy with each other and wanted things to remain that way.

But love was certainly in the air in the form of a particular of a song that Dean had recorded way back on 13th August 1953. "That's Amore" was re-issued as a single in May 1988, having been used as the theme for the new picture *Moonstruck*, starring Cher. It was marvelous to hear that song again 35 years later and was Dean's very first CD single.

Unfortunately and not wholly unexpectedly, it did not chart.

EMI Records, meanwhile, had created a series of albums entitled THE BEST OF THE CAPITOL YEARS and I was asked by the series producer Alan Dell (a prolific British radio DJ) to compile a selection of songs for the release featuring one of their most prominent signings. Some 45 years ago, Dean Martin had signed with them, so again it was somewhat of a task for me to choose a batch for this latest release. Once the songs had been selected and confirmed, they were to be digitally processed and the album was provisionally scheduled for the autumn release. It had to be a 'best of' compilation, of course, but I would have honestly preferred to compile something different, something of the rarer and unreleased items, but I had to more or less keep to the chart items and familiar songs that Dean had recorded.

I completed the work by September, again with my design, song choice and sleeve notes, but for reasons unexplained, EMI wouldn't be releasing it for the Christmas heavy-selling season. All three configurations were to be issued (CD, LP and tape cassette) which gave a much bigger spread of the market. There was a gradual withdrawal of new vinyl releases, so it was pleasing that the very last new LP of Dean's ever released (albeit another compilation) was one I had been directly involved in.

Dean's health continued to improve, and he made several appearances back in Nevada, plus a special four-night season in Chicago commencing 12th November, completing another year of mixed feelings, good and bad health, but above all, this displayed a return to his public. At this present time, there was a myriad of diseases and complaints that Dean was supposedly suffering from; half of them, if he had had them, would have killed him years before.

To help clarify the facts and dispel the gossip and fantasy surrounding these stories, we issued a bulletin at Dean's request to hopefully explain just how much Dean's health had improved. Meanwhile, the film magazine *Photoplay* featured the DMA in a half-page article and we continued to progress in our 28th year of existence.

Engelbert Humperdinck was the subject of the UK version of *This Is Your Life* on 30th November and Dean gave a small tribute via satellite from his home.

THE BEST OF THE CAPITOL YEARS was finally released on 9th January 1989, going on to sell in considerable numbers around the world. There was a possibility of more ideas that Capitol were going to think about, which was always something to look forward to!

At this time, since Dean had no intention of recording again, all of the song masters distributed on the Reprise label were lying dormant and secure under lock and key at the Warner

Brothers vaults, with a few songs appearing here and there in different parts of the world on various unusual releases (most of them on so called 'bootleg' issues). I asked them once more why there were no proper plans for these songs to be re-issued. Dean's office informed us that they would all be re-packaged and re-issued in the very near future. I did comment at the time that these songs could not just be left stagnating in the vaults but no one, not even Dean himself, seemed the slightest bit interested.

There were more appearances in Nevada again for Dean this year and he presented his usual act on stage for around 45 minutes, and on rare occasions he went to almost an hour, but this was the exception now. Although he was still the inimitable artist live on stage, he showed signs of strain and fatigue and was somewhat slower in his delivery and tone. In the closing moments of his show on the evening of his 72nd birthday, his former partner Jerry Lewis calmly walked on stage, pushing a trolley with a large birthday cake thereon.

Here's to 72 years of joy and happiness you have given the world, Jerry said.

Both had tears in their eyes as they looked at each other and embraced.

This was the first time that Dean and Jerry had been on the same stage since 1976 at Jerry's telethon with Frank Sinatra, yet Dean still had no interest in working with his old partner again. Director Peter Bogdanovich had attempted to get them together for *Paradise Road,* but the tentative idea for this comedy film never went further than that.

TWENTY-SEVEN

Have A Little Sympathy

In the autumn of 1989, a musicians' strike caused many a problem in the US, and Dean's appearances in Las Vegas were held over when he had to cancel his engagements indefinitely. The problem arose when Bally's announced they would use taped music instead of live musicians in lavish productions, although top status performers such as Dean Martin would still be able to use full orchestras. However, pickets still caused serious problems and Dean never approached the hotel as he did not wish to cross the picket line, becoming the first headliner to cancel because of these rules.

In a strange way, this gave him a break: he was not in need of more money or work, so he had spent these last few years steadily arranging a schedule so that he was definitely around, but not overworking in any sense of the word. His health had declined and he knew he had been advised to take things easier. Sometimes he ignored this advice and sometimes he actually behaved himself and took notice! His stomach and back problems seemed to be there more or less all the time now, but he just accepted this as part of life.

When Sammy was admitted to hospital with throat cancer, Dean's depression crept slowly back. Little Sammy was very ill, under extreme and extensive chemotherapy, and Dean was devastated. He had visited Sammy, and he spoke of some of those good times they had had together, but with such extensive treatment that famous voice could not even whisper a reply.

A short while later, Dean himself was admitted to the same hospital for an abscess in his throat.

Eventually, Sammy was sent home from hospital, taking further medication and being cared for by his wife Altovise and the children.

Meanwhile, there were movements with regard to some of Dean's albums seeing the light of day again: I was delighted that A WINTER ROMANCE was released in November, along with a bonus track "The Christmas Blues". Digitally remastered, we once again heard those wonderful renditions of winter and Christmas songs by Dean, sounding much richer and clearer than ever.

This same month, Dean suffered dental problems and underwent surgery, easily clearing this problem before he took part in the 60th Anniversary special tribute to Sammy. Introduced by Tony Danza, he read out a few messages to Sammy and looked very drawn and tired, joking to his old friend ...*roses are red, carnations are pink, if I had your talent, I wouldn't have to drink!* Dean had lost weight and his voice sounded weak and raspy, but he was still his old charming self.

But sadly, no matter how drawn and tired Dean looked, it was dear Sammy who brought everyone to tears. The tribute show was his last-ever appearance and, even though when you saw him on screen he was obviously in great pain, he still had that great smile for everyone and even got up on the stage for a short tap-dance sequence with Gregory Hines, with whom he had recently starred in the picture *Tap*.

But with the end of the 80s, Dean's health again was in question. He simply stayed at home, with Jeanne there quite frequently, keeping him as content as possible and trying to make sure he ate properly, because as he was now something of a recluse, he was not taking good care of himself. Living alone at his home, he would ignore family and friends on occasion, even declining the invitation to Frank's birthday party on 12th December. Occasional trips to his favorite restaurant La Famiglia or to some other eatery broke the routine, but he no longer drove anywhere himself. Dean, at 73, was deserving of better health. Perhaps he could have improved it more himself but, as I have said on numerous occasions, he was a very stubborn man and rarely took advice when it was given to him.

The following February he was admitted to hospital again with back and stomach problems, and was also suffering with muscle tightness in his hands. He had a minor operation because of an enlarged prostrate, but had delayed treatment because of his daughter Deana's wedding on 17th February. He presented the bride at the ceremony, but was in pain and very uncomfortable.

Whilst recovering in the hospital, he had visited Sammy there, who was now terminal. The fact that Sammy himself was so devastated by this appalling disease did not exactly make Dean feel any better, but he did his best to greet Sammy with words of affection and reassurance.

The DMA now entered its 30th year in 1990 and we were greatly saddened to learn from Sammy's management that the great man had died at his home on Wednesday 16th May. We issued a special tribute edition of the newsletter for May/June, featuring a whole array of photographs of Sammy with and without Dean. Sammy had been a wonderful person to know and had contacted us each and every time he had visited London, a good acquaintance who was always very pleased to talk with me.

Meanwhile, Dean himself had surprisingly returned to Nevada for more live appearances, but he now looked very drawn and shaky on stage, slurring his words and leaning on the piano very frequently. In the midst of his act, he spoke of his son Dean Jr and his friend Sammy, breaking down in tears every so often as he broke off singing. It was heart-wrenching to watch and I wondered why he had decided to return to cabaret. Almost staggering on the stage, he was met by hecklers asking him if he knew what he was doing and if he was drunk. I seethed at this disrespect: here was Dean trying to bring some normality back into life and these vile audience members saw nothing of, or simply didn't care about, his pain.

However, he carried on with his shows, but now took long breaks in between engagements, which made all the difference, because when he reappeared in the June, he looked much fitter and was back with his old jokes and patter with his audience.

Capitol records this year had released a Dean-related CD

within their COLLECTORS SERIES, a selection of 25 songs, approved by Dean himself when he had taken himself down to the Capitol Tower in Hollywood to watch the digital re-mastering of this selection in their studios. An intelligent collection of some of Dean's most popular items, together with a few released in stereo for the first time, it was all in all a good compilation. Dean even included a little note on the sleeve, mentioning that his 50th year in show-business was coming up (even though that actually fell in 1993!).

The media was still very content in telling everyone around the world that Dean Martin was drinking himself to death and falling over on stage all the time. But that was not true. He wasn't a well man, and did continue to take medication, some not always as prescribed, and sometimes mixed with alcohol, more than he had ever taken before.

We contacted every radio and television station in the UK, every film company that Dean had worked for in the past, and many others all over the world, letting them know of his upcoming 50th anniversary. But with typical appeal and excitement, no company bothered to even write back or contact us in any way, something I must say we experienced numerous times in the past. Although Dean was always very popular here in the UK, he had never been taken very seriously, being regarded as someone who didn't take himself or his work seriously. It seemed that no organization took the trouble to present anything particular and sadly, after so many years work, he was not recognized in any way. EMI Records here decided to delete THE CLASSIC DINO album we had compiled in 1979, but it had been a consistent seller and had remained in their catalog for over eleven years. I did suggest that this should be re-issued as a compact disc, together with a re-release of DINO – ITALIAN LOVE SONGS, but both of my ideas fell upon deaf ears at Capitol. The same silence came from Dean's management upon my suggestion that the Reprise issues should be re-released on CD, similar to all of the Frank Sinatra material, with additional and/or unreleased tracks on each disc. But jumping forward to 2001, the basic Reprise albums did eventually appear on CD, with two titles on one disc.

20th Century Fox released unseen footage of the ill-fated *Something's Got To Give* and Dean appeared at Las Vegas for a few more shows. Segments of him were seen on the *Crooners of the Century* special with Jerry Lewis and again in *Sinatra 75 – The Best Is Yet To Come*, screened in December.

Continuing his shows in Las Vegas however, he still managed to display the charm that was uniquely Dean, but it was painfully noticeable that he was chronically unwell. He was attacked again by intestinal influenza in March 1991 and had to rest. He also noticed something that had been creeping up on him: he was developing stage fright. He had always suffered from anxiety, but this was now becoming something that was spilling out into his professional appearances. But with medication, he managed to control this situation and carried on with only a selected few dates in Nevada.

Meanwhile, Capitol Records had re-released on CD the complete SWINGIN' DOWN YONDER plus eight extra tracks (one never before released). With the original sleeve notes and cover, this was a superb reissue and made me hope that many more were to come.

The DMA continued to promote Dean and his career and, even though he was not very much in the news now (if at all), we still had a growing band of admirers that joined us month after month.

Towards the end of this year, Dean had carried on with some occasional appearances in Las Vegas, but made a surprise move by announcing that he was to provisionally sign a two-year contract for appearances at the Desert Inn. This never came to fruition, for he did not engage any appearances there at all and completed his final shows for Las Vegas in July.

Dean Martin had finally called it a day.

TWENTY-EIGHT

Rain

Dean no longer wanted to appear in cabaret anywhere, bringing to an end an unprecedented career as one of Nevada's greatest ever crowd-pleasers. When Dean's name went up in lights in Las Vegas, or indeed anywhere, there was this solid gold guarantee that the crowds would come pouring in to see the man who had made a fantastic success out of everything he had attempted. The public could quite easily put someone down as easily as praise them, but Dean Martin had managed to get to the very pinnacle of success and life and had stayed there, not a small effort by any means.

When Dean worked with anyone in his career, without exception, he would play to that fellow artist and ignore the audience. Not that he didn't like the audience, he loved every one of them – but it was the art and talent within him that insisted he gave his all to the other person, in turn showing the watching audience just how good he was. Even in the most intimate surroundings, such as in cabaret or in small clubs, Dean always tended to look ahead and over the faces of those staring back up at him. This way, he got everyone there enthralled by him and so displayed no shyness whilst he was working in his own inimitable manner and unflappable style.

It was all part of his talent, and that was the way he worked, earning the respect and love of many fellow artists as well as people like Greg Garrison, Mort Viner and Mack Gray. These were the people behind this great entertainer who took away the worries of routine and complications just the way he liked it, enabling him to conquer the admirers by the multitude, making it all look so easy, but working hard at it every time!

Jimmy Bowen had begun to compile a set of songs for a double CD set of Dean's recordings to be issued on the Capitol label, a type of anthology of his songs for Capitol and Reprise, but owing to complications with Dean's ownership of Reprise sessions being married with the Capitol material, the entire project was shelved.

In 1991, John Chintala[7] (who had been a regular DMA member) was fortunate enough to meet and interview Jimmy Bowen as part of a radio special he was working on for Dean's 75th birthday.

Until his retirement due to health problems in 1995, Bowen was one of the most successful record producers in music history. He began his career as a member of the Rhythm Orchids, playing bass and co-writing the Buddy Knox chart topper "Party Doll" and cutting a Top 15 pop hit of his own, "I'm Stickin' With You." In the early 1960s, Bowen headed Chancellor Records' Los Angeles office and worked with such artists as Frankie Avalon and Fabian. In 1963, he was named A&R director for Reprise Records and scored his first hit for the label, Jack Nitzsche's classic "Lonely Surfer." But it was as the producer of Dean Martin's string of 20 Hot 100 singles between 1964 and 1969 that put Bowen's name on the map. During that time, he also produced major hits for Dean's fellow Rat Pack pallies Frank Sinatra ("Strangers In The Night" and "That's Life") and Sammy Davis, Jr. ("I've Gotta Be Me").

In the late 1960s, Bowen formed his own record label, Amos, which issued debut albums by two future members of the Eagles: Glenn Frey (*Longbranch Pennywhistle*) and Don Henley (*Shiloh*). After working as an independent producer (which resulted in such hits as "You Gave Me A Mountain" for Frankie Laine and Bobby Vinton's "Ev'ry Day Of My Life")

---

[7] *A long-time Dean Martin fan and collector, John Chintala is the author/publisher of the excellent and highly-recommended reference book* Dean Martin – A Complete Guide to the 'Total Entertainer', *which was originally published in 1998 and was revised and made available as an e-book in 2012. His writings have also appeared in* Goldmine, Filmfax *and* DISCoveries *magazines and the first two volumes of the highly-recommended Dean Martin CD box sets issued by Bear Family Records.*

Bowen became president of MGM Records in 1974. He joined MCA's Nashville division in 1977, became Vice President/General Manager of Elektra/Asylum Nashville a year later, and assumed those duties for Warner Brothers/Nashville when both labels merged in 1983. The next year, he was named president of MCA/Nashville and headed Capitol Nashville (later renamed "Liberty") from 1990 until his retirement five years later.

Bowen recalled his two decades spent as Dean's producer, A&R man, and close friend.

'I was a teenage idol for six months! In the seventh month, I was back to square one because Roulette Records wanted a follow-up to "I'm Stickin' With You" and I didn't have one! So I went back and worked in radio for a year in Colorado Springs, and I hate the cold. So I escaped from there, went to California and got a job as a songwriter and song plugger at American Music in Los Angeles. Then I ran the West Coast office of Chancellor Records. And in late 1962, a mutual friend of mine and Frank Sinatra's talked Sinatra into hiring me at Reprise. And when I looked over their artist roster, I said the one act I want to produce is Dean Martin. I loved him; I just loved what he did when he was with Jerry Lewis, the way he sang and the comedy and all.

'He had just done a country album called DEAN "TEX" MARTIN. And a few months after I met him, I produced DEAN "TEX" MARTIN RIDES AGAIN. I told him then that this was really good and all, but we gotta cut a pop hit. So Dean said, 'Well before we do that, I want to do an album called DREAM WITH DEAN, 'cause in Vegas, after the show, I go out in the lounge, get up with a quartet and sing a few of these old standards and people love it.' So I said, 'Good, we'll do that.' Well, in those days, you did 12 songs in an album; and I had 11 songs and about 30 minutes left. Dean was trying to do some song and he said, 'I don't want to do this.' And I came out of the booth and said, 'Well, we're one short, what else do you know?' And Ken Lane said, 'How 'bout my song?' So Dean walked over to the piano and started singing

"Everybody Loves Somebody" - I went, 'Oh shit, *that's* the pop hit!' Dean looked at me like I was nuts! So we did it with the four pieces as a mood thing, and I said, 'Let's recut this, I think this is a big hit.' The manager guy said, 'oh, I don't know.' Dean said, 'Hey, let the kid do what he wants.' I think I was 26 at the time.

'So a month later I got arranger Ernie Freeman and Hal Blaine on drums and a big orchestra and we went in and recut "Everybody Loves Somebody". We took it over to the company and nobody cared for it. They put it out, nothing happened and they took it off the priority list. Then this one Monday in Worcester, Massachusetts and in New Orleans, two radio stations added it. Within a week we had orders for 50,000 records, which was incredible for back then. And it was off and rockin' from then on.'

It hit number one in the summer of '64 at the height of Beatlemania and the British Invasion. Dean's next release, "The Door Is Still Open To My Heart" also made the Top 10.

'My best friend, a fella by the name of Don Lanier, who was the electric guitar player in our group in the '50s, and I roomed together then. I was going through this song-hunting process, 'cause the follow-up to the first big hit's the most difficult thing always. And I was saying, 'Damn, I can't find a song.' Don picked up a guitar and said, 'How 'bout this one, and started singing "The Door Is Still Open To My Heart".' I said, 'C'mon!' We got into the car and drove to 20th Century Fox where Dean was doing a picture, and when he got a break, Don played the guitar and we sang it for him and Dean said, 'That's great.'

It was Bowen's idea for Dean to remake "You're Nobody 'Til Somebody Loves You" which he had already recorded for Capitol.

'Yeah. It had been cut a hundred times, but had never been a hit single. And I had some version that a publisher had dropped off and I put it on the turntable and said, 'My God, there's one that'll fit him!'

The track was added to DEAN MARTIN HITS AGAIN as was

"Send Me The Pillow You Dream On".

'Right. That one was given to me by a guy named Dave Burgess who worked for 4 Star Music; they were primarily a country publisher. And in one of those many song hunts, he came in with three or four songs and that was one of them. It was very obvious when a song was right for Dean, and that was one that was right!'

Those songs, as well as most of Dean's Reprise hits, were arranged by the late Ernie Freeman.

'Oh, Ernie was an incredible musician and a brilliant arranger. I would sing him string lines and most arrangers hate that; they want to come up with their own. But Ernie had the ego-control and the talent that if I wanted something "dumb," he wouldn't do that. He'd fix it; he wouldn't let me hang myself. He'd come up with a string line that was just brilliant, or a harmony situation between horns and voices and strings that would just be marvelous. And he had a very commercial ear where many arrangers don't have that for radio. He was one of the first people to put strings on rock and roll and rockabilly records when he did arrangements for Snuff Garrett: "Dreamin'" by Johnny Burnette and Gene McDaniels' "A Hundred Pounds Of Clay." I loved working with Ernie; he was my favorite arranger ever.

'Lee Hazlewood came by Reprise Records around midnight one time. We had a little shot of Jack Daniels and he said, 'Well I got a song for Dean called "Houston." I had it out by Sanford Clark on Warner Brothers.' So we had to go break in the mailroom and decode the alphabetical system to find it. Got to bed about five that morning and had to get up at nine to go to Dean's house and played him "Houston" and he loved it. And that gave him a big hit.'

As for the follow-up, "I Will," which was written by Dick Glasser: 'Well, I was the head of A&R for Reprise and he was head of A&R for Warner Brothers. Our offices were right next to each other, we played golf together all the time. We were friends. And one of those nights, it was about 11 and as he's leaving to go home he asked me, 'What are you still doing here?' and I said, 'I'm hunting songs for Dean, I gotta see him in the morning.' In about 30 minutes, he came back with a demo of "I Will". He said, 'This is one of my songs; I think it would be good for Dean.' And again, you put it on and you go, 'Uh, oh, that's a killer thing!'

Dean's final easy listening hit was "Get On With Your Livin'". It was likely the first time he'd recorded with a fuzz-tone guitar.

'Probably! We did that at a studio called TTG in Los Angeles. And it had a hum in it; some of the inputs into the control room had this distortion. And that particular guitar sound, the guitar player was messing with it on his amplifier and then I ran it through this distorted input line and it made that sound. We all thought, 'Oh, this is marvelous.'

Dean's final LP, THE NASHVILLE SESSIONS, was the only time he recorded digitally.

'Yeah. Dean had been ill for a couple years and was recovering. He started feeling better and was working Vegas again. And his manager called and said, 'Dean would like to come down to Nashville and make an album.' I said, 'C'mon!' We found some songs here in town and used some of the Nashville musicians and it was great fun for everybody. We had several different bass players: Chuck Berghofer and Bill Pitman. My favorite keyboard player for Dean was Leon Russell. But Leon hated to play Dean's sessions 'cause I made him do all those eighth notes on the head. You know, the piano on a lot of Dean's stuff was just 'da da da, da da da, da da da.' And after about a minute and a half of that, a piano player's eyes start to cross! On a lot of the Dean Martin records, I had two piano players so they could alternate. One guy would play for six or eight bars, then the other guy would take over, 'cause it's a real hard thing to do. It got to where Leon wouldn't take my calls! So then I used different people. Don Randi could do it pretty good; he was a fine session player in L.A. On guitar: Glen Campbell played on a lot of them, also Tommy Tedesco and Al Casey. Strings were by the Sid Sharp String Section. And I used the Jack Halloran Singers, an eight-voice vocal group that did a lot of sessions in L.A.'

There is one particular song of Dean's that remains Bowen's favorite: "Everybody Loves Somebody". It was the highlight of everything he recorded as far as he was concerned. Dean had never sung with a big backbeat like that, with a big orchestra and a hip, modern rhythm section in it.

'He used to walk in the studio and in 15-20 minutes he'd have a song done. And it took me two hours to get the arrangement and the track ready. I kept walking by saying, 'I'll be with you in just a minute,' and he'd say, 'That's okay.' When it was all over, he said, 'That's the first time I ever sang with lead drums,' 'cause in that one room those drums just went everywhere. That performance he gave on "Everybody Loves Somebody" was just tremendous!'

John approached us for help with the same radio documentary for Dean's 75th birthday. In 2017, John said to Elliot, 'My first thought is how much [Bernard] helped with the show. Not only did he tape record answers for all the questions I wrote to him with - yes, 'wrote'…this was the pre-internet days! - but he transcribed his responses so I could have them in 'script form'. This made my job of editing his sound bites much, much easier. I did not ask him to do this; rather, he took it upon himself to go the extra mile and supply me with this information. Just one example of the generosity he showed towards me.'

Dean now had all the time in the world to do nothing, a somewhat precarious situation for someone who had chronic depression. With his health not particularly good, Dean was again advised to take more exercise, so for a while he took walks in various places with an assistant. This he found quite enjoyable, although he did not carry on for more than a few weeks. He knew he should look after himself better but never getting over the loss of his loved ones and friends, he realized in his heart that he had to be strong. His dear parents and his son (as well as his living family) would not like to see him so depressed and miserable, but his state of mind made his life now so dull and routine, in total contrast to his previous experiences.

But in order to try to get to the bottom of all the stories flowing out from the media about what was wrong with Dean, we contacted the man himself via his office. One of many of Dean's short hand-written notes came back eventually in July, joking that he was living the high life!

But then his management came back a couple of months later, telling me that because of increasing problems with his health, he'd been admitted to hospital on 16th September. Certain tests were carried out but as he refused any intensive checks on himself, the hospital was unable to completely clarify his situation. Nothing was ever officially released as a bulletin from the hospital or his doctors, but we learnt that in addition to being generally debilitated, he had cancerous tumors on both lungs, which caused him terrible breathing problems. This we sadly announced in our newsletter for October 1993, which naturally caused great concern to us and our devoted members.

Contacting Dean at his home, he replied by post, remarking that he was so thankful for our concern and that it was so pleasing to have had my support for so many wonderful years. As this letter had arrived in November, it was pleasing to have actually heard from him in this way and he still thought so highly of me after all this time, even taking time out to wish me a merry Christmas.

Over the years, Dean sent me numerous small hand-written notes, expressing various remarks and comments. Occasionally we had a typewritten letter, but they were all the same: Dean always expressed how grateful he was. Many items he had also sent me and my children over the years and, as well as those letters and notes, I can only assume that many times he did this on his own. But that was Dean, a kind person in so many ways, who never truly knew just how much his public adored him and his work. Admittedly, I was always so surprised and honored that he treated me in this way, and how he strongly expressed his feelings on paper whenever I informed him of good or tragic events within my personal life.

I was so proud and sometimes even shocked with his high opinion of me.

So many of the people who have worked with Dean will all tell you the same: that he was absolutely wonderful to know and to be with, was professional, sincere and brought much needed laughter and pleasure even to the most serious situation.

During the course of 1994, very little was seen of the man.

His visits to La Famiglia or Da Vinci's were less frequent and sometimes he would be seen eating alone or with Jeanne. His songs were played for him and perhaps a fellow diner would acknowledge him. Dean never ignored them and occasionally even signed an autograph.

He'd ceased smoking by now but continued to mix his medication with alcohol, doing nothing for his depression or general health overall. By the middle of the year, he'd lost a lot of weight, dropping from his usual 14 stone to a worrying 10. But with the cancer in his lungs, his weight would forever be dropping. Yet, as if still defying the odds, he spent New Year's Eve at Da Vinci's restaurant with Jeanne and Ursula Andress. When asked about his well-being from those nearby, he said quite brightly ...*yes, I feel quite a lot better now, thank you.*

Meanwhile, the DMA had been asked to assist with another compilation from Capitol, with an album titled SINGLES. I sneaked in some of my favorites from Dean's repertoire as well as a few never before released on CD! Capitol itself was also preparing a separate collection for the American market: called SPOTLIGHT it was a random selection of material taken from various LPs, again including some songs that had never been committed to CD before. This was pleasing as it meant that Dean's work was being discovered by a whole new audience.

I'd been toying with the idea of writing Dean's life story for some time but wondered what his take on that would be. So I asked him. In March 1995, he wrote back with his blessing.

Towards the autumn of that year, Dean suffered a further decline in health, his breathing had become worse than ever, and he and shut himself away. Yet I still received a letter here and there and always responded straight away, assuring him of my and the DMA's support for him. Sometimes he replied to my letters directly, sometimes he did not, but knowing how ill he was, I knew he was with his thoughts and his family. Who was I to expect him to respond to me?

It was November that his condition became critical. He remained in hospital for a few weeks but returned home in the December.

At 3.37am on the morning of Christmas Day 1995 in his Beverly Hills home, Dean Martin peacefully passed away from acute respiratory failure caused by lung cancer.

Without any exaggeration, I can only say I was devastated when his office called me late afternoon (UK time) that day. It seemed surreal.

For me, Dean Martin *is* Christmas…his seasonal ballads could be heard in our home throughout most of the holiday season every year. In fact, A WINTER ROMANCE was playing when I got the call.

Because of the time of year, postal communication would always be sluggish but I knew I had to issue a bulletin to the loyal DMA members, who were no doubt learning the news themselves throughout the building and, I'm pleased to say, highly respectful media coverage. Our home telephone didn't stop ringing with the press asking me for my thoughts and a few quotes. I managed to get a letter out to Jeanne and the family, expressing our sincere condolences, sending them our thoughts during their terrible sadness.

With a special invitation-only funeral, it was the family wish that no flowers be sent but a contribution to charity would be welcomed. This emotional event took place on Friday 29th December, and he was laid to rest in the Crocetti family mausoleum in Westwood Park, Los Angeles.

As a magnificent and unprecedented showing of respect, all the lights on the Las Vegas strip were switched off for ten minutes that afternoon. Jerry cancelled his stage performance in Denver to attend and bid his beloved Dino farewell. Sadly,

because of illness, Frank was unable to attend, his wife
Barbara going on his behalf instead. Sinatra was devastated:
first Sammy and now Dean.

He'd lost both of his closest friends.

TWENTY-NINE

Lay Some Happiness On Me

Jumping back to 1975, Dino had blocked Warner/Reprise from putting together a compilation but in 1976 he wrote to me out of the blue asking for a list of around twenty-four songs for inclusion on a forthcoming album he wanted released in the UK. He asked me if I'd also design the cover. He said he wanted my choices, my favorites, of his Reprise output. I jumped at the chance and sent the list of songs with a rough idea of the cover designs to his office.

Between us, via a few lengthy 'phone calls, we shuffled the songs around and played with the designs. This was the first time I really, truly worked with Dino himself on a commercial (and major) project.

Yes, I was nervous. Of course I was. I knew that if Dino got fed up with something or it became too complex, his interest would switch off. So I ensured I drove the project and I think he welcomed that. I wasn't bowing to his position and being just a 'yes' man if he suggested something I didn't necessarily like. I stood my ground and we worked at an even pace until he let me loose with Warners in the UK!

We'd whittled the twenty-four songs down to twenty, in this order:

Side 1:	'Everybody Loves Somebody'
	'Corrine Corrina'
	'Things'
	'Houston'
	'Lay Some Happiness On Me'
	'In the Chapel In the Moonlight'
	'Little Ole Wine Drinker, Me'
	'The Birds and the Bees'
	'King of the Road'
	'Send Me the Pillow You Dream On'
Side 2:	'I'm Sittin' On Top of the World'

'You're Nobody 'til Somebody Loves You'
'That's When I See the Blues'
'Tie A Yellow Ribbon'
'The Green, Green Grass of Home'
'The Door Is Still Open To My Heart'
'Ramblin' Rose'
'Amor Mio'
'In the Misty Moonlight'
'Detroit City'

I suggested to Dino we reproduce a small selection of previous album covers on the back of the sleeve to encourage back-catalog sales and when he said yes, I couldn't miss the opportunity to include GENTLE ON MY MIND alongside WELCOME TO MY WORLD, GREATEST HITS (VOLUMES 1 AND 2) and YOU'RE THE BEST THING THAT EVER HAPPENED TO ME.

The overall color scheme was blue (Dino's favorite color) and with typeface in orange and yellow, it was bright and would absolutely stand out in the record racks. After much deliberation, I named it TWENTY ORIGINAL HITS.

It was then all presented to Warner Bros., who changed the song list but kept the artwork.

I disagreed.

They disagreed.

I disagreed again.

They still disagreed.

Then I used my trump card.

Dino told them what songs we'd decided and that they would be staying.

They agreed.

The vinyl LP, tape cassette and 8-track cartridge tape were all allocated their catalog numbers and a synchronized release date of 20 October 1976.

We sat back and waited and, amazingly, the ALBUMS GENTLE ON MY MIND and GREATEST HITS (both volumes) received silver awards in the UK.

With this sudden success in mind I made a second ridiculously silly suggestion to a record company giant (if you recall elsewhere in this book I wrote about the 7' single release for "Gentle On My Mind").

'TWENTY ORIGINAL HITS needs to have nationwide television advertising,' I said cheerily.

They laughed.

I laughed nervously.

They laughed a bit more.

They said no.

Naturally, they thought this was insanity again from me but I kept on pushing for this because I felt that all the hard work Dino and I had put into this (and certainly Dino hadn't needed to at all), this release deserved full-blown adverts, and that meant, for me, television.

Much to my surprise, they eventually relented, saying that they would test the waters by advertising across the Tyne Tees area in the lead-up to the release date and, after just one week, album sales were in their thousands.

Warner Bros. were dumbfounded. So was I, to be honest.

They agreed national advertising and suggested I work with them further to promote the album.

I was offered an all-expenses paid nationwide campaign to speak to radio, TV and press but I turned it down, accepting instead just a visit to Manchester to chat with Piccadilly Radio. My hesitancy in going all-guns for the promotion was nothing to do with any ego I may have had nor my initial battles with Warner Bros over this album.

You see, my dear father Henry suffered a fatal heart attack just six days after the album came out and I was devastated and unable to function let alone embark on a promotional campaign. I simply couldn't leave my mother, my wife nor my daughter and son at this awful time. My mother insisted I go as both she and my father had seen how proud I was of getting this album out there. Against what I thought was a bad decision, I relented and Warner Bros. understood and were comfortable with the revised plans. Dino was supportive in his own way, telling me that my well-being was more important than his album.

So I commenced my journey to Manchester on 26 November with thoughts of my recently buried father and my family running around my head. The train ride was a blur as a result and I remembered little of it by the time I pulled into Manchester Piccadilly to be met by Warner Bros.' representative, a charming lady called Julie. She drove me to the Piccadilly Hotel and made sure I was booked in and had everything I needed. I had the weekend to myself but was to head to Piccadilly Radio for Monday morning, so I took in the sights.

On the Sunday morning when I went to the hotel reception to hand my key in for the day, there was a familiar face who came and stood next to me. Her Swedish accent and stunning looks were impeccable. I couldn't miss this opportunity to say hello, having admired her performances alongside Hammer veteran Christopher Lee in both *The Wicker Man* and *The Man With the Golden Gun*. As Britt Ekland said hello back, Rod Stewart sidled up beside us in his slippers.

For the next ten or so minutes Mr Stewart chatted with me, interested in my connection with Dean Martin. Surprisingly, he told me that he'd always wanted to record with the Count Basie Orchestra, a revelation that never fitted his rock star appearance! But here was a man who loved music, who was genuinely piqued by other styles of music beyond his own and was happy to chat in a hotel lobby with a chap trying to flog an American crooner's 'best of' LP! He offered me free passes to his King's Hall concert that night (his last performance there, I think) but I had to decline his kind offer as I knew I had to be up very early the next morning. I wish I'd said yes as I was and still am a great fan of his work.

Interestingly, Mr Stewart himself went on to record many years later a series of Grammy Award-winning albums of classic American big band and swing ballads.

Monday came and I was on-air on and off throughout the day talking about Dino, this new compilation and music in general. Some weeks later following this, I was offered a position as a DJ, but I turned this down as it would have meant relocating my family. Again, a regret? I wonder how life would have changed then.

With my time up, I headed back home on the Tuesday, subsequently happy with the knowledge that all my hard work had paid off.

TWENTY ORIGINAL HITS had gone Gold! In excess of one million copies!

Having met so many DMA members and the general public in my travels over the years, it was clear that the DMA had become larger than I had imagined. Promoting Dean Martin's career in the small way I did and continue to do has been incredibly rewarding and one letter we received was from an Elizabeth Hardy who lived in Blackpool. She wasn't a DMA member but was a huge fan of Dean Martin all the same and said that I was his greatest advocate, his greatest supporter and that if it wasn't for me, his name wouldn't be as half as well known in the UK as it was. Well, I'm not entirely convinced that is the case, but I am very proud of the work I did for him. So thank you, Ms Hardy, if you ever by chance read this, for your kind words.

Dino was overwhelmed, as we all were, with the phenomenal success of TWENTY ORIGINAL HITS and told me how grateful he was that I'd put so much hard work into it, especially when my father had passed away in the midst of everything.

As we entered 1977, the album continued to still sell well and in massive quantities and our membership was growing. In fact, we were so busy I did fear that we might not have been able to cope. We were a relatively small operation, remember, even though we had 4-figure membership numbers.

My concerns during the first half of the decade of Dino's wavering popularity had not just disappeared, they'd been vaporized.

Warner Bros. suggested I be flown to Las Vegas to present Dino with the Gold Award itself during one of his live shows. He'd agreed to this but the thought of me walking onto a Vegas stage in front of thousands of people made me shudder!

His office were in the throes of setting up flights and a hotel for me when I received a call from Warner Bros. advising that the award would simply be posted to his Beverly Hills home instead, with no pomp or fanfare.

I was very disappointed and I knew it was most probably Dino himself who had eventually decided he didn't want the fuss. But it was nice to know that he had it hung in his hallway.

Nevertheless, I do wonder where it is now.

THIRTY

Absence Makes
The Heart Grow Fonder

As 1996 began, the DMA had to continue. For the next few years we oversaw a number of compilations with Capitol, Reprise, Charly and Joker and after much persuasion from me, EMI agreed to release two of Dean's greatest albums together, remastered, on a single CD: DINO – ITALIAN LOVE SONGS and CHA CHA DE AMOR. Due to its success, EMI decided to introduce this 'two-on-one' series for many of its other artists, something which I was quietly proud of.

Our working relationship with Charly began shortly after they had obtained the rights under license to Dean's Reprise material and their intention was to release it all over a series of new CD-only compilations. After releasing (in January 1996) THE BEST OF DEAN MARTIN 1962-1968, they approached me to consult with them on two follow-up sets that would become DEAN MARTIN SINGS THE ALL-TIME HITS (August 1996) AND DINO - THE GOLDEN YEARS (December 1996). They sold very well so there was no reason why their output wouldn't continue.

They asked me if I would like to begin preparing, long-term, for the entire catalog to be made available going forward. I, of course, said yes! The team at Charly gave me *carte blanche* to bring all the material together in any way I felt relevant (as long as it wasn't in the format of the original Reprise albums themselves).

FAR AWAY PLACES WITH DINO was the first and it took a good few months from concept to pre-production. A tentative release for 1997 was scheduled with a retail price of £17.99.

Then a spanner hit the works.

A $60million golden spanner!

The Dean Martin Family Trust had bought the complete and exclusive rights from EMI for the Reprise masters.

That meant that Charly was no longer in a position to release any material of Dean's and my plans were scuppered.

I wondered as time went on if the Family would do anything with the masters because there was simply no sign of any albums.

But my fears that Dean's work would never see the light of day on CD were unfounded when Collectors' Choice Music eventually began issuing fantastic two-on-one-disc complete albums in chronological order with original album artwork - licensed by The Dean Martin Family Trust ironically *back* to EMI! Our friends over at The Dean Martin Fan Center were involved and I was very happy that the releases were in safe hands and that Neil Daniels would do Dean proud.

The following, then, is an abridged version of the unpublished sleeve notes written by me that would have been included in the FAR AWAY PLACES WITH DINO set.

This double album set of 40 songs from Dean Martin is the latest in a series of releases from the great entertainer in which his recorded repertoire from 1962 has been digitally re-mastered. By the time this series is complete, there will be a comprehensive library of his work enabling all admirers to up-date their own vinyl collections on re-mastered compact discs, and for those of you who have just 'discovered' Dino, there is the golden opportunity to experience these excellent recordings, and his unique style of singing.

The title of FAR AWAY PLACES WITH DINO might be otherwise misleading, for in an entertainment and a very entertaining career of over 50 years, this man was not prone to frequent travelling!

This collection of songs recorded by Dean Martin over a ten-year period (1962-1972) takes you on an imaginary and romantic journey to places around the world. With a tongue in cheek approach to so many songs, Dean sings of romance, travel and such places as Paris, Phoenix, Houston as well as his family homeland of Italy, and taking in some other spots along the way.

Changing record labels in 1962, the French-styled songs here were all recorded in one session on February 26th with that highly creative musical arranger, Neal Hefti. It was to be the birth of a new era in Dean's recordings, but his success with the new label did not come overnight as some had predicted. Commercially, he was going through a thin period, but with his 1964 hit record "Everybody Loves Somebody", Dino was back in the charts again. The disc proved so popular that he was offered his own TV show, which was [initially] called by the same name. The shows were to last for many years on TV, during which time he had the very best artists from the entertainment world as his guests.

He was kept busy in the recording studios, and in three years had cut well over a hundred song titles.

The song, "South of the Border" appears twice on these CDs, but each is from a totally different session. The first version appeared on an early album, with a Latin-styled arrangement from Don Costa, where Dean ends up 'soused at the Border. A completely different recording appears on Disc Two, which came from the first of four Matt Helm stories that he made for Columbia Pictures, entitled *The Silencers*. The combined orchestras of Gene Page and Ernie Freeman made this version more powerful musically in its presentation.

His regular recording dates continued and in 5 years had issued no less than 16 solo albums. He began to slow down this rate during the 1970's, but a new Dean Martin album was always welcome.

After a protracted and painful illness, Dean Martin died on Christmas Day 1995, and we had lost a great personality, unique in his field who seemed to epitomize something we would all like to do, and that was not to take life too seriously. This happy and carefree nature was reflected in all his work, especially his music.

The Dean Martin Association will continue with the legacy of his work, and I hope that this song collection will give you much lasting pleasure. There are many more compact discs of his still to be issued on Charly, and they will be a fine tribute to a much missed entertainer.

Following our rewarding working relationship with John Chintala, he came to us again, this time with regard to a reference book on Dean he was preparing. John said in 2017: 'Bernard took the time to answer, or at least try to answer, every question I directed toward him. In those pre-internet days, researching someone's career was much more difficult than it is today. Bernard opened up his 30+ years of files for my perusal, and even supplied his [personal contact details] so that we could correspond directly. The book would have been much less complete without his help and assistance.'

As I started slowing down my work with the DMA, Elliot began to get more involved, but after much discussion and pondering, we saw that the very nature of a society such as the DMA was intrinsic to the old style of 'fan club', one that couldn't compete with the online-based appreciation groups that were springing up quickly for any number of artists, actors and movies and so on. We dabbled with an online presence but it didn't suit the DMA's approach...or perhaps it didn't suit mine?

In 2009, we started a working relationship with Mark Adams, who had approached us as he was about to embark on a tour portraying Dean Martin as part of a series of Rat Pack shows. That working relationship became a friendship and Mark's performance, along with his co-stars George Daniel Long as Sammy and Stephen Triffitt as Frank, was phenomenal and we are immensely proud and honored to still lend our support to Mark and his incredibly talented co-stars all these years later.

That same year, Dean posthumously won a Lifetime

Achievement Award at the Recording Academy's 51ˢᵗ Annual Grammy Awards on 8 February. His daughter, Deana, accepted the honor at the live event. The Recording Academy had previously nominated him for Best Vocal Performance, Male for the album EVERYBODY LOVES SOMEBODY (THE HIT VERSION) in 1965.

We met up with George in April 2018 in the Matcham Room of London's Hippodrome Casino (where *The Definitive Rat Pack* had a regular slot) for a chat about his career after we were approached to write the group's souvenir booklet. We'd seen George perform as Sammy many times before, of course, as part of Flying *Music's Frank, Dean and Sammy: The Rat Pack Live from Las Vegas* and what struck us on meeting him backstage was how effortless he was able to transform himself into the role. We've got to know him since over the years following that first meeting and can attest to him being a warm and generous person who always makes people smile.

We asked him how important was it for him to be approachable.

'Oh, being approachable is *really* important for me. Of course, we all get it wrong sometimes but you have to be nice to people you meet along the way. Occasionally you can be really busy or stressed and the audience member who wants a chat with you isn't always aware of that, but a smile and a thank you goes a long way. The same goes for your work colleagues. You get more out of people if you treat them kindly.'

George channeled Sammy almost perfectly so we wondered if there were any preparations he went through.

George laughed infectiously.

'Preparations? What's that?,' he replied, tongue in cheek. 'I have small routines that I go through in a certain order depending on the show, maybe the order in which I get dressed, always do my hair last, check the bowler hat is on stage and so on. I never get ready too early, which Sammy himself was known for. He would just disappear, have a nap and not warm up before a show. I tend to have a think about any new things that have cropped up, stage entrances and exits in a new venue, maybe go over song lyrics in my head if I haven't sung a particular one for a while. I find that if you overthink things then that's when they can go wrong.' George could be his own critic, however, and he considered that his preparations were perhaps based on what he did or how he fared in a previous performance. 'I note myself after a show. I go away and think about any mistakes I made or things I may do differently and then put them into practice the next time.' Clearly, he wanted to always hone his portrayal, his performance and ensure that he was the best he can possibly be when his cue to go on stage begins – but he had to have started somewhere so we were intrigued about his very first time auditioning for Sammy.

'Telling you when that was will give away my age!' laughed George with a twinkle in his eye. 'It was in 2000, I believe. I had to brush up on my tap dancing with the help of Jo Kempton who was resident director on the Flying Music production and also a good friend of mine. It was being filmed for UK Living TV, something now I regret as they edited a lot of things out of context to make it better viewing which, unfortunately, didn't represent me as well as it could have. For example, I was pretending to cry on the stairs as a joke to say 'I really hope I get this,' then they used it as real footage and didn't add the bit where I was laughing immediately afterwards, so revealing it was fake! I must be the Donald Trump of show business with all this fake news!'

George, Stephen and Mark did all perform together previously for Flying Music's *Frank, Dean and Sammy: The Rat Pack Live from Las Vegas* and after hundreds of shows, they came together again to form *The Definitive Rat Pack* ' which is us, our show,' said George. 'We get to be in control of all creative elements, we work together developing it and we are all free to change what we want to do and experiment more. It makes everything looser and the essence of what any Rat Pack show should be is fun and camaraderie. The more natural you are, the more the audience warms to you.'

Frank, Dean and Sammy all had their own individual acts and any number of Dean's over the years follows the same basic structure (you can watch one of his from the 60s, right up to his last performances in 1988 and he'd always start with the same opening song parody gag ['Drink to me only...that's all I aks...ask...'] but from then on, it varied slightly depending on the venue, the year and who was in the news. With that in mind, George said of *The Definitive Rat Pack*'s interpretation: 'If it's terribly scripted then it loses the main ingredient that made them so popular.' And that main ingredient he was referring to was the laid-back approach, the notion that the original Frank, Dean and Sammy seemingly made it up as they went along.

George has travelled the world with *The Definitive Rat Pack* and we asked him if he had any stories he could share with us.

'I'd have to kill you first!' he replied with that laugh again. 'I love travelling with the show and have seen some wonderful places and met some lovely people, so it's a privilege. I can't think of many stories without saying what's not mine to say. I'm not one to gossip so you haven't heard it from me but...'

The three artists embodied the spirit of the trio they portray so much that we never perceived *The Definitive Rat Pack* as a 'tribute act'. It was always so much more than that: Stephen, Mark and George were performers *recreating* a show that now exists in show-business history.

Did they feel any weight of responsibility as a result? Bearing in mind their audiences (who absolutely loved what they do by the standing ovations they regularly received) would likely have never seen the real Frank, Dean and Sammy, how faithful did they need to be to the original act?

'You are incredibly responsible for the portrayal as you wouldn't want the audience going away with a slight on each of the character's legacy. People sometimes do forget that what you say is in the spirit of them and not you and perhaps can't distinguish that. Fans also have their favorites and it can be hard if you get a bad review or response as they may not have really been into the person in the first place and then you either make them like them or they don't like you either! It's all subjective, but all we can do is portray them to the best of our abilities as you can't please everyone.

'Much of the material has just morphed over time. I try to think as Sammy when in character, so before I say something I ask myself would he have said anything like it? You can't spend the whole show stuck in 1963 so we can make modern references as long as it's in character. For example, if a mobile 'phone goes off you can make a joke of it. There would have been no 'phones so rather than say something like 'What is that strange contraption?' it's easier to accept that no one cares if you make out-of-era choices as long as it's apt. We don't do many race or Jewish gags as they aren't really necessary with what we do. I do occasionally make relevant statements but have the advantage of being in control of what is said and not have to say anything that would make anyone uncomfortable, including myself. The other problem is that if the audience don't know Sammy was Jewish and if you don't set it up, then any script relevant to that can make you look a little racist. I didn't want to spend all my time pointing out those aspects of Sammy just so the audience get the references and in-jokes. I have had a few incidents where they thought it was me saying it personally and completely missed Sammy's subtle stabs at racism. I overheard one lady call me racist and misquoted what I'd actually said on stage in character.' George's respectful and protective nature of the original shows is clear and Stephen and Mark follow suit. 'We used to smoke on stage, too, and now we don't. It's much easier anyway and after not being able to do it due to legislation, we actually have gotten so used to not smoking. As for the drinking...no comment!'

The camaraderie he had with Mark and Stephen on stage was clear.

'Of course, with any group there will be times when you rub each other up the wrong way, you are in each other's pockets a lot and you have to make decisions that suit everyone - but we never take our disagreements on stage. The good thing is once we have been on stage we have so much fun that most stuff is forgotten. I guess my role in that is being the diplomat. We have many different layers of relationships with each other so we will be different when it's all of us as opposed to when I spend time one on one with either of the other two. I'm a good go-between for the guys, too, and I am very organized, so I tend to be the person who they call to get information.' And with that mischievous smile, he adds, 'And at their time of life, the memory goes a bit!'

The Definitive Rat Pack has a number of CDs available and they're absolutely well worth a listen[8]. They're not live recordings of their stage act, however, so we asked George if he enjoyed studio work as much as live performances.

'I prefer live as vocally I need to move around to really get into character. A live performer tends to adopt a 'studio voice' which can be softer, so I know I sound different in studio than on stage. It's a bit restrictive in the studio as you have to stay on the microphone but on stage as I can make a bigger sound when moving as well as phrase things to movement.

'I have two songs I'm not too keen on singing: "Mr Bojangles" and "The Candyman". I just don't like singing "The Candyman" and neither did Sammy apparently, because it's pop and not much you can really do with it. It's not a great song to perform as I prefer something with a bit more sentiment. "Mr Bojangles" can be something of a struggle mainly at private events. It's a really hard song to sing as I really want to tell the story and because I get so emotionally involved, I have been known to cry by the end, I invest a lot into it. If audiences aren't really paying attention or are drunk and rowdy it makes it impossible to sing and you have to motor through it which doesn't do the song justice without pathos. Some clients request it but as it's slow, if you are doing

---

[8] *For more information on* The Definitive Rat Pack, *including international tour dates and purchasing copies of their CDs and souvenir booklets, please visit* thedefinitiveratpack.com.

a dinner and dance event people sometimes prefer something with more swing all evening and "Mr Bojangles" can, as lovely as the song is, bring the mood down. Add the to the fact that it's the longest song I sing, even with the cut verses it runs at over four and a half minutes, so a long time to be up there wishing you weren't!'

George trained at the London Studio Centre but his informative years were thanks to local groups and a great music teacher at secondary school who transformed theatre there and mentored him a lot. ('Thank you, Mr David Hebden!') But why did he want to perform in the first place?

'I enjoyed it and some people said I should try it as they had spotted something in me. I recall I wanted to be an accountant or lawyer when I was younger and spent a lot of my teens around horses which I had to let go to progress in theatre. My first role was in *Showboat* for Oxford Operatic Society when I was 12. Over my career I've been lucky enough to be in many West End productions including *Sister Act, Miss Saigon, Porgy & Bess* and *Carmen Jones*. I was even lucky enough to be the first death in Stephen Sommers' *The Mummy Returns* in 2001. I died my socks off but didn't get a credit!'

George nodded when we asked him if he would have done anything different in his performing career.

'Of course, but I'm not sure all of it was within my control. I see a few places where I swerved to another path by a snap decision or courage to stick to my principles but ultimately I have had a successful and lengthy career. I'd like to think I'd be here anyway even if I had made changes, so I can't look back - it's all been a wonderful experience.

'There were roles I just missed out on due to a variety of circumstances but I never think of the as the ones that got away. I'd like to take on something again at some point, just for fun but it would have to be something I knew I could do and was comfortable with. I've never been much of a typical actor striving for roles, I would generally go up for stuff that I knew I could do and say no to being seen for something I was less confident with. I've not always had the greatest confidence with my ability and always wanted to be consistent instead of push any boundaries but I find new ways of pushing myself with Sammy. He keeps me on my toes. I don't always have time for anything else as *The Definitive Rat Pack* schedules can get quite busy, so I won't do any long West End runs again but I still go up for TV, film, commercials or other short term stuff. It also means I can work on other ventures.'

As well as transforming into Sammy, George made transformations of other well-grounded things, about as far as one can get from the smell of the grease-paint and the roar of the crowd. As a horticultural consultant he taps into a different side of his creativity[9].

'I love being around nature, it's not the same as performing as I can't really dance into my meetings, but I guess you still have to be a showman to sell the design or yourself as a designer. I didn't always have an interest in gardens but decided to study horticulture with the Royal Horticultural Society and see what happened. I then realized that I liked the idea of design and so took my training further. I wasn't enjoying longer contracts on shows any more, too, so wanted a quieter, more normal life. I haven't really done much 9-5 and wanted to try something that gave me flexible hours and that I could do at any age. It gives me the freedom to down the drawing board and pens and go off and join the guys on a gig.'

In 2023 George picked up a well-deserved RHS Award.

We've talked about this with George before, but we put it to him again what he thought Sammy would make of someone taking on his persona? 'I hope he would be happy about it. I don't ever pretend to be a carbon copy of him: he is Sammy, I'm George. It's more about the essence, so I'd hope he would respect me as a performer and maybe see a little of him in me. If I'd had the chance to meet Sammy himself, I don't think I'd have the words to say to him. I can get pretty tongue-tied. I

---

[9] *For more information on George's exceptional landscape gardening, please visit* gardens.wellgroundedgroup.com.

think all I'd ask if he could give me some of his talent as he had enough to spare!'

In 2011, on our 51st anniversary the DMA put on hiatus its *Just Dino* newsletter and we formally ceased operations as a fee-based, membership-driven organization. The DMA still continues today, however, primarily as a non-profit body with a regular podcast and a social media presence. In March 2022, we became part of the advisory board for The Rat Pack Music Alliance[10].

You may have gathered by now that I am one of Dean's greatest admirers and yes, you're quite right. But I am not blinkered or naïve about him to say that everything he did was perfect. Far from it. He treated people abominably sometimes, but equally, treated others with such grace and respect.

However, I have always thought myself as being very fortunate indeed regarding my association with the man, and I honestly hope that this literary effort of mine will be considered as it was intended: as a work of genuine sincerity and affection, and that my small contribution to his life and career will be perhaps something that will be remembered and referred to in the future. He was a very large part of my life and will remain so, treating my children as if he were an uncle and making such a positive difference to my own career and that of my son's. How many words have I written about Dean since 1960? And this biography, this recollection, would likely be the very last thing I would ever personally write about Dean…a coda to an incredible six decades.

You will have your own opinions about the kind of person I am and the type of man Dean was, but the fact remains that no other performer has given me so many years of sheer pleasure with his style of entertaining.

It has been a great pleasure to work for and with him in my

---

own way and if everything was as pleasing as his charm and talent, the way he projected such happiness and contentment to his millions of fans across the world (and still does long after his death), wouldn't it be a perfect world? He left behind such a legacy of work and memories that he's not truly gone, not as long as we remember him.

Thank you, dear Dino, for all you have done for me and this crazy world we live in.

And I'll let the man himself have the last word:
I've had a special request…but I'm gonna sing anyhow.

How Do You Speak To An Angel?

Shortly before Bernard Thorpe passed away in 2015, he wrote: '[Dino] took to me so much with his utter personal support and friendship...little, ordinary me! He gave me an incredible amount of backing and confidence with all the albums, gifts, opportunities and much more over the years. He was unfailing in his connections with me, all off his own back. Dino himself had the most wonderful show business life and, with my very small part in his career, I hope did assist him. He was a genuine human being who had so much natural talent, linked with lots of luck and self-determination. I am extremely proud to have worked for Dino for so many years and did my very best to keep his name alive, even after his death in 1995, and promote his career as an important milestone in entertainment history.'

Bernard's daughter Carole added this: 'Having grown up listening to Dean, watching his films and TV shows, it was easy to see the respect and admiration my dad had for him and continued to do so for the rest of his life. His love for Dean the performer and the man never waned and he has passed that onto myself, perhaps even from my birth when Dean sent me the doll from one of his album covers[11]! So, thank you Dad and Dean for the love and entertainment shared by myself and millions across the world.'

His son Elliot continued: 'The amount of time Dad had dedicated to both Dean and the DMA was astonishing and I don't think my sister or I truly realized to what extent. I hope I have done Dad's biography of Dean justice and that it is ultimately something both my parents (and Dean himself) would have been proud of. It sad to think that the three of

---

[11] HAPPINESS IS...DEAN MARTIN (Reprise, 1967)

them never saw it published in their lifetimes.'

The Dean Martin Association itself has gained new ground in recent years, relaunching its regular newsletter *Just Dino* (now as a digital magazine) in 2023 and taking the lead in organizing the annual Dean Martin Hometown Festival in Steubenville. We have also formed close ties with the Muscular Dystrophy Association, The Harmonium Project, the Steubenville Cultural Trust and the Ohio Valley Health Center. We avidly support societies, artists and entertainers who are dedicated to keeping Dean's music, peers and era alive.

Dean would occasionally send notes to the DMA for us to reproduce in future editions of the newsletter. The one that follows was his first such correspondence, undated, but his filming references indicate he wrote it in late 1961 or early 1962 and was included in 'A Letter from Dino', Vol 2, No 8, August 1962.

> Dear Friends
> I am pleased to be able to write this journal letter personally to you. I'd also like to express my deep gratitude to each and every one of you for your loyalty and friendship.
> Your own club president over in London and myself are really getting together to make the British club for me really great.
> It's a wonderful feeling when people like you thousands of miles away take the trouble to be interested in me.
> Together, the two of us hope to really got to town and do many more great things for you all.
> I've just finished a role in *Sergeants 3* and enjoyed working on this film very much. I hope that you will all see it and enjoy it as much as we did filming it. Also in the cast are Frank Sinatra, Sammy Davis Jr, Peter

Lawford, Joey Bishop, Henry Silva, Ruta Lee and the Crosby Brothers. Sounds like I'm a critic! But I really must say that they all are a great crowd of people to work with – really the tops.

Anyhow, it's a Western and we all think it will be enjoyable film fare for everyone.

I have another movie currently in release, which most of you have most probably seen already and know about. It's *Ada*, which I did for MGM. I had the good fortune of working with the very charming and lovely Susan Hayward - also a very fine actress, I might add. MGM adapted this film from the popular novel titled *Ada Dallas*.

I had a bit of time off after the wind-up of *Sergeants 3* for a little rest and a little travelling.
Next, I'll be doing a film for Paramount titled *Who's Got the Action?* and I'm looking forward to working with Lana Turner.

I have several other things lined up on the board, but nothing definite that I can mention at this time.

My wife and children are all in good health, for which I am most grateful. The children are growing more and more with each passing day.

I hope that all of you had pleasant summer vacations.

Should any of you wish to send me letters, I would be pleased if you would forward them to Bernard Thorpe in London, who will then forward them to me.

I would like to thank you for your interest in me and I hope that all of my future efforts continue to please you.

Until next time…

All the best,

APPENDIX

The Oldest Established

Notable events, year-by-year, of The Dean Martin Association since 1960.

1960

November, founded by Dean Martin and Bernard Thorpe as Dino's Fan Club; December, Dean changes the name to The International Dean Martin Club

1961

Dean starts regular contact with Bernard, sharing career information and insights into his life as the years progress; Dean's office begins regularly supplying merchandise as and when it is released

1962

Dean makes Frank Sinatra, Sammy Davis Jr, Joey Bishop and Peter Lawford honorary members; Dean wants only one world-wide official organization, so he closes unofficial fan-clubs in Germany and Chicago, transferring membership to the club

1963

January 19, featured in pop magazine *Cherie*

1963

Dean changes Bernard's position to be President with Dean himself acting as Honorary President

1964

June, LET'S BE FRIENDLY (EMI) compiled, produced and sleeve design by Bernard. Bernard interviews Dean for World Record Club magazine

1966

Dean changes his title from Honorary President to Chairman; attends UK premiere of *The Silencers* at London's Odeon Leicester Square, with the Matt Helm 'Slaygirls' in attendance; Pop magazine *Diana* runs article on the club and 'super-agent' Matt Helm.

1967

January 25, attends 20th Century Fox's private showing of *Murderer's Row*; joint release with Pye Records 7" single of "I'm Not the Marrying Kind" with a special introduction by Dean; attends UK premiere of *Rough Night In Jericho*

1968

BBC Radio's *Roundabout* program runs major feature on Dean, scripted by Bernard; attends UK premiere of *The Ambushers*

1969

January 24, at Bernard's suggestion Pye Records release "Gentle On My Mind" as a single from the album of the same name. It reaches No.2 in the UK charts on March 1 and remains high in the charts for 23 weeks. It is also the most played single of that year; Bernard meets with Dean's recording manager Jimmy Bowen; October, holds first ever members' meeting

1970

Bernard compiles 6xLP box set DEAN MARTIN (EMI); April 23, the DMA attends UK premiere of *Airport* at Odeon Leicester Square

1972

Dean makes Jack Lord an honorary member; July 31, BBC Radio starts a 'Dean Martin Week' in which the DMA features; November, profiled in music publication *Listen Easy*

1973

April 2, Dean changes the name to The Dean Martin Association

1974

July, profiled in music publication *Melody Maker*

1975

Compiles MEMORIES ARE MADE OF THIS (KODAK/EMI); Deana Martin contacts the DMA, expressing how pleased the family is with the continued hard work on Dean's behalf; Dean makes his god-daughter Nancy Sinatra an honorary member

1976

Produces 20 ORIGINAL DEAN MARTIN HITS (Reprise) with input from Dean himself. It becomes Dean's only UK Gold Award album, reaching No. 2 on November 13

1979

Compiles THE CLASSIC DINO (Capitol). The album goes on to remain in EMI's catalogue for 11 years); August, profiled in both the lifestyle magazine *Weekend* and newspaper *Croydon Advertiser*

1980

Celebrates 20th Anniversary; EMI publicizes THE CLASSIC DINO as the recommended Dean Martin album of the year; May, Dean gives Bernard the moniker Chief Executive

1982

July, final members' meeting held (withdrawn because of increasing venue costs)

1983

June, attends Dean's London concerts at Apollo Victoria

1985

Celebrates 25th Anniversary

1987

September, monthly newsletter undergoes a major revamp, renamed *Just Dino*

1988

Compiles THE BEST OF THE CAPITOL YEARS (EMI), Dean's first UK CD release; Bernard begins work on collating a comprehensive discography of Dean's output

1990

Celebrates 30th Anniversary

1992

Takes part in a Dean Martin 75th birthday radio special, Pennsylvania, USA

1994

Compiles SINGLES for EMI

1995

March, Bernard receives permission from Dean to write his biography; contributes to *Biography* documentary on Dean for A&E; December 25, Dean passes away and, the DMA issues notice of his death following the call from his office

1996

Jeanne Martin contacts the DMA thankful for all the support and hard work over the years; August, produces DEAN MARTIN SINGS THE ALL-TIME HITS (Charly Records); suggests to EMI a 'two on one' CD release of THIS TIME I'M SWINGIN' with PRETTY BABY and DINO ITALIAN LOVE SONGS with CHA CHA DE AMOR. This format instigates similar highly-successful releases for other artists by EMI

1998

Compiles THE VERY BEST OF DEAN MARTIN: THE CAPITOL AND REPRISE YEARS (EMI)

1999

Compiles AGAIN (Joker Records)

2000

Celebrates 40th Anniversary; compiles SOMEONE LIKE YOU (Joker Records); writes liner notes for concert program for *Frank, Dean and Sammy: The Rat Pack Live from Las Vegas*; May, writes article on *Frank, Dean and Sammy: The Rat Pack Live from Las Vegas* for theater publication *Encore*; August, selects songs for THE VERY BEST OF DEAN MARTIN: THE CAPITOL AND REPRISE YEARS VOLUME 2 (EMI)

2003

Writes Bob Hope obituary for *Encore*; November 17, compiles songs for exclusive hmv release THE DEAN MARTIN COLLECTION

2007

November 25th, attends stage show *Christmas With the Rat Pack* in London

2009

July, writes for concert program for Mark Adams' 2009 tour of *That's Amore: A Celebration of Dean Martin and Friends*; August, interviews Mark Adams as part of the promotional material for *That's Amore: A Celebration of Dean Martin and Friends*; August, contributes to concert program for the 2009/2010 tour of *Frank, Dean and Sammy: The Rat Pack Live from Las Vegas*; September, DMA allowed exclusive access to rehearsals of *That's Amore: A Celebration of Dean Martin and Friends*

2010

Celebrates 50th anniversary.

2011

Formally ceases as an active, fee-based organization; publication of *Just Dino* goes on hiatus

2014

Discussions begin between Bernard and his son Elliot regarding the Dean Martin biography that Bernard started in 1995, with a view for potential publication to tie-in with Dean's centenary year in 2017.

2015

February, Bernard gives permission for Elliot to solely work on the biography; March, Bernard passes away after a short illness; Chinbeard Books commissions publication of the biography

2017

Elliot relaunches the DMA as an online presence only, without an active membership; Chinbeard Books releases the biography in paperback as *Just Dino - A Personal Recollection of Dean Martin*

2018

The rights to *Just Dino - A Personal Recollection of Dean Martin* revert to the DMA; website undergoes a redesign; Grosvenor House Publishing releases a revised and expanded edition of the biography in hardback, retitled *Dean Martin - Recollections*

2020

Bernard's discography of Dean's work is finally published as *Dean Martin – A Discography*

2021

Ron Iveson joins the DMA team as Association Consultant

2022

March, joins the advisory board of The Rat Pack Music Alliance; December, Cindy Williford joins the DMA team (research/social media); relaunches as a member-driven (non-profit, non-fee-based) organization; Bernard posthumously wins the ARSC Award for Excellence for *Dean Martin – A Discography*

2023

May, attends ARSC Awards, Minnesota; June, attends The Dean Martin Festival, Steubenville; July, Thomas Brady joins the DMA team (research/social media); September, Marisa Lavins joins the DMA team (research/social media); October, *Just Dino* resumes regular publication (now as a free digital-only magazine)

2024

June, attends The Dean Martin Festival, Steubenville; July, Cindy appointed DMA Vice President; same, Ed Krzan joins the DMA team (research/networking); same, attends soundcheck and stage show *The Rat Pack Live In Concert*, Southend, UK; September, attends the MDA *Show of Strength* telethon, St. Louis, Missouri; together with The Harmonium Project, appointed lead organizer for the 2025 Dean

Martin event (now rebranded as The Dean Martin Hometown Festival), Steubenville; sets up The Annual Dean Martin Association Charity Golf Scramble, Steubenville; October, writes for concert program *The Rat Pack – Swingin' At the Sands*; November, sponsors the Dean Martin nutcracker figure for the Nutcracker Village, Steubenville; December, hosts live event *Joe Scalissi Sings Dean Martin* at Froehlich's Classic Corner, Steubenville

2025

Jimmy Bowen takes the role of DMA Honorary Chair while Mark Adams, Michelle Della Fave, Mark Halliday, George Daniel Long become honorary members; June 12-14, the DMA leads and hosts The Dean Martin Hometown Festival in Steubenville; August, The Dean Martin Association of America is formed, supporting the DMA in the US with events, sponsorships and fundraising; Michelle Della Fave becomes the DMAA's first endorser; September: Cindy Williford is appointed DMA/DMAA President; Ed Krzan is appointed DMA/DMAA Vice President; Elliot Thorpe becomes DMA Executive Chair; November, the DMA celebrates 65 years